Introduction to Sport Marketing

Books in the Sport Management Series

Sport Governance
Russell Hoye and Graham Cuskelly

Sport and the Media
Matthew Nicholson

Sport Funding and Finance
Bob Stewart

Managing People in Sport Organizations
Tracy Taylor, Alison J. Doherty and Peter McGraw

Introduction to Sport Marketing

Aaron C.T. Smith

AMSTERDAM • BOSTON • HEIDELBERG • LONDON • NEW YORK • OXFORD •
PARIS • SAN DIEGO • SAN FRANCISCO • SINGAPORE • SYDNEY • TOKYO

Butterworth-Heinemann is an imprint of Elsevier

ELSEVIER

Butterworth-Heinemann is an imprint of Elsevier
Linacre House, Jordan Hill, Oxford OX2 8DP, UK
30 Corporate Drive, Suite 400, Burlington, MA 01803, USA

First edition 2008

British Library Cataloguing-in-Publication Data
A catalogue record for this book is available from the British Library

Library of Congress Cataloging-in-Publication Data
A catalog record for this book is available from the Library of Congress

ISBN: 978-0-7506-8685-3

For information on all Butterworth-Heinemann publications
visit our website at elsevierdirect.com

Typeset by Charon Tec Ltd., A Macmillan Company. (www.macmillansolutions.com)

Printed and bound in Hungary

08 09 10 10 9 8 7 6 5 4 3 2 1

Contents

Series Editor

Dr. Russell Hoye is an associate professor in the School of Sport, Tourism and Hospitality Management, La Trobe University, Victoria, Australia. Russell has been involved in sport management education since 1993, working in Australia at La Trobe University, Griffith University and Victoria University, and in China, with The University of Hong Kong and Tsinghua University. He is a board member of the Sport Management Association of Australia and New Zealand (SMAANZ). He was the guest editor for the inaugural special issue of *Sport Management Review* on professional sport in Australia and New Zealand published in 2005.

Russell's areas of expertise include corporate governance, organisational behaviour, volunteer management and public sector reform within the sport industry. He has acted as a consultant for the Australian Sports Commission, Sport and Recreation Victoria and a number of local government and non-profit organisations. His research interests focus on examining how governance is enacted with sport organisations and how volunteers engage with and are managed by sport organisations. He has published papers on these topics in journals such as *Nonprofit Management and Leadership*, *Sport Management Review*, *European Sport Management Quarterly*, *Society and Leisure*, *International Gambling Studies*, *Third Sector Review*, *Sporting Traditions*, *Managing Leisure*, *Football Studies*, *Annals of Leisure Research* and the *Australian Journal on Volunteering*.

List of figures

List of tables

Preface

Many millions of people around the globe are employed in sport organisations in areas as diverse as event management, broadcasting, venue management, marketing, professional sport and coaching, as well as in allied industries such as sporting equipment manufacturing, sporting footwear and apparel, and retail. At the elite level, sport has moved from being an amateur pastime to a significant industry. The growth and professionalisation of sport has driven changes in the consumption and production of sport and in the management of sporting organisations at all levels of sport. Managing sport organisations at the start of the 21st century involves the application of techniques and strategies evident in the majority of modern business, government and non-profit organisations.

The **Sport Management Series** provides a superb range of texts for the common subjects in sport business and management courses. It provides essential resources for academics, students and managers, and is international in scope. Supported by excellent case studies, useful study questions, further reading lists, lists of websites, and supplementary online materials such as case study questions and PowerPoint slides, the series represents a consistent, planned and targeted approach which:

- Provides a high-quality, accessible and affordable portfolio of titles which match management development needs through various stages
- Prioritises the publication of texts where there are current gaps in the market, or where current provision is unsatisfactory
- Develops a portfolio of both practical and stimulating texts in all areas of sport management

The **Sport Management Series** is the first of its kind, and as such is recognised as being of consistent high quality and will quickly become the series of first choice for academics, students and managers.

1 Sport marketing introduction

Overview

The principles and tools of sport marketing represent the essential knowledge sport managers require in order to position their sport, association, club, team, player, code or event in the highly competitive sport market. This chapter explains the principles and tools of marketing sport organisations (professional and amateur), sport leagues and codes, players/athletes, sporting equipment and merchandise, and sport events. The purpose of this chapter is to introduce the core philosophy and process of sport marketing. It will introduce some basic marketing concepts, and will outline the Sport Marketing Framework that will be used as the guiding structure for this text.

At the end of this chapter, readers should be able to:

- Explain what the terms marketing and sport marketing mean.
- Describe how sport marketing can be represented by a philosophy, a process, a set of principles, and a suite of tools.
- Identify the two different angles of sport marketing.
- Understand the relationship between the philosophy, processes, principles, and tools of sport marketing.
- Identify the components of the Sport Marketing Framework.

What is sport marketing?

The term 'marketing' tends to be used in a variety of ways. Some think of marketing as the use of advertising, publicity and personal selling techniques to make others aware of a product, or to attract more consumers to buy it. However, marketing is much more comprehensive than this narrow interpretation. Put simply, marketing means to be focused on satisfying the needs of customers or consumers. In turn, this means that sport marketing is focused on meeting the needs of sport customers or consumers, including people involved in playing sport, watching or listening to sport programmes, buying merchandise, collecting memorabilia, buying sporting goods like clothing and shoes, or even surfing a sport-related website to find out the latest about their favourite team, player or event. The terms 'consumer' and 'customer' are used throughout this text. A sport consumer is someone who generally uses sport products or services. A sport customer is someone who pays for the use of a specific product or service. It is legitimate to use the terms interchangeably to refer to those people who use and pay for sport products and services.

> *Chapter Principle 1.1*: Marketing is more than promotion, advertising, personal selling or sales gimmicks.

Satisfying the needs of consumers obviously involves more than just putting together a slick advertisement or offering a temporary discount. For example, marketing involves making decisions about what different groups of consumers may need or want: the most effective way of selling a product or service, the best way of making the product or service available, the idea behind a product or service, the unique features of a product or service, and ultimately, its price. Marketing demands a process where a range of issues are considered in order to maximise the likelihood that a customer is satisfied by the product or service it consumes. These issues can be combined in order to construct a definition of marketing.

Marketing

Marketing is generally described as the process of planning and implementing activities that are designed to meet the needs or desires of customers. Marketing pays attention to the development of a product, its pricing, promotion and distribution. It aims to create an exchange, where the customer gives up something (usually money), for a product or service that is of equal or greater value. Although the term 'product' directly refers to tangible items, it is quite common to use it to represent the entire offering to consumers including services. Thus, it is conventional to speak of the 'sport product' in a global sense as a representative term for all offerings associated with sport, whether in physical form, like sport equipment, or as a service, such as entertainment.

A simpler definition of marketing was provided by Smith and Taylor (2004, p. 5), who wrote 'Marketing is selling goods that don't come back to people who do'. At first this definition seems to only focus on the selling part of marketing. On the other hand, if products 'don't come back', it means that customers' needs have been satisfied and they do not want to return what they purchased in order to secure a refund. This definition implies that marketing leads to satisfied customers who will continue to use the same product in the future. Marketing aims to entice people to try products or services and then keep them as long-term customers.

> *Chapter Principle 1.2*: Marketing aims to create an exchange where the customer gives up something for a product or service.

Sport marketing

Sport marketing is the application of marketing concepts to sport products and services, and the marketing of non-sport products through an association to sport. Sport marketing therefore has two key features. First, it is the application of general marketing practices to sport-related products and services. Second, it is the marketing of other consumer and industrial products or services through sport. Like any form of marketing, sport marketing seeks to fulfil the needs and wants of consumers. It achieves this by providing sport services and sport-related products to consumers. However, sport marketing is unlike conventional marketing in that it also has the ability to encourage the consumption of non-sport products and services by association. It is important to understand that sport marketing means the marketing of sport as well as the use of sport as a tool to market other products and services.

The two angles of sport marketing are central to understanding the full range of ways in which sport is used. The weakness, however, is that they tend to emphasise the selling part of sport marketing. Before any transaction can occur, a lengthy strategic analysis must be performed in order to determine what sport consumers want and what are the best ways of delivering it. As a result, sport marketing should also be seen as the collection of planning and implementation activities associated with the delivery of a sport product or service.

Prior to any sales, a sport product or service must hold a place in the mind of a consumer. In practice, this demands that a consumer is aware of the sport product or service and has responded to it in some way. The process of cultivating such a response is known as *branding*, and when a sport brand has grasped a firm place in consumers' minds, then it is said that it is *positioned*.

The consequence of successful branding and the acquisition of strong market positioning is not merely a single transaction. Rather, sport marketing reflects the establishment of an ongoing relationship between a sport brand and its users.

With the introduction of these three further points, it is possible to devise a simple working definition of sport marketing.

> *Chapter Principle 1.3*: Sport marketing is the process of planning how a sport brand is positioned and how the delivery of its products or services are to be implemented in order to establish a relationship between a sport brand and its consumers.

Two angles of sport marketing

With a working definition of sport marketing specified, it is useful to return to the idea that there are two angles to sport marketing. To repeat, the first is that sport products and services can be marketed directly to the consumer. The second is that other, non-sport products and services can be marketed through the use of sport. In other words, sport marketing involves the marketing *of* sport and marketing *through* sport. For example, the marketing *of* sport products and services directly to sport consumers could include sporting equipment, professional competitions, sport events and local clubs. Other simple examples include team advertising, designing a publicity stunt to promote an athlete, selling season tickets, and developing licensed apparel for sale. In contrast, marketing *through* sport happens when a non-sport product is marketed through an association to sport. Some examples could include a professional athlete endorsing a breakfast cereal, a corporation sponsoring a sport event, or even a beer company arranging to have exclusive rights to provide beer at a sport venue or event.

> *Chapter Principle 1.4*: Sport marketing has two angles: one is the marketing *of* sport products and services, while the other is marketing *through* sport.

Interactive case

Have a look at the Ducati website, http://www.ducati.com, as an example of the marketing *of* sport.

Consider the following questions:

1. How does Ducati market its product *to* sport consumers?
2. What sort of sport consumers do you think would be interested in Ducati products?
3. How does Ducati emphasise that its product is a sport product?

Now have a look at the Shell website, http://www.shell.com, as an example of marketing *through* sports.

Go to 'Shell Motorsport', then select 'Shell and Ducati'.

Consider the following questions:

1. How does Shell market its motorcycle oil products to sport consumers?
2. How does the Shell association with Ducati influence sport consumer perceptions about Shell motorcycle oils?
3. What promotional techniques have Shell used to market their products?

Points to consider.

1. The products offered by Ducati are not limited to bikes. It also sells merchandise, promote Ducati clubs, organise the 'Ducati Week' for motorcycle enthusiasts and provide sport information such as the 'Desmoblog' and Press releases. Some of these may not be designed to make money (the most obvious example is the sport information it provides), but it indirectly encourages consumers to become enthusiastic about Ducati products.
2. Note that the Shell website offers many 'products' to the sport consumer. It also advertises its range of oils and provides 'How To' and bike travel guides, bike tips, downloads and entertaining Ducati videos. These could be persuasive to sport consumers who value technical knowledge about motorcycles, or who are committed fans of the Ducati race team.

Sport marketing as a philosophy, a process, principles and tools

While thinking about what sport marketing encompasses, it is helpful to understand that it is a hierarchical concept. That is, there are levels at which sport marketing can be considered. At the most fundamental level, sport marketing embraces a general *philosophy* or a set of beliefs about how to go about marketing. It is not just marketing managers or the marketing department of a sport organisation that can think in marketing terms. A marketing philosophy is about putting the needs and wants of the customer at the centre of all decisions. It is important to add that the needs of the customer must complement the goals of the enterprise. In business, the goal is to make a profit, but in sport organisations the most important goal is usually to win or attract attention to the sport or organisation. Marketing philosophy is concerned with creating a win-win situation for both the organisation and sport consumers, but it recognises that no one will win if consumers' needs are not met. This sport marketing philosophy is adopted in this text, and is used as

5

a basic assumption throughout. For example, each chapter provides a reminder of the importance of understanding and targeting customers' needs, and working out the best alignment between an organisation's goals, consumers' needs, and the features of a sport product.

> *Chapter Principle 1.5*: The *philosophy* of sport marketing is to satisfy the needs of sport consumers.

At a second level, sport marketing may be considered a *process.* It is a process because it involves a series of activities and steps. For example, sport marketing involves research, analysis, planning, development, implementation and evaluation. These processes are a common property of sport marketing and feature as the structural framework around which this text is written.

> *Chapter Principle 1.6*: The *process* of sport marketing is the series of steps required to find opportunities, devise strategy, plan the tactics, and implement and evaluate a sport marketing plan.

At the third level, sport marketing may be summarised as a set of principles because it adopts numerous ideas and concepts that provide specific guidance to those undertaking sport marketing activities. In each chapter, a set of sport marketing principles are highlighted in order to provide clear guidance as to how the processes of sport marketing can be used in practice.

Finally, at the most operational level, sport marketing principles can be implemented with the aid of tools, which are analytical devices and specific activities used in day-to-day practice.

> *Chapter Principle 1.7*: *Sport marketing* can be described as a philosophy (an attitude towards marketing), a process (a series of activities), a set of principles (general rules and guidelines) and tools (recommended techniques).

To summarise, this text adopts the sport marketing *philosophy* that consumers' needs are met when they match features of a product or service where the ultimate goal is to cultivate a relationship between a sport brand and consumers. The text structures this philosophy around a sequence of sport marketing *processes* which reflect the organisation of the chapters. Within each chapter, sport marketing *principles* are presented to help steer the implementation of sport marketing processes. In addition, *tools* are offered as specific, recommended techniques. The four levels are represented in Figure 1.1.

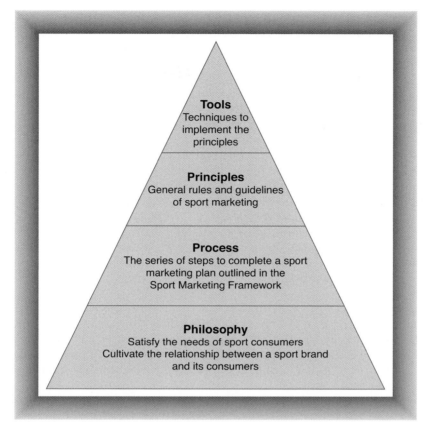

Figure 1.1 The Structure of Sport Marketing.

Chapter Principle 1.8: The *principles* of sport marketing provide the rules and guidelines for the implementation of the Sport Marketing Framework *process*, while the *tools* of sport marketing are specific activities designed to help execute the *principles*.

Structure of the text

The marketing of sport may appear at first to be similar to general marketing. However, sport marketing does have differences to other forms of marketing. For example, the sport product is often highly inconsistent and unpredictable because it is not possible to predict the outcome of a sporting match or control the quality of play. In many other industries, the failure to guarantee the quality of a product would be disastrous. Another significant difference is that few products can evoke the emotional attachment and personal identification that sport commands. To be successful in sport marketing, it is necessary to understand general marketing as well as the unique circumstances of sport.

There are two aspects of sport which are pivotal to understanding its unique circumstances: the sport market and the sport consumer. Chapter 2 introduces the special features of sport with an emphasis on the three sectors associated with sport: the government, the not-for-profit, and the corporate sectors. Chapter 3 introduces the various types of sport consumers including those who utilise sport as a consumer product and those who actively engage in sport. The chapter will also reveal the idiosyncratic motives and behaviours of sport consumers as well as the factors that influence their behaviour.

Once the sport market and the sport consumer are described, it is possible to move onto the process of sport marketing. Chapter 4 provides an overview of the four stages of the sport marketing process: (1) identify sport marketing opportunities; (2) develop a sport marketing strategy; (3) plan the marketing mix; and (4) implement and control the strategy. Figure 1.2 illustrates the Sport Marketing Framework. It is helpful because it offers a structure through which the logical sequence of sport marketing is implemented. A detailed guide to stage one is contained in Chapter 4. Stage two is provided in Chapter 5.

Chapter Principle 1.9: The *Sport Marketing Framework* provides a detailed explanation of the four stages of the sport marketing process: (1) identify sport marketing opportunities; (2) develop sport marketing strategy; (3) plan the marketing mix; and (4) implement and control the strategy.

Chapter 6 explores the first elements of the sport marketing mix. It introduces the key elements of the sport product, and outlines product-related marketing strategies. Chapter 7 specifies the second element in the sport marketing mix. The chapter is structured around a step-by-step pricing approach. Chapter 8 tackles the third dimension of the sport marketing mix. It highlights the basic concepts and issues of sport distribution and pays particular attention to the centrality of the sport venue, and media and broadcasting. Chapter 9 highlights the final component of the marketing mix. The chapter identifies the purpose of promotions, reviews its key elements, and describes promotions planning. Building on the promotion of sport, Chapter 10 presents the process of locating sponsors, the nature of sponsorship associations, the management and leveraging of relationships, and the evaluation process. Chapter 11 augments the sport marketing mix by examining sport services. This chapter introduces the specific aspects of services marketing and the idiosyncrasies of the sport service. It describes the techniques of quality service and customer satisfaction management as well as customer relationship marketing.

The world of sport marketing is changing rapidly, and the way in which the marketing mix and sponsorship are deployed is subject to constant new media platforms, technologies and opportunities. Chapter 12 focuses on the current marketing context relevant to sport. This includes the key media

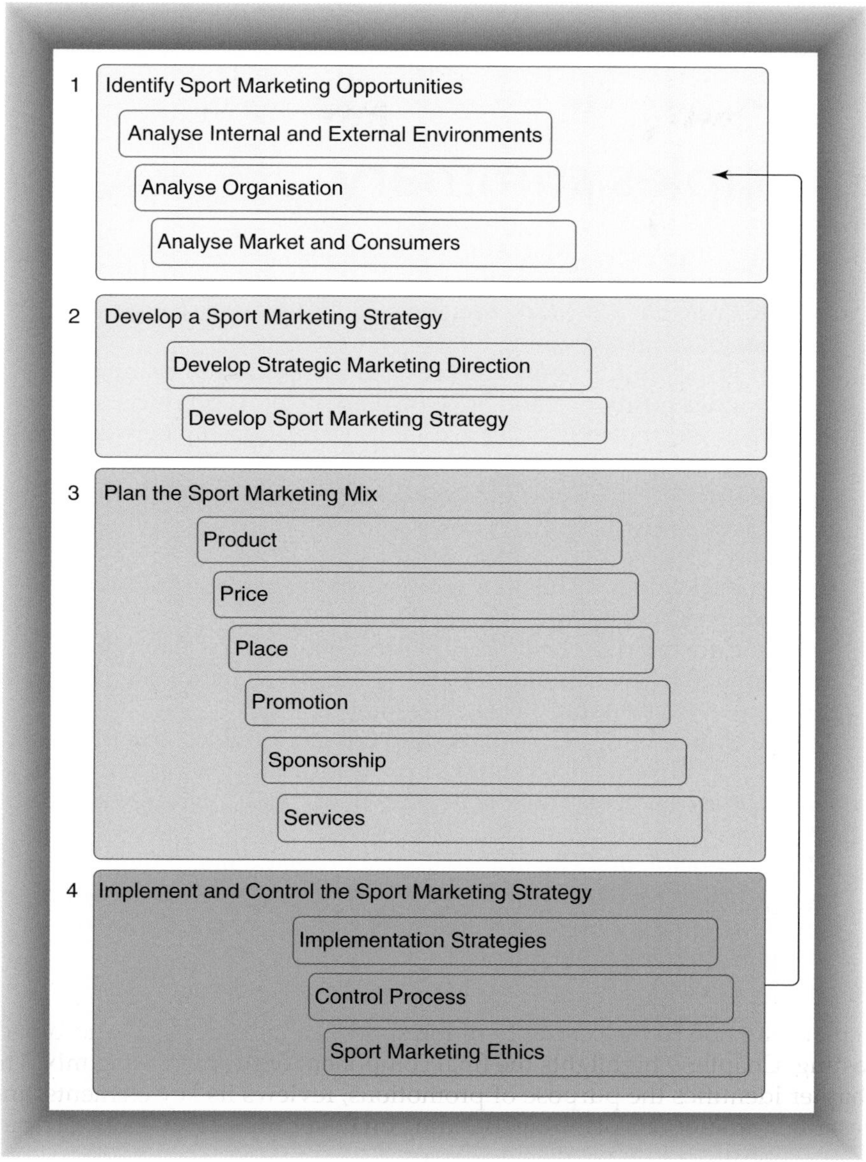

1 Identify Sport Marketing Opportunities

> Analyse Internal and External Environments

> Analyse Organisation

> Analyse Market and Consumers

2 Develop a Sport Marketing Strategy

> Develop Strategic Marketing Direction

> Develop Sport Marketing Strategy

3 Plan the Sport Marketing Mix

> Product

> Price

> Place

> Promotion

> Sponsorship

> Services

4 Implement and Control the Sport Marketing Strategy

> Implementation Strategies

> Control Process

> Sport Marketing Ethics

Figure 1.2 The Sport Marketing Framework.

technologies and their implications for the way in which sport consumers engage in the marketing process.

Chapter 13 explains the final stage of the Sport Marketing Framework. It introduces readers to the activities associated with setting up feedback mechanisms for determining whether the implementation process is successful. Chapter 13 also summarises the key processes and principles which are addressed in the text. It concludes with a discussion of the ethical responsibilities of sport marketers.

Principles summary

- Chapter Principle 1.1: Marketing is more than promotion, advertising, personal selling or sales gimmicks.
- Chapter Principle 1.2: Marketing aims to create an exchange where the customer gives up something for a product or service.
- Chapter Principle 1.3: Sport marketing is the process of planning how a sport brand is positioned and how the delivery of its products or services are to be implemented in order to establish a relationship between a sport brand and its consumers.
- Chapter Principle 1.4: Sport marketing has two angles: one is the marketing of sport products and services, while the other is marketing through sport.
- Chapter Principle 1.5: The philosophy of sport marketing is to satisfy the needs of sport consumers.
- Chapter Principle 1.6: The process of sport marketing is the series of steps required to find opportunities, devise strategy, plan the tactics, and implement and evaluate a sport marketing plan.
- Chapter Principle 1.7: Sport marketing can be described as a philosophy (an attitude towards marketing), a process (a series of activities), a set of principles (general rules and guidelines) and tools (recommended techniques).
- Chapter Principle 1.8: The principles of sport marketing provide the rules and guidelines for the implementation of the Sport Marketing Framework process, while the tools of sport marketing are specific activities designed to help execute the principles.
- Chapter Principle 1.9: The Sport Marketing Framework provides a detailed explanation of the four stages of the sport marketing process: (1) identify sport marketing opportunities; (2) develop sport marketing strategy; (3) plan the marketing mix; and (4) implement and control the strategy.

Review questions

1. What is the basic philosophy of all marketing?
2. How is sport marketing different from general marketing?
3. Explain the difference between marketing *in* sport and marketing *through* sport.
4. What are the steps in the Sport Marketing Framework?
5. Provide a definition of sport marketing in your own words.
6. What do you think is the ultimate goal of sport marketing?

Relevant websites

http://www.ducati.com   (Ducati)

http://www.shell.com   (Shell)

http://www.eose.org   (The European Observatoire of Sport and
Employment)

http://www.sportengland.org   (Sport England)

http://www.ausport.gov.au   (Australian Sports Commission)

Further reading

Hoye, R., Smith, A., Westerbeek, H., Stewart, B. & Nicholson, M. (2006). *Sport Management: Principles and Applications*, Elsevier, Oxford.

Shilbury, D., Deane, J. & Kellett, P. (2006). *Sport Management in Australia: An Organisational Overview* (3rd ed.). Strategic Sport Management, Melbourne.

Summers, J., Gardiner, M., Lamb, C.W., Hair, J.F. & McDaniel, C. (2003). *Essentials of Marketing,* Thomson, Melbourne.

Reference

Smith, P.R. & Taylor, J. (2004). *Marketing Communications: An Integrated Approach* (4th ed.). Kogan Page, London, p. 5.

2 Sport markets

Overview

This chapter provides a summary of the sport market, noting the role of its three industrial sectors: government, not-for-profit and corporate. A review of the size and scope of the sport market and a description of the special features that make sport a unique marketing challenge is included in this chapter.

At the end of this chapter, readers should be able to:

- Describe the size and scope of the sport industry.
- Identify the differences between the three sport sectors and their roles in sport marketing.
- Explain the unique features of sport as a product.
- Describe how the special features of sport impact upon sport marketing.

The sport industry

What is an industry?

To understand what the sport industry is, it is necessary to first discuss what an industry is. The term industry can be defined as a market where similar, or closely related, products and services are offered to consumers. Industries are often categorised according to the types of products and services they offer. The result is that there can be a wide range of organisations involved in an industry, including commercial or corporate entities, non-profit organisations, associations, manufacturers, wholesalers, retailers, government agencies and small businesses. From a sport marketing perspective it is useful to remember that in a single industry the products and services that are produced satisfy similar consumer needs and wants. As a result, the sport industry includes all the suppliers of products and services that satisfy the needs of sport consumers. The important point is that the sport industry is a marketplace where consumers can acquire products and services that are associated with sport in some way.

It is easy to get caught in the trap of thinking narrowly about what the sport industry comprises. For example, on first impressions the sport industry may appear to be little more than sport venues, gymnasiums, clubs and teams, leagues, athletes, sporting apparel and shoes, merchandise, sporting associations, the Olympic Games and government sport departments. While this is a good start, there are many other organisations which are part of the sport industry. Some examples include:

- Government departments of sport and recreation, at state or county and federal or national level.
- The media, including print, television, cable, satellite and the Internet.
- Education, such as universities and private providers, which teach sport management.
- Researchers who study the sport market or consumers, as well as exercise physiology and sport medicine.
- The transport and construction sectors which contribute to the building of venues.
- Corporations and private enterprises which contribute to sport through sponsorship.
- Volunteers who support sport clubs and associations.

One way of thinking about the composition of the sport industry is to imagine it as a series of steps from supplies and raw materials that make up sport products and services, through to their delivery and marketing. Figure 2.1, devised by Westerbeek and Smith (2004), provides an example of a 'value chain' for the sport industry. It is called a value chain because at each step there is the addition of new value to the sport product (see Porter, 1985). This diagram shows that government has a broad impact across all areas of the sport industry. Not only do they provide money to support sport organisations, they also help to create many of the physical facilities and venues in which sport activities take place. In addition, governments create legislation and policies which affect sport in many ways. For example, they set laws which regulate how and when media can cover sport events. Many other types of government legislation can affect the individuals and groups involved in the sport industry, such as company law, taxation, patents and copyright, contract law and income tax law.

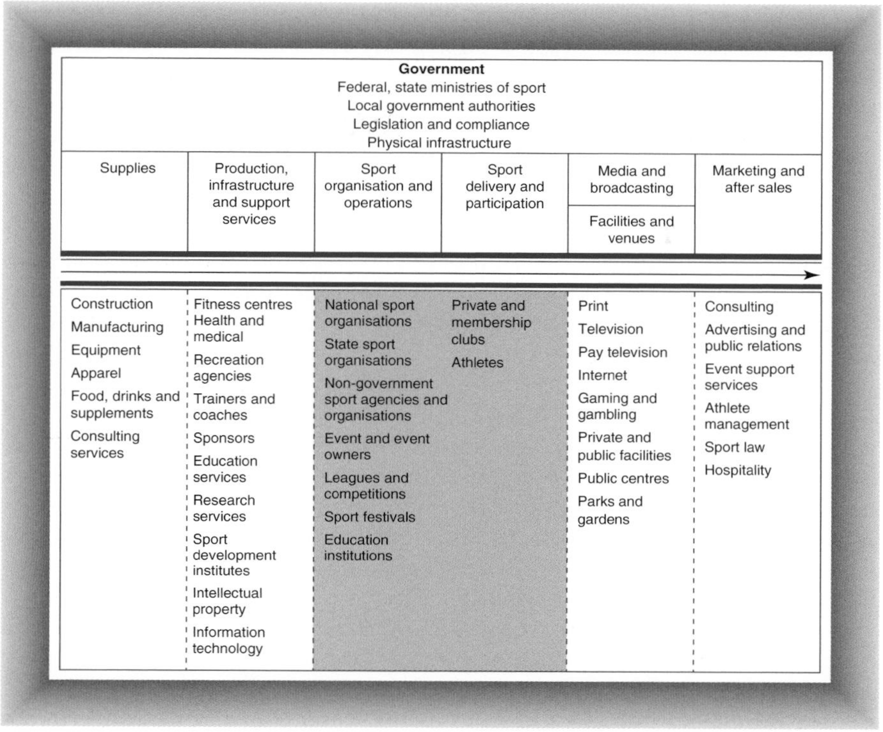

Figure 2.1 Value Chain of the Sport Industry.

The next level down in the diagram shows seven different categories of producers, suppliers, consumers and others who are involved in the sport industry. Underneath each is a list of examples for that category. The shaded area shows the activities and groups that are most commonly associated with the sport industry. These may be seen as the core sport products and services. Figure 2.1 shows that there is a lot more to the sport industry than just the core. For example, to the left of the shaded core are input activities which contribute to the development of the core sport products and services. To the right of the shaded area are activities related to the distribution and marketing of sport products and services.

Three sectors of sport

In looking at the sport industry value chain, it should become clear that three different kinds of industrial activities are involved. First, there are those associated with the government, which are collectively referred to as the public sector, including national, state/county/provincial, regional and local governments, as well as quasi-government institutions and agencies that are involved in the development of sport, determining government sport policy, bolstering competitive performance or in health promotion or

15

drug compliance. The second kind of activity is undertaken by the non-profit or voluntary sector. This group is made up of local clubs, community-based associations, governing organisations and international federations. In the non-profit sector, the focus is on the development of sport through organised competition and participation, with a heavy emphasis on the regulation and management of sport. The final set of activities is the purview of the professional or corporate sport sector. This group is commercially focused, comprising professional clubs, leagues and major events. In addition, this group includes a vast number of corporations which have a financial interest in sport, such as equipment and apparel manufacturers, sport retailers, broadcasting companies, telecommunications providers and sponsors. In fact, any organisation whose primary purpose is to make a profit from an association with sport may be placed in this category.

As Figure 2.1 shows, the three sectors mix and mingle, their activities intersecting regularly. In fact, sport could not be produced without the collusion of all three sectors. To begin with, the government or public sector provides the context in which sport is undertaken. Often this includes financial support and the provision and maintenance of sport venues and facilities for non-profit sector activities. Equally, non-profit sport is expected to deliver social and community benefits. The regulatory environment created by government also affects corporate sport because professional leagues generally require the use of public venues. Of course, corporate sport only exists because the playing, coaching and administrative talent is cultivated by non-profit sport clubs, leagues and associations. Reciprocally, parts of the corporate sector seek marketing benefits through an association with non-profit sport by providing much needed funding through sponsorships. In general, it is important to remember that the activities of the three sectors bleed into each other. For example, some high-profile non-profit sport organisations are professionally managed and behave as corporate entities. There is also some ambiguity about where large non-government, non-corporate entities such as the International Olympic Committee fit in. An excellent overview of these three sectors is provided in Hoye et al. (2006). The next sections focus on the marketing implications that are connected with each of the three sectors and their primary activities.

Government sport sector

In general, governments get involved in sport because of its potential for social, economic and political benefits. For example, sport can provide health benefits for participants as well as social cohesion. It can also stimulate economic activity and bolster civic pride. For some governments, sport is advantageous because it can cultivate national identity and solidarity, which tends to be helpful for re-election and general national spirit. Although the policy approach taken by a government towards sport can change radically depending on its ideological orientation, all governments influence sport in at least four ways.

First, governments at various levels provide funding and facilities for sport. This includes funding for national sport organisations and Olympic campaigns, and the construction and maintenance of major and local sport, recreation and leisure facilities. Second, governments can be directly involved in the development of sport via training institutes and elite testing facilities. Third, governments can deliver sport-, health- or physical activity-related programs, or just promote lifestyle campaigns. Finally, governments can take responsibility for aspects of sport compliance, like anti-doping, as well as the composition of the general regulatory environment. A few further comments on this last element are warranted.

The term regulatory environment refers to the nature of competition within an industry. Unlike more traditional industries, the sport industry is often allowed by government to pursue anti-competitive practices, including significant restrictions on the rights of players. This occurs because many governments accept that sport performs poorly under normal market conditions. As a result, although league regulation may be anti-competitive, it is generally not considered unreasonable, or against the public interest. While member teams are highly competitive and concerned with on-field dominance, they also understand that their long-term viability depends on a high-quality and well-balanced competition where teams are of comparable strength and ability.

Governments regularly employ marketing principles to support their sport objectives. Typically, governments do not get directly involved in marketing sport, but often spend considerable money on promoting the benefits of sport or its locations. For example, governments use marketing to attract large sport events to specific cities. They also employ marketing to promote the social and health benefits of sport participation or an active lifestyle.

Non-profit sport sector

In the Western world, it is generally accepted that all sport products and services cannot be provided by the government. The result has been the emergence of non-profit sport organisations, which make up the gaps in between profit-oriented business and government. Non-profit sport organisations are therefore concerned with the public good rather than making money. However, since they are not administered by the government, non-profit sport organisations must find resources and expertise for themselves, and must comply with government regulations about their legal status and conduct. As a rule, non-profit sport organisations are highly specialised in that they tend to evolve to fit a particular community sporting need. They are also administered mainly by volunteers. Non-profit sport organisations are the backbone of sport.

Non-profit sport organisations develop communities, social networks and local groups through the provision of specialised sport products and services. Typically, these services revolve around the organisation of sport competitions and the subsequent development and management of players, coaches, administrators, along with the code itself. However, there are also professional service organisations, lobby groups, event organisers and governing bodies. Sport and recreation organisations can be classified into three different kinds of non-profit groups. The first includes amateur sport, training, fitness and sport facilities, and sport competitions and events. The second includes recreation and social clubs, such as country clubs and leisure clubs. The third includes service clubs which use sport as a vehicle for social development. Of these three groups, the first is the largest as it incorporates a vast number of sport clubs and their associations. In some countries, and particularly in the United States, school and college sport is the most prevalent form of non-profit sport.

Non-profit sport organisations face numerous marketing challenges. To begin with, they are often cash-poor, which means that they cannot pursue expensive advertising or other major promotional activities. Another challenge is that they do not necessarily have access to sport marketing expertise as they heavily rely on the goodwill and service of volunteer staff. A final problem is that many non-profit sport organisations have rich but cumbersome amateur traditions, which do not lend themselves to attractive marketing. Non-profit sport organisations consequently focus their marketing initiatives on low-cost activities that emphasise the benefits of participating in sport. Some have recognised the importance of differentiating their products and services from others, and work hard to create a relationship between their brand and sport consumers. In addition, some non-profit sport organisations are taking advantage of new technology and new media platforms to inexpensively position themselves distinctively in a cluttered sport marketplace.

Corporate sport sector

The corporate or professional sport sector is characterised by the commercial imperative; the desire to make a profit from sport. As Figure 2.1 demonstrates, there are numerous places in which commercial enterprises can provide value-adding products or services associated with sport that can generate money. At the hub of corporate sport are professional clubs and teams that compete in large national or international leagues, or athletes and teams that participate in large events. Although these organisations and athletes may not be profit-seeking, they nevertheless provide the core content that other profit-based businesses wish to associate with.

Professional sport teams produce a product that is sold to four groups: first, fans who support leagues by attending games, following games on television and other media and purchasing league- and team-related merchandise; second, television and other media or broadcasting companies, which purchase the right to show games as a programming option; third, communities which build facilities and support local clubs; and fourth, corporations which support leagues and clubs by increasing gate monies, purchasing teams outright or providing revenues through sponsorships or other associations.

Corporate sport also includes the manufacturers of sport-related products and services like stadium builders, equipment manufacturers, sport apparel fashion labels, advertisers, athlete and player managers, sport nutrition and supplement developers, sport physicians and physiotherapists, event and sport tourism promoters, hospitality services, sponsors and team franchise owners.

The core of corporate sport is branding, given the importance of establishing lasting relationships with sport fans and consumers. For example, sport equipment and apparel manufacturers need to convince consumers that using their brand has benefits over using a competitor's brand. Much of the branding emphasis of corporate sport revolves around the spectacle and entertainment value of the sport experience.

The size of the sport industry

The size of the sport industry can be measured in a number of ways. For example, one way is to count how much money is spent on sport, such as sporting goods, the building of venues and organised sporting activities. Another approach is to determine how much money government and private organisations like corporations contribute to sport, such as grants and sponsorships. Another approach still would be to examine how much consumers spend on sport-related products and services per year, how many people participate in sport, how many people are employed in the sport industry and even how many volunteers provide their services. However, it is extremely difficult (if not impossible) to calculate accurate statistics on these aspects of sport. The sport industry is just too large, and it is also so fragmented that it is not practical to locate and study them all. It is possible, however, to consider estimates, or approximate calculations. These provide a hint of how large and significant the sport industry is both from an economic and social viewpoint.

In Australia, it was estimated that during 2003–2004 Australians households spent an average of AUS$887 per week on sport and physical recreation goods and services (National Centre for Culture and Recreation Statistics, 2004). In Europe it has been suggested that in each European Union member state, sport represents between 1.6 per cent and 2.5 per cent of each country's gross domestic product, or the sum of what they produce in a year (Vocasport, 2004). The entire US sport market has been estimated at $390 billion in 2006 (Plunkett Research Limited, 2007), including $5.6 billion in National Football League revenue and $61 billion in sales of sporting apparel and shoes. The golf market in the United States in 2002 was estimated to be worth $62.2 billion (SRI International, 2002), with 502.4 million rounds of golf played per year (National Golf Foundation, 2003).

In terms of sport participation in England, it has been estimated that 21 per cent of the adult population (around 8.5 million people) take part in sport at least three days per week (Sport England, 2006). It is also estimated that 4.7 per cent of the adult population (around 1.9 million people) give at least one hour of their time a week to volunteering in sport. In Australia, it was estimated that 9.1 million adults participated in physical activities for recreation, exercise or sport (The Australian Bureau of Statistics, 2006). The Australian Bureau of Statistics also found that seven million people (49.2 per cent of the adult population) attended at least one sport event during the same year, and at the end of June 2001 there were approximately 90,000 people working for organisations in the sport industry (excluding government, manufacturing and sales).

Research in Europe supported by the European Commission estimated that nearly one million employees work in sport as their main professional activity (Vocasport, 2004). The Vocasport project also suggested that there are almost 10 million volunteers in sport-related organisations in the European Union.

Interactive case

Europe

Download a copy of the Vocasport 2004 report from the website of EOSE (the European Observatoire of Sport and Employment). Log on to http://www.eose.org and follow the links. Read pages 38–43 of the document which talk about the economic impact of sport in Europe, and the participation rates.

England

Log on to the Sport England website, and look at the results of their recent survey into sport participation in England. Log on to http://www.sportengland.org and follow these links: Get Results→Research→Active People Survey.

Australia

Go to the Australian Sports Commission website, and look at the report *Household Expenditure Survey on Sports and Physical Recreation, Australia 2003–2004*. Log on to http://www.ausport.gov.au and follow these links: Information and Research→Topics in Sport→Statistics.

The special features of the competitive sport product

Sport has an extraordinary ability to command attention, interest, loyalty and, even abhorrence. Some people feel that sport is almost sacred, that it is character-building and its purpose is far loftier than business and profit. For these people sport is special, and that it is not like any other activity. Some believe that when sport becomes a business it loses its most important qualities like passion, history and the centrality of the fan. Sport managers who take this view tend to believe that managing sport is a difficult task, and that standard business and marketing practices do not translate easily. This is because the emotions inherent in sport forces managers to avoid decisions that could compromise long-standing traditions, cause fan dissatisfaction or reduce volunteer participation. People who believe sport is unique sometimes argue that the commercialisation and professionalisation of sport has damaged its community and participation foundations.

On the other hand, to some, sport is just another business. To these people, sport is a form of leisure or entertainment experience that can help organisations to make money by keeping customers happy. From this viewpoint, good business practices are needed to help keep sport organisations alive; any benefits that sport might confer (e.g. health benefits, character-building opportunities, belonging) will be lost forever if an organisation cannot remain profitable by operating in a business-like manner. Those who believe sport is just another business take the view that standard management practices are appropriate. Instead of seeing sport as a unique enterprise, they believe that sport is a client-based service business, operating within a specific, but not necessarily unique business marketplace. They often take a corporate view of volunteers and traditions. For example, volunteers are a 'human resource' of an organisation who must be inducted, rewarded, trained and counselled like any other member of staff.

Both of these perspectives are true. Sport is a special kind of product, but it still operates in a business context that demands professionalism and accountability. Most sport marketers hold the view that sport organisations, whatever their size or scope, can no longer be managed as fun and games, or separated from the wider commercial world. Even non-profit clubs, for example, must perform financially if they want to survive in the highly competitive world of sport and alternative entertainment products. Sport is not so unique that it cannot be put in a commercial framework. But it is not just another form of commercial entertainment either. Sport is business, but it is a special form of business. The key is to understand the special features of sport and their relevance to meeting the needs of sport consumers.

In the next section, the special features of sport are described with an emphasis on those factors that make sport appealing to consumers, but would normally be considered unattractive in most products. These features are important for sport marketers to understand because of the need to balance the potential to dissatisfy sport consumers by overemphasising marketing and commercial gain, against the attraction of keeping the unique characteristics of sport alive for them.

Chapter Principle 2.1: Sport is a special form of business. A standard marketing approach does not always work in sport, so sport marketers must also understand the special features of the sport market.

Emotion and passion

Sport can stimulate an emotional response in its consumers of the kind rarely elicited by other products. Imagine bank customers buying memorabilia to show allegiance with their bank, or consumers identifying so strongly with their car insurance company that they get a tattoo with its logo. We know that some sport followers are so passionate about players, teams and the sport itself that their interest borders on obsession. This addiction provides the emotional glue that binds fans to teams, and maintains loyalty even in the face of on-field failure.

While most managers can only dream of having customers that are as passionate about their products as sport fans, the emotion stimulated by sport can also have a negative impact. Sport's emotional intensity can mean that organisations have strong attachments to the past through nostalgia and club tradition. As a result, they may ignore efficiency, productivity and the need to respond quickly to changing market conditions. For example, a proposal to change club colours in order to project a more attractive image may be defeated because it breaks a link with tradition. Similarly, a coach or manager can be appointed on the basis of his/her previous loyalty to the club rather than because of a capacity to manage players better than the other applicants.

> *Chapter Principle 2.2*: Sport can elicit an emotional response in its consumers that is rarely found in other businesses. It can stimulate immense loyalty, but also strong attachments to nostalgia and club tradition.

On-field versus off-field success

One of the most significant differences between not-for-profit sport organisations (at least those that participate in competitive sport) and business is the way in which they measure performance. Commercial businesses may have many goals, but their main purpose is to maximise profits. For example, British Petroleum and Shell are fierce retail competitors, but in the same year they could both produce a profit, and claim it a success. However, a large annual profit might not seem like a success to a sport club if they finished the season at the bottom of the ladder. Sport club members and fans judge performance on the basis of trophies, championships, premierships, pennants, cups and rankings. It is important to note that on-field and off-field successes do not always go together. A sport club may bankrupt itself by paying high salaries for players and coaches in an effort to secure a championship. On the other hand, they may succeed financially but not perform on the field of play.

Competitive sport clubs and organisations have to manage competing demands. On the one hand, they need to maximise profit in order to invest in their competitive activities. On the other hand, they need to perform on the field of play no matter what the cost. However, as the sport and leisure industry becomes increasingly competitive, and more alternative entertainment options are available to sport consumers, sport organisations become increasingly pressured to focus on profits and cash flow. Marketing is one avenue to help support revenue without compromising an emphasis on sport performance.

> *Chapter Principle 2.3*: Sport organisations measure their success both on and off the field of play. On-field success refers to achievement within sport competition. Off-field success refers to financial stability and profitability.

A level playing field

In most business settings it is desirable to put competitors out of business. Naturally, fewer competitors mean more available customers. However, this is not always the case in sport. In fact, sport organisations that compete in leagues actually rely on the health of their competitors for their own success. For example, fans are often more attracted to a game where there is a close contest, and the winner is unknown in advance. Dominating a league or competition can be self-defeating, because the interest of fans can fade.

When it is difficult to predict who will win a match, sport leagues attract higher attendances and viewers. Ironically, in order to remain successful, leagues and competitions need as many of their clubs to be competitive as possible. When the outcome of a match is highly predictable, it will not attract large crowd numbers and eventually it will reduce ticket, media and sponsorship revenue. It is important for sport that there is a healthy, competitive balance between teams. This leads to uncertainty about who will win a contest, and encourages fans to watch.

Chapter Principle 2.4: Sport organisations that compete in leagues and competitions rely on the health of their competitors for their own success. Sport consumers are more attracted to attend games where there is a balanced competition.

Interactive case

Read the full report *'Competitive Balance in Football: Trends and Effects'* in the *English Premier League* by Professor Jonathan Michie and Professor Christine Oughton, available at:

http://www.football-research.org/papers/competitivebalance-paper.htm

Collaboration and cartels

Teams and clubs depend on the continued on-field and off-field success of their opponents. If a league is divided into two groups, one group of wealthy and high performing teams and another group of poor and low performing teams, this will ultimately damage all the clubs involved and the competition in general. In practice, clubs must cooperate with their rivals in order to deliver what their consumers want. Sport organisations need their opposition to remain successful, and may cooperate to share revenues and trade player talent to maintain competitive balance. In most industries, businesses would not be allowed to cooperate in this way; it is considered anti-competitive, or *cartel* behaviour, and there are often laws that prohibit it. But in sport, cartel arrangements are common. For example, clubs may share revenue, prevent other clubs from entering the market, collectively fix prices and generally limit the amount of competition.

Some sport codes and leagues have pursued a balance in their competition, and have implemented policies to encourage it. Sport regulators commonly believe that a balanced competition will produce exciting and close results, which will increase the level of public interest in the sport and generate larger attendances and broadcast rights fees. For example, salary caps for players, rules about sharing revenues and regulations regarding how players are to be drafted to teams are all designed to maintain a competitive balance between teams.

The idea of regulating sport leagues in order to keep a fair and balanced competition is a common one in sport. To achieve this, regulators often adopt three key structural principles. First, they establish an independent decision-making body to regulate the member teams or organisations, like the Federation International de l'Automobile (FIA) for motor sport, and the English Football Association for football. This decision-making body makes rules that address how players or teams are recruited and allocated, the number of teams allowed in the competition, where the teams are located, the length of the playing season, the design of the fixtures, and admission charges. Such rules can help to ensure that no one team monopolises the best players, and that each team has a reasonable chance of winning. Other regulations set by the central body may even involve changing the rules of the game itself to make the sport more attractive to new markets or different forms of distribution (such as free-to-air or pay television). For example, the Atlanta Organising Committee for the Olympic Games in 1996 infamously decided to schedule the marathon in the hottest part of the day in order to maximise prime-time television viewing. The regulating body is usually able to enforce disciplinary action upon those who breach the regulations.

Second, sport regulators impose rules that are designed to minimise costs and maximise profits. For example, they enforce policies to restrict the ability of teams to bid for players, set limits on player salaries and determine the distribution of shared revenues like broadcasting rights. In principle, policies are designed to ensure that teams cannot only acquire their fair share of quality staff, coaches and players, but can also retain them.

Third, sport regulators aim to increase revenue through marketing efforts. They may try to expand the consumer base for their sporting product, improve the overall attractiveness of the product or generally try to improve the image of the league in the community. The market, for example, could be expanded by admitting new teams to the league, extending the playing season, or playing games at different times of the week. Regulators may also spend money on improving the quality of the game through programs to develop player skills, or by upgrading venues to make them more fan-friendly, or safer for athletes. Governing sport bodies also use their market power as sole owners of the sport competition (or monopolists) to maximise broadcast and sponsorship rights fees by negotiating as a single entity rather than through individual teams.

> *Chapter Principle 2.5*: Sport leagues and competitions implement policies to encourage competitive balance. Policies often include salary caps for players, rules about sharing revenues and regulations regarding how players are to be shared between teams.

Variable quality

Commercial businesses aim for predictability and certainty, especially when it comes to product quality. But predictability and certainty are not always valued in the sporting world. The sport experience is better when it is unpredictable, and sport organisations actually depend on that unpredictability in order to be attractive. When the results of games cannot be predicted, attendances at sporting contests are likely to be higher, as are the profits of leagues. However, the lack of predictability also leads to significant variability in the quality of sporting performances. Many factors can contribute to the variability of the sport product, including the weather, player injuries, the venue, the quality of the opponents, the closeness of the scores and even the size of the crowd. A cricket match can be exhilarating, boring or even frustrating, but fans still have to pay the same price. Sport marketers may attempt to overcome this by 'improving' the product in systematic ways, such as including a star player, offering premium seating or providing other forms of entertainment and attractive facilities. The uncertain nature of sport contests is just one element of a total experience, although it is an important element for financial success.

Chapter Principle 2.6: Unpredictability can be advantageous in the competitive sport product because it makes sport more attractive.

Product and brand loyalty

Loyalty to sport products and brands is strong due to the emotional attachments that sport consumers develop for their favourite teams, events, players and equipment. A good test of product loyalty is whether consumers are prepared to keep purchasing the product, even when the price of competing products falls. Fans invest an enormous amount of time and energy in their favourite sport products, and this can create a lifetime bond. In fact, sport fans often see their team as an extension of themselves; it becomes part of their self-identity.

When sport consumers passionately support a particular kind of sport, a specific competition or a specific team (or brand), there is low cross elasticity of demand. This is an economic term that means it is difficult to substitute (or replace) one sport product for another. Most sport competitions have an inelastic demand and a high degree of product loyalty. Even if fans are unhappy about the result of a game, the winning margin or the standard of refereeing, it is unlikely that they would change their sporting preferences. If, for instance, a supporter's football team is playing interstate and the match is not televised, it is unlikely that he/she would go to a hockey or bocce game instead, regardless of whether the venue was attractive and the ticket was free. The situation is quite different for most other products. If a consumer bought a computer and discovered that he/she was not satisfied with its quality, he/she would be likely to change brands or retail outlets next time. In sport, it is not so easy to substitute products.

It might seem that the low degree of product substitution in sport could only be an advantage to sport organisations. However, there are drawbacks. For example, it can be difficult for a new sport, team or brand to enter the marketplace and wrestle fans away from their existing loyalties. Another obstacle is that sport consumers are unlikely to increase their sport watching as a result of reduced ticket prices, or increased personal income levels. This means that marketing efforts need to be innovative about how to attract and convert fans as some conventional marketing tactics are ineffective.

> *Chapter Principle 2.7*: In competitive sport there is a low cross elasticity of demand where it is difficult to substitute (or replace) one sport league, team, brand or competition for another.

Identification

Some sport consumers identify so strongly with their sporting heroes that they seek to emulate them. Supporters may wear the same club 'uniforms', colours and sport clothing brands as their heroes. Many businesses such as sport equipment and clothing manufacturers have recognised the power of sporting identification, and regularly market their products through successful athletes. Of course, sport identification is the driving power behind sport sponsorship. By seeking an association with sport, sponsors try to claim some of the loyalty that fans possess for sports, teams and players. The issue of fan identification is discussed further in Chapter 3.

> *Chapter Principle 2.8*: Product loyalty is strong due to the emotional attachments that sport consumers develop to sport products and brands.

Blind optimism

Despite their allegiance to tradition and history there are some situations where sport consumers and marketers have a high tolerance for change, particularly when they involve personnel (such as players and coaches) and competitive success. For example, even when a star player moves from one club to another, his/her supporters are likely to remain loyal to the original club. For example, even though David Beckham has moved from Manchester United to Real Madrid to Los Angeles Galaxy, the majority of supporters from each club have remained loyal. However, this is not to suggest that there are no 'true' Beckham supporters, but their loyalty was never to any of the clubs that he played for. Usually, the emotional bond that joins fans to their clubs means that they will put up with countless changes to its personnel. Sport organisations rarely pass up the opportunity to trade players and remove coaching and support staff where it might lead to more competitive performance.

> *Chapter Principle 2.9*: Sport consumers identify with teams, clubs, brands and athletes, and see them as extensions of themselves.

Fixed supply schedules

A supply schedule refers to the ability of a business to change their production rates to meet the demand of consumers. Some businesses are able to increase their production level quickly in order to meet increased demand. However, sporting clubs have a fixed, or inflexible (inelastic) production capacity. They have what is known as a *fixed supply schedule*. It is worth noting that this is not the case for sales of clothing, equipment, memberships and memorabilia. But clubs and teams can only play a certain number of times during their season. If fans and members are unable to get into a venue, that revenue is lost forever. Although sport clubs and leagues may have a fixed supply schedule, it is possible to increase the number of consumers who watch. For example, the supply of a sport product can be increased by providing more seats, changing the venue, extending the playing season or even through new television, radio or Internet distribution.

Chapter Principle 2.10: The competitive sport product is restricted by a fixed supply schedule making it difficult to change production rates in order to meet the demand of customers, but can be overcome through alternative distribution channels.

This chapter observed that sport requires professional management, but with an appreciation of the special features of the sport market. The financial and business sides of the sport product need to be balanced with an understanding of its emotional power. Sport is a business, but a special kind of business. It is important for sport marketers to understand the unique features of the sport market because they have an influence on the development of a marketing program.

Case Study—The Sport Industry Working Together

by Sharyn McDonald

The sport industry includes an enormous web of teams from a vast array of sports globally: 'Sport takes place in a wide variety of settings—from mountains and oceans to state of the art stadiums and arena. Whether it is a local club or a professional team, sport is enjoyed regardless of national borders or social divides' (Global Sports Alliance, 2006a). With diverse interests emerging from such a wide range of sports and countries, and across all three sectors of sport, one group thought it advantageous to create a global voice to secure a healthy sport environment for future generations.

NPO Global Sports Alliance aims to meet this challenge and has recruited support from sport enthusiasts, consumers and participants from 23 countries around the world in order to participate in the Ecoflag Movement. In addition, there are several important partners working with the Global Sports Alliance in order to promote their initiatives, including the United

Nations Environment Programme (UNEP) and the International Olympic Committee. There are three main projects devised by the Global Sports Alliance. The first is the Ecoflag Project, which involves a flag flown at sport events ranging from school sports days to world championships as a symbolic environmental message. The second is the Sports-Eco.Net Project, which promotes the 'reduction, reuse and recycling' of sport equipment. The third is the Global Forum for Sports and Environment Project (G-ForSE), which is designed as a site for dialogue about the ways in which sport can be a vehicle for environmental awareness and sustainability.

G-ForSE holds a large database on global environmental initiatives in sport and seeks to provide a platform for the industry 'to determine their roles in increasing environmental action and awareness in sports' (Global Sports Alliance, 2006a). G-ForSE organises events such as Global Forums, 'Dream Matches' and 'Dream Camps'. The G-ForSE Global Forum 'is held every two years and brings together the representatives of sports federations, sports facilities, professional athletes and the sporting goods industry to assess progress and develop new channels for increasing environmental action and awareness through sport' (Global Sports Alliance, 2006b). One such initiative developed jointly by Global Sports Alliance and UNEP was a soccer match held between a Japanese domestic team and the Brazilian national team. This match was to celebrate the establishment of Global Sports Alliance Brazil and all the proceeds of this match went towards 'Nature and Sports Camps'.

Nature and Sports Camps otherwise called Dream Camps provide an opportunity to improve environmental awareness in children through sport. The first successful camp was trialed in Nairobi, Kenya. Approximately 100 children took part in soccer and tennis activities, and the children received recycled tennis rackets from Global Sports Alliance. In addition to the sport activities, the camp included participation in tree planting, recycling and clean-ups. Organisers see the benefits of utilising sport in raising environmental awareness and hope this helps to shape a new sports culture. The Global Sports Alliance is a positive arena for members of the sport industry, regardless of their role and sector, to unite in a common and important cause.

For further information see:
Ecoflag 'What is the Ecoflag?'
http://www.ecoflag.com/what/index_e.html

G-ForSE 'Dream Match G-ForSE Events'
http://www.g-forse.com/event/DreamMatch.html

G-ForSE 'Dream Camps G-ForSE Events'
http://www.g-forse.com/event/DreamCamps.html

Global Sports Alliance (2006a) 'GSA Projects'
http://www.gsa.or.jp/English/GSA/Actions.html

Global Sports Alliance (2006b) 'G-ForSE'
http://www.gsa.or.jp/English/G-ForSE/G-FroSE.html

Principles summary

- Chapter Principle 2.1: Sport is a special form of business. A standard marketing approach does not always work in sport, so sport marketers must also understand the special features of the sport market.
- Chapter Principle 2.2: Sport can elicit an emotional response in its consumers that is rarely found in other businesses. It can stimulate immense loyalty, but also strong attachments to nostalgia and club tradition.
- Chapter Principle 2.3: Sport organisations measure their success both on and off the field of play. On-field success refers to achievement within sport competition. Off-field success refers to financial stability and profitability.
- Chapter Principle 2.4: Sport organisations that compete in leagues and competitions rely on the health of their competitors for their own success. Sport consumers are more attracted to attend games where there is a balanced competition.
- Chapter Principle 2.5: Sport leagues and competitions implement policies to encourage competitive balance. Policies often include salary caps for players, rules about sharing revenues and regulations regarding how players are to be shared between teams.
- Chapter Principle 2.6: Unpredictability can be advantageous in the competitive sport product because it makes sport more attractive.
- Chapter Principle 2.7: In competitive sport there is a low cross elasticity of demand where it is difficult to substitute (or replace) one sport league, team, brand or competition for another.
- Chapter Principle 2.8: Product loyalty is strong due to the emotional attachments that sport consumers develop to sport products and brands.
- Chapter Principle 2.9: Sport consumers identify with teams, clubs, brands and athletes and see them as extensions of themselves.
- Chapter Principle 2.10: The competitive sport product is restricted by a fixed supply schedule making it difficult to change production rates in order to meet the demand of customers, but can be overcome through alternative distribution channels.

Review questions

1. What does it mean to say that sport is a special form of business?
2. In what ways can sport products be differentiated from other products?
3. Why is it important for sport competitions to have competitive balance?
4. What are some of the ways in which sport organisers can encourage competitive balance?
5. Why are some sport products unpredictable?
6. Explain why corporate sponsors want to be associated with sport.

7. What does it mean to say that sport has a low cross elasticity of demand where it is difficult to substitute (or replace) one sport league, team, brand or competition for another?

8. What are some of the ways in which sport organisations can get around the fixed supply schedules associated with sport competitions?

Relevant websites

http://www.thefanatics.com (the Fanatics website)

http://www.fansvoice.com (The Fans Voice website)

http://football.guardian.co.uk (*Guardian Unlimited*, online newspaper)

http://www.timesonline.co.uk (*Times Online*, online newspaper)

http://www.football-research.org (Football Governance Research Centre)

http://www.msnbc.msn.com (MSN and NBC online news page)

http://www.youtube.com (YouTube consumer media company watching and sharing original videos)

http://www.latimes.com (*Los Angeles Times*)

http://en.wikipedia.org (*Wikipedia* online encyclopedia)

Further reading

Boyle, R. & Haynes, R. (2000). *Power Play: Sport, the Media and Popular Culture*, Longman, London.

Downard, P. & Dawson, A. (2000). *The Economics of Professional Team Sports*, Routledge, London.

Shilbury, D., Deane, J. & Kellett, P. (2006). *Sport Management in Australia: An Organisational Overview* (3rd ed.). Strategic Sport Management, Melbourne.

References

Hoye, R., Smith, A., Westerbeek, H., Stewart, B. & Nicholson, M. (2006). *Sport Management: Principles and Applications*, Elsevier, UK.

National Centre for Culture and Recreation Statistics (2004). *Household Expenditure Survey on Sports and Physical Recreation, Australia 2003–2004*, Australian Bureau of Statistics, Canberra.

National Golf Foundation (2003). *Rounds Played in the United States* (2003 ed.). National Golf Foundation, Florida.

Plunkett Research Limited (2007). *Sports Industry Overview.* Available at: http://www.plunkettresearch.com/Sports/SportsStatistics/tabid/273/Default.aspx (accessed 10th January 2007).

Porter, M. (1985). *Competitive Advantage: Creating and Sustaining Superior Performance*, The Free Press, New York.

Sport England (2006). *Active People Survey: Headline Results.* Available at: http://www.sportengland.org/index/get_resources/research/active_people/active_people_survey_headline_results.htm (accessed 10th January 2006).

SRI International (2002). *The Golf Economy Report: Golf 20/20 Vision for the Future*, SRI International, California.

The Australian Bureau of Statistics (2006). *Sport and Recreation: A Statistical Overview, Australia, 2006* (1st ed.). (Cat. no. 4156.0), ABS, Canberra.

Vocasport, (2004). Vocasport 2004: *Vocational Education and Training in the Field of Sport in the European Union: Situation, Trends and Outlook.* Available at: http://www.eose.org/sect/proj/ProjCD.php?uid=4 (accessed 10th January 2007).

Westerbeek, H. & Smith, A. (2004). *Sport and Leisure Exports: Industry Definition and Statistical Modelling.* Department of Communication, Information Technology and the Arts, Canberra.

3 Sport consumers

Overview

Sport consumers are motivated by a range of factors and benefits to attend games, buy merchandise and watch sport on television. This chapter explains these different motivations with the intention of revealing how to best communicate with consumers through marketing. In addition to the internal motivations of sport consumers, this chapter also addresses the external factors that can influence their buying behaviours. External factors are important in understanding how circumstances can sway sport consumers' decisions to use particular sport products.

At the end of this chapter, readers should be able to:

- Identify the different motives consumers have for buying sport products and services.
- Explain the effects of each motive on sport consumption.
- Highlight the external factors that can influence the behaviour of sport consumers.
- Specify how the external factors can be influenced by sport marketers to enhance product usage.

Who is a sport consumer?

Chapter 2 observed that sport consumers can come in many forms including spectators, participants, serious fans and business sponsors. There is no simple formula to describe how and why sport consumers behave as they do. For example, some sport fans may use teams and players to help them construct a sense of self, but others may only follow sport to fill in their spare time with a pleasurable form of entertainment. Sport consumers can be remarkably loyal, but they can also be fickle and critical. The best starting point is to identify the different kinds of sport consumers, and in doing so, highlight which have motives in need of further exploration.

Kinds of sport consumers

There are numerous valid ways of defining sport consumers, most of which revolve around identifying different kinds of sport products or services. However, the first point to make is that there is a difference between sport consumers and sport stakeholders. A consumer is an individual or group who use a sport or sport-related product or service in exchange for a direct (like cash to buy a ticket to a game) or indirect (like purchasing a television in which sport is one form of entertainment) payment. A stakeholder is an individual or group who have an interest or agenda in a sport product or service. For example, the government and corporate sponsors are stakeholders in that they have an interest in sport products and services, but they are not consumers. Sport consumers are the end users. Here, sport consumers are differentiated into four categories.

First are *sporting goods consumers*. These retail consumers buy sport products including, for example, equipment, apparel, books, magazines, nutritional and health supplements, games, merchandise, memorabilia and licensed products. A sporting goods consumer is anyone who purchases a physical product that has a sport-related aspect or purpose. This may range from the direct, such as a tennis racquet, to the indirect, such as a computer game like *Madden NFL 08.*

Second are *sport services consumers*. These consumers utilise a sport-related service or experience excluding viewing or participating in sport directly. Sport-related services include education, gambling, specialised coaching, medical services and recreational and health activities such as those offered by pools, gymnasiums and leisure centres.

Third are *sport participants and volunteers*. These consumers are actively engaged in sport as participants or in unpaid organisational and support roles. This includes all participants in school, recreational and organised club sport.

Fourth are *sport supporters, spectators and fans*. These consumers take an active interest in the performance of sport mainly, but not confined to, the elite or professional level. The activities of sport supporters, spectators and fans include attendance at live sport, or viewing sport on television, the Internet or DVD. This group of sport consumers are very complex because they may use sport products and services in ways that other, less intense consumers do not. For example, fans may actively engage in online chat rooms or fantasy league games about sport. In some instances, particularly committed fans may become 'fanatical' when their behaviour and level of engagement steps outside of normal social expectations. Of course, most sport participants and volunteers are sport fans as well, and also utilise different kinds of sporting goods and services. For this reason, it is best to assume that sport consumer motivations are complex. It is easier to categorise kinds of sport consumption than kinds of sport consumers. Furthermore, based on these categories of consumption, it is clear that the motives of sport supporters, spectators and fans are the most complex, and need to be explored further.

> *Chapter Principle 3.1*: A sport consumer is an individual who purchases sporting goods, uses sport services, participates or volunteers in sport and/or follows sport as a spectator or fan.

Sport consumer motives

Even though the topic of sport consumer motives is complex, it is pivotal to understanding sport marketing in the current, competitive environment. Sport marketers need to appreciate the many reasons why consumers are motivated to buy sport-related products and services. Without this knowledge it is more difficult to tailor products to consumers' needs. The more that is understood about sport consumers, the easier it is to approach them with enticing marketing.

Sport consumers attend certain games, follow certain sports and buy certain products for a multitude of reasons. As a result, it is possible to look at sport consumer behaviour from a range of perspectives. One common approach in business, but typically outside of a marketing orientation, is to consider sport consumption behaviour from an *economic* viewpoint. This view suggests that people behave rationally and use sport products and services that meet their quality and value needs. The problem with this view, of course, is that sport consumers do not necessarily behave in rational ways because they have an emotional connection to the sport products they consume. For this reason it is productive to consider consumer behaviour from a *psychological* and *social* point of view. A psychological perspective suggests that people's attitudes and motivations (or desires) will predict what they buy. A social perspective suggests that people may be influenced by their social circumstances. The forthcoming section examines sport consumer behaviour mainly from a psychological and social perspective. It also focuses on the fourth group of consumers identified in the previous section because their consumption decisions are the most complex and furthest removed from rational expectations based on economic factors. This group of sport supporters, spectators and fans will simply be referred to as sport fans.

Becoming a sport fan

There are many possible benefits that sport fans may experience through watching, talking, reading and thinking about sport. This section considers what it is about sport that has captured the attention and passion of so many people for so long. There has been a considerable amount of research examining the psychological and social reasons (often called *psycho-social* motivations) why sport fans consume sport products. Some of this excellent research is given in the Further Reading section at the end of the chapter. Here, the reasons are summarised into three different groups of motives: (1) psychological motives, (2) socio-cultural (social and cultural) motives and (3) self-concept motives.

Chapter Principle 3.2: Sport fan motives for consuming sport products and services can be summarised into three categories: (1) psychological motives, (2) socio-cultural motives and (3) self-concept motives.

Psychological motives

The psychological reasons (or motives) that drive sport fans to consume sport products and services are connected to the interest and enjoyment that they derive from sport. Sport can fulfil a number of emotional and intellectual needs for the sport consumer. For example, sport can be stimulating, can help to release stress, can be an escape and can provide entertainment and visual pleasure. In other words, sport can stimulate positive feelings and thoughts for the sport consumer. Each one of these motives is explained further next.

Stimulation

Sport can be a stimulating, psychologically energising activity. It generates excitement and even anxiety, both of which can encourage the body to produce adrenaline. It also allows fans to shout and vent aggression in a socially acceptable way and to experience intense sensory stimulation.

Escape

The stimulation provided by sport can provide consumers with an escape from the ordinary routine of everyday life. The collisions, body contact and action offered by many sports can attract fans that want to escape from their highly organised and regulated work environments into a world of passion, spontaneity and uncertainty. After all, sport gives spectators an acceptable place to shout, scream and sing or dance, where their normal work or family roles might not. Sport can also provide a release and a distraction from a stressful lifestyle. For many fans, sport watching is the ultimate 'escape experience'.

Aesthetic (visual) pleasure

Sport watching offers aesthetic (or visual) pleasure to fans. Sport fans are often prepared to pay to witness excellence, such as skilful play or memorable moments. In some sports (although not all) fans may also be attracted by the 'sex appeal' of the participants; bikini-clad beach volleyball players are an obvious example of this, as are the physique-hugging Lycra uniforms worn by track and field athletes.

Drama and entertainment

Sport can provide entertainment and drama. Through watching an engaging contest, fans can be part of a theatrical experience. The scale of many sporting venues, the sight of thousands of fans in club colours and the use of lively half-time entertainment all enhance sport's dramatic qualities. Some events, like horse racing, for example have blended sport performance with fashion, theatre and a carnival feel to maximise the dramatic atmosphere.

> *Chapter Principle 3.3*: Psychological motives for sport fans include the opportunity for stimulation, escape, aesthetic pleasure and a sense of dramatic entertainment.

Socio-cultural motives

In addition to the psychological interest and pleasure that sport fans receive from consuming sport, they may also experience social and cultural benefits. Sport encourages fans to gather into groups, such as families, fellow team supporters, and state and national 'cheer' squads. It provides fans with a social gathering place, as well as activities to share and common topics to talk about.

Family and social interaction

Sporting events and activities provide an opportunity for families and friends to spend time together in an organised and pleasurable way. A sport experience can help sport fans fulfil family needs, or to spend time with friends. It is important for sport marketers to realise that if a spectator is motivated to attend a match because of these reasons, then the type of game they attend or the teams which are playing may be irrelevant. Alternative activities may easily substitute for the sport experience, and still allow the consumer to meet their family and social needs.

Cultural connections

Fans use sport as a form of cultural connection and celebration. Sport can help fans connect to their national, racial or ethnic culture, or even a subculture that they belong to (a social group which shares beliefs and behaviours). Spectators may like to attend games that are relevant to their heritage, or where the majority of athletes are from ethnic or racial group they identify with. Sport can also provide meaningful symbols, rituals and 'mythical images'. The Olympic Games, for example uses a number of important rituals and symbols, such as the lighting of the flame, the Olympic oath and the closing ceremony, all of which have special meaning to participants and spectators. For sporting clubs, the theme song, club colours, insignia and mottos fulfil the same function by providing powerful images which represent a common belonging to the group. Watching, reading and talking about sport can create a feeling of familiarity that comes from participating in a seasonal ritual. There are also weekly cycles, which include the dramatic match, the post-game argument, the mid-week review and pre-match media analysis, which are repeated reliably from season to season.

Economic benefit

Another kind of socio-cultural benefit for sport fans is the possibility of gaining money through gambling on sport. This is a potential advantage that is not part of the game itself, but one of the 'extras', or an external benefit that needs a social and cultural system to operate.

> *Chapter Principle 3.4*: Socio-cultural motives for sport fans include the opportunity for family and social interaction, cultural connections and even economic benefit.

Self-concept motives

While psychological and socio-cultural motives help describe why a fan is attracted to sport, it is clear that not all fans experience the same degree or strength of identification. The degree to which a fan identifies with a team is an important issue, since it may predict their loyalty. It is therefore useful to differentiate between psychological and self-concept motives, as the former describes attraction, and the latter strength of sport identification. Psychological motives are internal to individuals whereas belonging motives are a function of a sport consumer's interaction with sport. Fans with a stronger identification have sport more deeply embedded in their self-concept. A fan's identification with a team could be motivated by a need to belong to a group or a tribe, or by a desire for vicarious achievement.

Belonging and group affiliation

Sport consumers may feel a need to belong to a group. They may also be motivated to develop a sense of identity that is connected to the group, or to identify with something bigger than themselves. These fans want to feel part of a tightly bound community that shares a common interest. They may also develop a sense of personal identity partly through a connection to teams and athletes. If a sport fan develops a strong feeling of connection to a successful team or player, they may use that success to pretend that they too are successful; they share the warm after-glow of victory. It is important to note, however, that the depth of identification fans possess can vary significantly. On the one hand, there may be 'fair-weather' fans whose attendance at events will vary. On the other hand, there are the passionate supporters who will remain loyal to their favourite teams and clubs even when the teams are performing poorly.

Tribal connections

Sport fandom can also be used to recreate ancient ceremonies and primitive social rituals. For example, team sports like football provide strong tribal connections, with athletes acting as the tribal heroes, and rituals like pre- and post-game ceremonies. The fans themselves are the tribal followers who have conflicts with other tribes (other team's fans) and show their tribal colours and loyalty by wearing club colours. Of course, there are also tribal chants and team songs, which help to bind the fans together, and to intimidate rival tribes.

Vicarious achievement

Sport fans can develop a psychological attachment to sports, teams and players. This connection can assist fans to develop a feeling of being strong, important and successful. The term vicarious achievement refers to a sense of accomplishment that is felt second hand, through the success of someone else. Some fans may experience an increase in self-esteem when their team is winning. Others may feel a sense of confidence and skilfulness by learning team statistics and club history. Given that sport fans feel successful when their team is successful, the reverse occurs when they must deal with the disappointment of scandals and poor team performance. In these situations fans may be a little less eager to publicly announce their support of the team, and they might even downplay the failure of the team. Fans can compensate for a team's poor performance by developing strong feelings of closeness with fellow fans, being very critical of other successful teams, voicing criticism of umpiring or refereeing decisions, or by being blindly optimistic that things will get better.

Chapter Principle 3.5: Self-concept motives for sport fans include the opportunity for belonging and group affiliation, tribal connections and vicarious achievement.

Look at the following sport fan websites:

1. The Fanatics website
    Look at the pages http://www.thefanatics.com and
    http://www.thefanatics.com/gallery.php
    The Fanatics began in 1997 with the aim of forming an organised, passionate
    and patriotic support group that would follow Australian teams anywhere.
    It organises international travel and group seating for like-minded fans.
2. The Fans Voice website http://www.fansvoice.com
    Look at the 'Sports Fan Bill of Rights' page.

Influences on sport consumer motives

The motives just described help to explain why a fan may be driven to consume sport. But it is clear that not all sport fans will be motivated by the same reasons. Some may be motivated by a desire for entertainment while others may be motivated by deep feelings of connection to a group.

Research on sport consumer behaviour has revealed some of the variables that influence the motives that fans' hold. This research indicates that a sport fan's reasons for buying a sport product may be affected by demographic variables, or their age, education, income, gender and race. For example, older fans are less likely to be motivated towards sport through the desire to belong to a group than younger fans. Fans with higher levels of education are less likely to be motivated for economic gain, bolstering self-esteem, stimulation or group affiliation.

Other research suggests that males and females may be motivated to consume sport for different reasons. Males, for example, are more likely to be motivated by economic factors than females, as well as reasons of escapism, psychological stimulation, aesthetic pleasure and self-esteem. Females, however, are more strongly motivated to consume sport for family and social reasons.

While research into these kinds of factors can be informative, as a sport marketer it is important to remember that not all research provides the same result. For example, not all researchers agree that gender makes a significant difference to fan motivation. In addition, some researchers have found that gender differences may be more pronounced in some cultures or racial groups than others. There may also be other reasons to think carefully about the results of research. After all, it is likely that the sport fans targeted in one research study are different to the ones that have been studied in others.

The key issue to remember is that different sport fans will be motivated to consume sport for different reasons. Some reasons for consuming sport will lead to greater loyalty than others. Self-concept motives, in particular, may stimulate stronger feelings of allegiance. Also, fans' reasons for buying a sport product may be affected by their age, education, income, gender and race, although there is enough evidence to suggest that these demographic variables do not influence motivation in a uniform way. One approach to assist in understanding sport fans better is to examine and classify their behaviour rather than their motivations. This is easier because behaviour is tangible and measurable irrespective of the motivation that stimulated it.

Chapter Principle 3.6: Fan motives for consuming sport are affected by their age, education, income, gender and race, but these demographic variables do not always influence motivation in a uniform or predictable way.

Understanding spectator behaviour

Some fans go to sport for no other reason than to see their favourite team contest the game. These *passionate partisans* are loyal to their team and get despondent when their team loses and elated when it wins, and are prepared to incur inconvenience (a wet day, or a long, slow trip to the stadium) to savour the fruits of success. They form the hard-core support base of sport, and their moods and identity are bound up with the successes and failures of their favourite team. They are heavy purchasers of memorabilia and club merchandise and will be great defenders of club history and traditions. They also possess a significant personal investment in their preferred club and its season-to-season performance.

There are also many sport fans who are more interested in supporting a winning team than blindly following their team through 'thick and thin'. These *champ followers* share some of the emotional highs and lows of the passionate partisan, but are less reliable and fanatical. The champ follower's allegiance will change according to whatever team happens to be the top performer. Alternatively, champ followers often remain hidden from public view (are non-attendees) until their favourite team starts winning and they become vocal and active supporters, until such time as their team begins to lose again.

A third category is the *reclusive partisan*, whose interest in the game and commitment to the team is strong, but who attends infrequently. The reclusive partisan is opinionated, and apparently loyal to his or her team, and could become a passionate partisan again if others can influence them or through media-saturation coverage of the event.

The common motive shared by each of the above categories is the desire to see their team win. Their dominant concern is not whether it is likely to be a close contest or whether it will be skilful, dramatic or entertaining, but the likelihood of success. They are attracted to team performance or team quality. Such sport fans are parochial.

There are at the same time many sport fans who, while notionally committed to a particular team, are more interested in the game or sport itself, and attend more frequently than the reclusive partisan, but less frequently than the passionate partisan. These fans may be considered *theatregoers*. The theatregoer is motivated to seek entertainment through a pleasurable experience. However, entertainment from this viewpoint involves more than drama and half-time shows. It also includes comfortable and proximate viewing conditions, easy access, the availability of complimentary services, a close contest and the participation of star performers. The theatregoer is attracted to comfort, enjoyment, excitement, sensory stimulation and uncertainty of outcome. Since their team and game loyalty is initially low, most theatregoers will attend less frequently than passionate partisans unless the likelihood of exciting and pleasurable contests continues throughout the season. At the same time, a few theatregoers will put such high value on their sporting experiences that they will become regular patrons. In this respect, theatregoers may be described as either *casual* or *committed*.

Like the theatregoer, the *aficionado* will be attracted to games which are expected to be exciting, and contain star performers. However, unlike most theatregoers, aficionados attend frequently because of their strong attachment to the structure of the game and its athletic practices. They will attend games that provide high skill levels, tactical complexity and aesthetic pleasure, even if they are likely to be one sided or unexciting. Some aficionados would call themselves purists because they would attend their match of the day, which may or may not include the top performing teams. The aficionado will also be attracted to a quality venue since it will accentuate a quality performance. Both the aficionado and the theatregoer will show only moderate concern about who wins or loses. Their dominant concern is game performance or game quality, and not the likely success or failure of a particular team.

While each of the fan categories has an interest in the game or sport, there are significant differences in the ways in which their interest is expressed. Different incentives will activate different segments. A change to the structure or conduct of the competition which attracts more of one type may be resisted by another type. While theatregoers are likely to attend more games where the stadiums are comfortable, games are expected to be close and competitive, and where complimentary entertainment is provided, passionate partisans and champ followers may think that such changes undermine the essential nature and traditions of the game, and lessen the expectation of success. Similarly, while theatregoers may be excited about the sensory delights that they see arising from new rules designed to speed up the game, an expanded league or the relocation of one team to another city, passionate and reclusive partisans are likely to view such adjustments as treachery, and in extreme cases sever their relationship with their club. It should be noted that all fans can vary according to their personal profile and depending on the sport in question. Thus, one individual may be a casual theatregoer when it comes to cricket, but a passionate partisan when observing volleyball. Table 3.1 summarises the five categories of spectators, their motivations and behaviour. It was originally devised by Stewart (Smith & Stewart, 1999).

Table 3.1 Sport Fan Categories

Type of Spectator	Motivation	Behaviour
Aficionado	Seeks quality performance	● Loyal to game rather than team, although will usually have a preferred team ● Attends on regular basis ● Puts emphasis on aesthetic or skill dimension
Theatregoer (casual and committed)	Seeks entertainment, close contest	● Only moderate loyalty to team ● Frequent losses create disinterest only in team ● May attend other games
Passionate partisan	Wants team to win	● Loyal to team ● Short term loyalty undiminished by frequent losses ● Strongly identifies with, and responds to, team's success and failure
Champ follower	Wants team to win	● Short-term loyalty ● Loyalty a function of team success. Expects individual or team to dominate otherwise supports another team or spends time elsewhere
Reclusive partisan	Wants team to win	● Loyalty not always translated into attendance ● Strong identification but provides latent support only

Marketing implications

For the sport marketer, the above categories highlight the different segments that comprise the sport fan market. In particular, it reinforces the importance of supporting the passionate partisan and the aficionado. However, it is clear from the categories that the motivations of partisans and aficionados are quite different. The categories also demonstrate the potential for increased attendances provided by the theatregoer, champ follower and reclusive partisan. In each case, the provision of appropriate incentives may be used to generate greater frequency of attendance. The theatregoer would be attracted to comfortable seating arrangements, colour and drama, the availability of appropriate food and drink, and the expectation of an exciting contest, whereas the reclusive partisan and champ followers would be most attracted to games in which their teams had a good probability of winning and were in the championship race. For champ followers to maintain interest, in contrast to passionate partisans, it would be necessary to have a competition where playing talent was distributed equally among the teams, and where the championship race was close for most of the season. Reclusive partisans would also be influenced by the social context in which the sport operates, and a strong media campaign which emphasises the cultural significance and fashionability of the event may be effective in this case.

Sport marketers are faced with the difficult task of ensuring that the sport product provides for good watching conditions, a balanced competition, uncertainty of game and seasonal outcome (exciting high-quality games played in attractive surroundings), and that the loyalty of partisan fans is maintained (by ensuring the ongoing viability of teams within strategically positioned regions and districts which fans can use to establish a sense of identity and community). While changes to the structure of a sport competition (like new recruiting laws, the relocation of teams or the merger of clubs) are likely to weaken the loyalty of partisan supporters, it must be weighed against the attraction that such changes have for the other spectator categories, particularly the theatregoers.

Chapter Principle 3.7: Sport fans can be classified according to the sources and dimensions of their attraction to the sport, and their frequency of attendance.

External factors that influence sport consumption

Even when fans are strongly connected to their team or club, they will not always regularly attend games or watch them on television. The reasons for attending matches and events may also be influenced by other factors, such as the type of sport involved, the balance of the competition, the uncertainty of outcome and the likelihood of a certain team winning. Other important factors include the venue and facilities, weather conditions, prices, income levels, special experiences, promotional factors and the availability of alternative activities. Each of these factors will be briefly examined along with its potential influence on sport fan behaviour.

Type of sport

Different sports attract different types of fans, and different fans are motivated by different factors. The type of sport that a fan is interested in reveals something about their motivations. Fans of individual sports like tennis and motor racing are more likely to be motivated by an interest in particular athletes, compared with fans of team sports such as football, soccer and volleyball who are more likely to be motivated by a sense of personal belonging to a team. In addition, fans who prefer non-aggressive sports such as baseball are more likely to be motivated by aesthetic concerns than fans of aggressive sports such as American football and boxing who are more interested in vicarious escapism.

Balance and uncertainty

Some fans will be influenced by the anticipated closeness of the competition. More fans will attend games when they expect a close contest, which will be affected by the quality of the opposing team or athletes. Closer contests tend to be expected later in the season or event when semi-finals and finals are played. Generally, the closer the expected result of the match, the more attractive a game will be to fans. When fans are uncertain about who might win, they are likely to be more enthusiastic about attending, and tend to have more intense experiences when they do.

The likelihood of winning

Although some fans appreciate a close contest, others are preoccupied with winning. Since fans can receive a sense of personal satisfaction in identifying with a winning team, they will attend or watch games more frequently if they believe their team has a strong chance of winning. In contrast, a team that consistently loses will have difficulty attracting a large following. In general, winning teams and athletes will attract more spectators than losing teams and athletes. There are some instances, however, where fans enjoy watching teams lose that they dislike.

The venue

Sport venue features and facilities can have a strong impact on a fan's decision to attend a sport event. A facility will attract fans if it is able to provide an attractive setting, a convenient layout, good signage, a visually appealing scoreboard, comfort, a better view of the contest and easy accessibility. Parking, the quality of food and beverages, child-care facilities and other entertainment options can also have an effect on a fan's decision to attend. The expectation of a large crowd can also be a motivating factor.

Weather

The weather can affect match attendances by influencing both the conditions under which fans watch the game, and the quality of the game itself. A waterlogged ground will not only inconvenience many fans, but may also produce slow-moving and boring games. This has encouraged many venues in rain-prone cities to construct retractable roofs or provide under-cover seating. However, good weather may also be a problem if it means that people may be attracted to alternative leisure activities. For example, a temperate climate and close proximity to water-based activities may lure fans away from sport.

Interactive case

Log on to the following website to look at the biggest stadium in the world with a retractable roof.
http://www.millenniumstadium.com/

Price

To some extent admission prices to sport events can have a predictable effect. While admission prices are typically fixed during the regular season, between seasons and during finals they can change significantly, which can impact on a fan's decision to attend. Broadly speaking an increase in admission prices will lead to a reduction in crowd numbers. However, there is evidence that price increases have only a minor influence because sport fans are unusually loyal consumers. This relates to the point made earlier that sport has a low cross elasticity of demand. Sport fans may be unlikely to substitute one sport league, team or competition for another, even if the price of their preferred competition rises.

Income levels

The income levels of fans can have a direct effect on what kind of leisure they prefer. As the income of fans rise, there is often a decrease in match or event attendances. More income usually means people have more choices to participate in alternative leisure activities, such as travel, restaurants and the theatre.

Special experiences

Special experiences will generally gain the attention of fans. The experience may involve the participation of a star player or personality, or the likelihood of a record-breaking performance. It may also involve the expectation of a dramatic or even violent encounter, or the anticipation of highly skilled and aesthetically pleasing play. These experiences can give sport fans a feeling that they are getting value for money. Special experiences can also include the availability of reserved seating, access to a private box and the opportunity to meet a celebrity. The contest itself is just part of the total package.

Promotional factors

Promotional strategies, particularly when accompanied by admission concessions, sales vouchers and merchandising discounts, are important influences on fans' decisions to attend sport. Advertising, direct mail outs, give-away prizes, the promotion of upcoming games, entertainment and the provision of premium seating can increase crowd sizes.

Alternative activities

The availability of alternative activities will also influence sport fan decisions. While this factor is unlikely to explain week-to-week variations in attendances, it can explain a decline in attendance over a longer period of time. Fans have become increasingly mobile and are able to choose between a huge number of leisure and entertainment alternatives. In addition, home entertainment options such as computers, game consoles and pay television are the biggest threats to live sport. The choice between competing leisure activities has never been more expansive.

Chapter Principle 3.8: Fans' decisions to attend or view sport may be influenced by external factors, such as the type of sport involved, the balance of the competition, how uncertain the outcome is, the likelihood of their team winning, the venue and facilities, weather conditions, prices, personal income levels, special experiences that are being offered, promotional factors and the availability of alternative activities.

Case Study: The Barmy Army

by Sharyn McDonald

Although in the 1994–1995 Ashes series the English Cricket team were not achieving great success against Australia, they had a loyal group of English fans willing them to win and who attracted a significant amount of media attention. The Australian media labelled this lively group *England's Barmy Army*, which became a registered trademark in March 1995 (Barmy Army, 2007). This entourage is a colourful ensemble of fanatical cricket supporters who liven up the game with their songs, merchandise and banter, and who are prepared to travel to all of England's overseas matches in support of their team.

The combination of a large gathering of sport fans and the over-abundance of alcohol encourages critics of sport to focus on the negative side of fandom. The passionate vocal support can be considered as intimidating, disruptive behaviour resembling a kind of mob mentality. A large group of sport fans, dominated by males, in a stadium environment, projecting insults at the opposition and their supporters replicates the unpleasant traits usually associated with soccer fans (Parry & Malcolm, 2004). However, the Barmy Army have tried to project a different identity.

Regardless of race, age or gender, any fan of English cricket can be a part of the Barmy Army. Although there is no official membership scheme, there is a mailing list of 25 000 subscribers. Barmy Army marketing focuses on recruiting people using the attraction of the fun of being involved, and the vibrancy and colour of the way in which they are dressed. Barmy Army emblazed cricket merchandise has become a successful business venture and the group has enhanced their exposure with guest appearances on television.

The entrepreneurial activities associated with the evolving Barmy Army have been criticised, but they nevertheless provide a unifying influence. Cricket is a commercialised commodity and its coverage on television focuses not only on the game but on the overall atmosphere. The animated Barmy Army is easily identified by broadcasters and their guaranteed attention is an attractive location for perimeter advertisers. Realising the potential to attract media attention, the Barmy Army have progressed beyond commercial interests, and have assumed a benevolent persona, demonstrating social sensitivity through charity work.

One of their publicised acts of charity was support for the victims of Pakistan's earthquake in 2005. Operating through the Islamic Relief Organisation, the Barmy Army played in charity matches and used the funds from shirt sales to support those in need. In the United Kingdom, they donated 6000 Barmy Army bottles of water during the Leukaemia Research Fund's fun run. They are also opportunistic in their charity fund raising, such as collecting for tsunami victims at the Boxing Day test in South Africa in 2004, and optimistic pre-planned victory parties, with proceeds going to charity (see Wark, 2007).

The Barmy Army has grown into an organisation that attracts its own sponsorship and is capable of contributing to social change. Although some of their antics will remain questionable, the Barmy Army seem to have created their own style of supportership that is highly appealing.

For further information see:

Barmy Army (2007). *History of the Barmy Army*.
http://www.barmyarmy. com/history.cfm

Parry, M. & Malcolm, D. (2004). England's Barmy Army commercialization, masculinity and nationalism, *International Review for the Sociology of Sport*, 39(1): 75–94.

Wark, P. (2007). An Admirable Army That's Far from Barmy.
http://www.timesonline.co.uk/tol/life_and_style/article1289328.ece (accessed 5 January 2007).

Summary principles

- Chapter Principle 3.1: A sport consumer is an individual who purchases sporting goods, uses sport services, participates or volunteers in sport and/or follows sport as a spectator or fan.
- Chapter Principle 3.2: Sport fan motives for consuming sport products and services can be summarised into three categories: (1) psychological motives, (2) socio-cultural motives and (3) self-concept motives.
- Chapter Principle 3.3: Psychological motives for sport fans include the opportunity for stimulation, escape, aesthetic pleasure and a sense of dramatic entertainment.
- Chapter Principle 3.4: Socio-cultural motives for sport fans include the opportunity for family and social interaction, cultural connections and even economic benefit.
- Chapter Principle 3.5: Self-concept motives for sport fans include the opportunity for belonging and group affiliation, tribal connections and vicarious achievement.
- Chapter Principle 3.6: Fan motives for consuming sport are affected by their age, education, income, gender and race, but these demographic variables do not always influence motivation in a uniform or predictable way.
- Chapter Principle 3.7: Sport fans can be classified according to the sources and dimensions of their attraction to the sport, and their frequency of attendance.
- Chapter Principle 3.8: Fans' decisions to attend or view sport may be influenced by external factors, such as the type of sport involved, the balance of the competition, how uncertain the outcome is, the likelihood of their team winning, the venue and facilities, weather conditions, prices, personal income levels, special experiences that are being offered, promotional factors and the availability of alternative activities.

Review questions

1. Identify and describe the different kinds of sport consumers.
2. Define and distinguish between (1) psychological motives, (2) socio-cultural motives and (3) self-concept motives.
3. Choose one variable from age, education, income, gender or race, and speculate on how it might influence sport consumption.
4. Why are sport fans often distinguished on the basis of their consumption behaviour?
5. List the five different types of sport fans and provide a brief comment on the best way to market sport to each.
6. What is the difference between an internal factor and an external factor when it comes to their influence of sport consumption?

Relevant websites

http://www.thefanatics.com (The Fanatics)

http://www.millenniumstadium.com/ (Millennium Stadium)

http://www.barmyarmy.com/history.cfm (Barmy Army)

http://www.timesonline.co.uk/tol/life_and_style/article1289328.ece (*The Times Online*)

Further reading

Bernthal, M.J. & Graham, P.J. (2003). The effect of sport setting on fan attendance motivation: The case of Minor League vs. Collegiate Baseball, *Journal of Sport Behaviour*, 26(3): 223–239.

Downard, P. & Dawson, A. (2000). *The Economics of Professional Team Sports*, Routledge, London.

Stewart, B., Smith, A.C. & Nicholson, M. (2003). Sport consumer typologies: A critical review, *Sport Marketing Quarterly*, 12(4): 206–216.

Szymanski, S. (2003). The economic design of sporting contests: A review, *Journal of Economic Literature*, 41: 242–258.

Wiley, C.G., Shaw, S.M. & Havitz, M.E. (2000). Men's and women's involvement in sports: An examination of the gendered aspects of leisure involvement, *Leisure Sciences*, 22: 19–31.

Reference

Smith, A. & Stewart, B. (1999). *Sport Management: A Guide to Professional Practice*, Allen and Unwin, Sydney.

4 Sport marketing opportunities

Overview

This chapter overviews the Sport Marketing Framework, which comprises identifying sport marketing opportunities, developing a strategic marketing strategy, planning the sport marketing mix, and implementing and controlling the sport marketing strategy. This chapter provides detailed guidance for undertaking the first stage of the Framework: identifying sport marketing opportunities. Included are details on the three parts of stage one: (a) analyse internal and external environments; (b) analyse organisation; and (c) analyse market and consumers.

At the end of this chapter, readers should be able to:

- Identify the key marketing activities required to identify sport marketing opportunities.
- Explain the elements and purpose of a SWOT analysis.
- Conduct a macro and micro environmental analysis.
- Describe the process and importance of a competitor analysis.
- Identify some of the introductory issues associated with market research, including its application and importance to identifying marketing opportunities.

The sport marketing framework

The Sport Marketing Framework is the process that describes the stages and activities of sport marketing. It is the backbone of all sport marketing efforts. The Sport Marketing Framework is made up of four stages and is illustrated in Figure 4.1, with stage 1 of the process, 'Identify Sport Marketing Opportunities', highlighted. Stage 1 involves three parts. First is the analysis of conditions in the external marketplace (such as competitors' activities, technology, legal restrictions and the economic climate) as well as the internal environment of a sport organisation (such as its strengths and weaknesses). Second is the analysis of the sport organisation's unique position, such as its mission, vision, objectives, performance measures and stakeholders. Third is the analysis of the market and its consumers via market research.

Once stage 1 is completed, the assembled information is used to undertake stage 2 of the sport marketing framework—'Develop a Sport Marketing Strategy'. Stage 2 involves making key decisions about the strategic direction a sport marketing program should take in light of the analysis performed in stage 1. During this stage, it is important to establish the strategy within the boundaries of both objectives and performance measures in order to later evaluate whether the marketing program has been successful. Stage 2 also involves determining the specific tactics that will be used during the strategy, such as how it will distinguish (differentiate) the sport product or service in the market, exactly who it will be targeted towards (segmentation), and what marketing mix decisions (this is a term covering the elements of product, pricing strategies, promotional strategies and distribution systems) will be employed to implement the strategy. In stage 3 of the process, the sport marketing mix is documented in detail. Finally, stage 4 involves putting the plan into action and making sure it remains on track.

> *Chapter Principle 4.1*: The Sport Marketing Framework describes the four stages of sport marketing: identifying sport marketing opportunities, developing a sport marketing strategy, planning the sport marketing mix, and implementing and controlling the sport marketing strategy.

Stage 1: Identifying sport marketing opportunities

The first step of the Sport Marketing Framework recognises that it is important to conduct preliminary research and analysis before it is possible to make sensible marketing decisions. It is important, for example, to know what

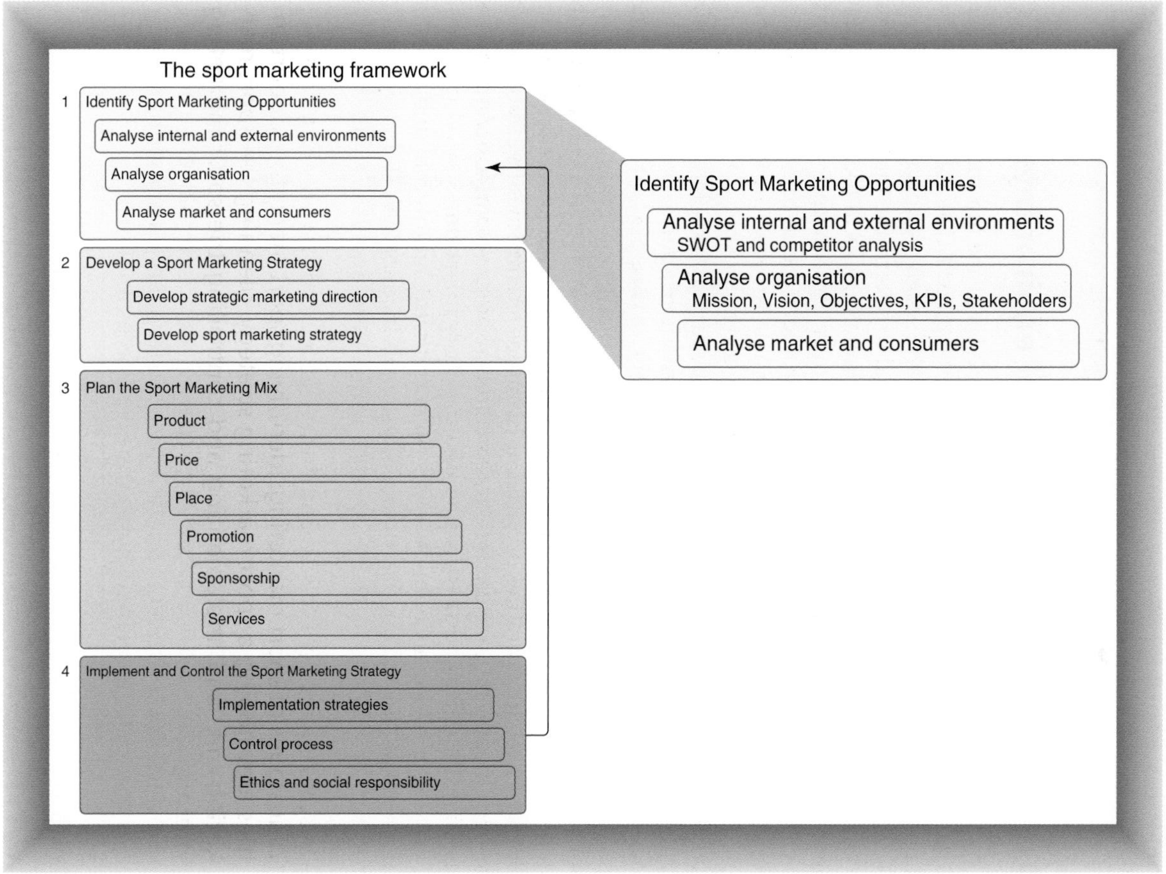

The sport marketing framework

1 Identify Sport Marketing Opportunities
   Analyse internal and external environments
   Analyse organisation
   Analyse market and consumers

2 Develop a Sport Marketing Strategy
   Develop strategic marketing direction
   Develop sport marketing strategy

3 Plan the Sport Marketing Mix
   Product
   Price
   Place
   Promotion
   Sponsorship
   Services

4 Implement and Control the Sport Marketing Strategy
   Implementation strategies
   Control process
   Ethics and social responsibility

Identify Sport Marketing Opportunities

Analyse internal and external environments
SWOT and competitor analysis

Analyse organisation
Mission, Vision, Objectives, KPIs, Stakeholders

Analyse market and consumers

Figure 4.1 Identify Sport Marketing Opportunities.

opportunities exist in the marketplace, what competitors are doing, what a sport organisation is good at doing, and what consumers actually want. The first stage of the sport marketing process is therefore to identify sport marketing opportunities. This involves analysing the market and consumers, as well as the organisation for which the plan is being constructed. It is important to realise that the three parts of stage 1 should be conducted at approximately the same time, as the three analyses are interconnected.

Analyse internal and external environments

The first activity in stage 1 prescribes an analysis of the internal and external environments in which a sport organisation is placed. The internal environment refers to the unique circumstances of the sport organisation for which the plan is developed. It is therefore essential to determine the strengths and weaknesses of the sport organisation. For example, a local football club may be strong in terms of its positive community profile and the support it receives from a regional association which provides access to a well-organised competition structure. However, the club may be weak in financial terms and may have difficulty in attracting young players.

The external environment refers to the marketplace in which a sport organisation operates. This includes the immediate sport industry as well as the national and international context. In fact, it is important to understand the industry-related external environment, the nature of competitors, and the broad national and global environment. In the example of a local soccer club, an analysis of the external environment may reveal that soccer is not a popular sport in the region, or that there is limited government support for its development. These external factors may also have a strong influence on the specific strengths and weaknesses of a sport organisation.

In the following section, the tools for conducting an internal and external analysis will be explained in detail. These tools include SWOT analysis (with external environment analysis) and competitor analysis (with the Five Forces analysis).

Chapter Principle 4.2: The first step in identifying sport marketing opportunities is to analyse the internal and external environment using the tools of SWOT analysis (with external environment analysis) and competitor analysis (with the Five Forces analysis).

SWOT analysis: An analysis of the internal and external environments

One of the basic tools in this stage of the sport marketing process is known as the SWOT analysis. The term SWOT is an acronym for the words *strengths, weaknesses, opportunities, threats*. A SWOT analysis is used to examine the strategic position of an organisation from the inside (strengths and weaknesses) and the outside (opportunities and threats).

The SWOT analysis can be divided into two parts. The first part represents an internal analysis of an organisation, which can be summarised by its *strengths* and *weaknesses*. An organisation has control over its strengths and weaknesses. The strengths of an organisation include those things which an organisation does well, and can be considered capabilities. The weaknesses of an organisation can include those things which it does poorly, and can be seen as deficiencies. The second part of the SWOT technique is concerned with external factors. These are elements which the organisation has no direct control over and can be summarised as *opportunities* and *threats.* Opportunities include environmental circumstances which can be used to an organisation's advantage, while threats include unfavourable situations in the external environment that need to be avoided.

The strengths and weaknesses of a sport organisation, along with the opportunities and threats it faces, will influence the options available for a marketing plan. As a result, SWOT analysis is used to identify the major issues that mitigate strategic options. A good rule of thumb is to look for no more than five factors under each of the four headings so that the most important issues are given the highest priority. One of the most common mistakes made when conducting a SWOT analysis is getting caught in needless detail, and losing sight of the 'big picture'. It is also important not to focus only on sport-related matters, but to consider general organisational and business factors.

Strengths and weaknesses

The analysis of strengths and weaknesses should be focused on present-day circumstances. To recap, strengths can be defined as resources or capabilities that a sport organisation can use to achieve its strategic direction. Common strengths may include committed coaching staff, a sound membership base, a good junior development program, or management staff with sound business skills and knowledge. Weaknesses should be seen as limitations or inadequacies that will prevent or hinder the strategic direction from being achieved. Common weaknesses may include poor training facilities, inadequate sponsorship, a diminishing volunteer workforce or a weak financial position.

Opportunities and threats

While strengths and weaknesses should be focused on the present-day situation, opportunities and threats should be future oriented. Opportunities are the favourable situations or events that an organisation can use to its advantage in order to enhance its performance. For example, common opportunities include new government grants, the identification of a new market or potential product, or the chance to appoint a new staff member

Table 4.1 SWOT Guidelines

Strengths	• Resources (e.g. finance, staff, volunteers) • Skills (e.g. talents of management, staff and volunteers) • Advantages (compared with competitors)
Weaknesses	• Lack of resources (e.g. finance, staff, volunteers) • Lack of skills (e.g. among management, staff and volunteers) • Disadvantages (compared with competitors)
Opportunities	• Favourable situations in the external environment • Weaknesses of competitors
Threats	• Unfavourable situation in the external environment • Unfavourable trends in leisure and entertainment

with unique skills. Threats, in contrast, are the unfavourable situations which could make performance more difficult for the organisation in the future. Common threats include inflating player salaries, potential new competitors, or unfavourable trends in the marketplace such as the increased popularity of gaming consoles. Table 4.1 summarises the SWOT technique.

The next section will introduce the many factors that need to be considered when evaluating the external environment in order to determine the opportunities and threats an organisation faces. This is followed with an explanation of how to perform a competitor analysis and Five Forces competitor analysis.

External environment analysis

The external environment is made up of a number of factors, including an organisation's competitors, the sport industry, and the wider environment. These are illustrated in Figure 4.2.

The largest circle in Figure 4.2, the macro (or broad) external environment, is made up of the political, economic, legal, technological, social and physical environments. Imagine for example that there has been a change over time in the demographic make-up of a region. Such changes may impact the kinds of sports that are considered most popular and likely to attract participants. In a population with a greater proportion of older people, sports such as lawn bowls and golf may have an improved opportunity to expand their participation bases.

Figure 4.3 summarises the six factors that form the macro external environment of a sport organisation. It is important to understand the demands, constraints and possibilities that each of these elements might bring to the sport organisation. Each of these will be described next.

Political environment

Government policy influences the ways in which sport organisations are able to operate. For example, sport policy in some countries like Australia

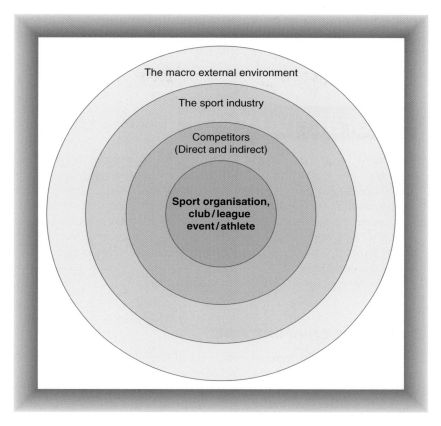

Figure 4.2 External Environments of a Sport Organisation.

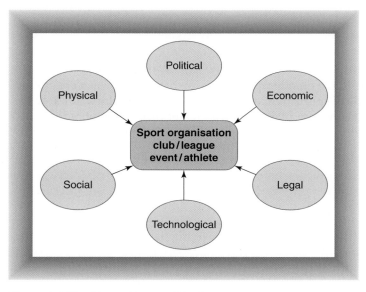

Figure 4.3 The Macro External Environment.

put a high priority on the development of elite sport, which may be supported by millions of dollars of funding. Government influence can also be relevant in attracting major events to cities.

Interactive case

Log on to the Sport Canada website (see link below). Sport Canada is a branch of the Canadian government that manages sport programs, sport policy and major games and event hosting in Canada. Look at the funding programs that are discussed on the website and think about what kinds of sport is supported by the government. Where does the money go, and what does this say about the priorities that the Canadian government has for sport? Consider what this says about the political environment in Canada with relation to sport.
http://www.pch.gc.ca/progs/sc/index_e.cfm

Economic environment

The economic environment is made up of two elements: the macroeconomic and the microeconomic. Macroeconomic elements represent the big picture; they describe the economy on a national level. Microeconomic elements represent the detailed picture at the organisational or consumer level.

Macroeconomic factors are used to provide a broad picture of economic issues that might affect a sport organisation. When employment levels and consumer spending are higher (in times of prosperity), consumers are more likely to spend money on sport. During times of recession or depression, consumers may not be as likely to spend money on sport. However, it is possible that during these low economic times consumers will still choose to spend money on sport for entertainment and distraction. The way that sport organisations will be affected may vary greatly from one organisation to another.

One of the most important microeconomic elements relevant to sport organisations is consumer income levels. Naturally, a consumer's income level will have an influence on whether they can afford to purchase a sport service or product. When economists talk about income, they often use the terms gross income, disposable income and discretionary income. Gross income is how much money people earn before any tax or expenses are taken out. Disposable income is how much money is left over after tax has been paid. Finally, discretionary income is what is left over after tax had been paid and all the necessities of living have been bought (e.g. rent, food, transportation). As sport is not a necessity of life, consumers pay for sport products out of their discretionary income. Therefore, the greater the amount of discretionary income that a consumer has, the more money they have to potentially spend on sport if they wish. It is true, however, that some sport fans are so dedicated that they consider spending on sport as important as spending on the essentials of living.

Legal environment

The legal aspect of the macro external environment can include legislation passed by government, as well as the regulations set down by sport associations, and national and international sporting bodies. Governments create legislation (laws), which are designed to implement and enforce the policies they set (see Political Environment section). For example, government sets laws which regulate how and when broadcasters can cover sport events. Many other types of government legislation can also affect the individuals and groups involved in the sport industry, such as company law, taxation, patents and copyright, and contract law. The smaller regulatory bodies which are relevant to sport organisations can include associations, leagues and international federations. The International Olympic Committee, for example, sets rules about how Olympic competitions should be run. WADA (the World Anti-Doping Agency) is another international example. WADA sets regulations regarding the types of substances allowed to be used by athletes in sanctioned sport competitions, and also establishes the standards of punishment.

Technological environment

Technology has had a substantial impact on the way sport organisations operate. For example, e-mail has revolutionised communication, medical technology has improved sport medicine techniques and webstreaming has made sport accessible from almost anywhere in the world. Technological developments are so important to the marketing of sport that Chapter 11 is dedicated to exploring its implications.

Interactive case

Consider the case where BBC webstreamed the entire FIFA World Cup in 2006. Look at the following web link:
http://news.bbc.co.uk/sport1/hi/football/world_cup_2006/bbc_coverage/5060332.stm

Social environment

The social environment can include the culture of a region as well as its prevalent social trends and demographics. Different cultures and changing cultural trends can have an influence on whether sport is a valued activity, what kind of sport is appreciated, and even how sport and competition should be organised. Cricket, for example, is strong in England, Australia, New Zealand, India, South Africa and the West Indies (all previous colonies of the British who introduced the game). It is common for sport consumers from other countries, however, to report that the game is too slow and boring. Social issues may also include demographic trends which refer to the changing composition of a population in an area.

Physical environment

The physical environment can include the unique geographical features of a region, the weather and the built facilities available. On the east coast of the United States, for example, the temperate climate and accessible coastline mean that there is substantial opportunity to participate in water sports. In many European countries, the Alpine formations and cold environment during winter provide ample opportunity for a variety of snow sports to be enjoyed. Weather factors, such as the availability of water, can directly impact the kinds of sporting surfaces that can be easily managed; golf courses and other turf surfaces require significant water resources to be maintained. Changing weather patterns may represent a significant threat to sport grounds and events, with drought being an obvious example. Finally, the availability of sporting facilities can also present unique opportunities and threats to a sport organisation. In a country such as England, for example, there are numerous facilities and grounds available for Polo to be played, whereas only few such facilities exist in China.

Interactive case

Log on to the website for Ski Dubai.
www.skidubai.com
www.visit-dubai-city.com/dubai-ski-resort.html

This is an unusual case study which shows how a sport facility is trying to provide a service that is in direct contrast to the geographical features and weather of the local environment. This is an example of a ski resort in a desert! The average daily temperature in Dubai is 24°C/75.2°F in January, rising to 41°C/105.8°F in July. This hardly seems like the kind of environment for snow sports, but a 400-metre indoor ski slope has been built. There are 23 massive air conditioners to help keep the temperature about 2°C/30°F. Obviously the major drawback of building and maintaining a facility like this is the extraordinary costs involved in 'fighting' the natural temperature and environment.

The sport industry environment

Sport organisations should look at how the general external environment influences their specific industrial environment. Figure 4.4 provides a

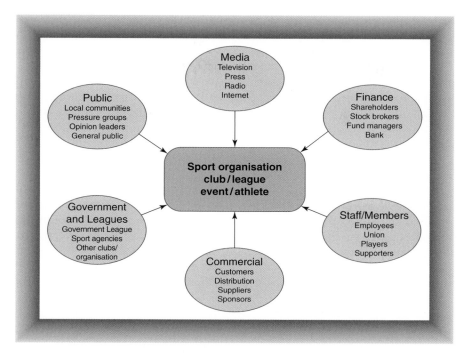

Figure 4.4 The Sport Industry (Micro) External Environment.

summary of the specific sport industry environmental factors that may influence a sport organisation's marketing decisions. The combination of an analysis of broad, external environmental factors and the sport industry external environment should complement the opportunities and threats component of the SWOT analysis.

Chapter Tool 4.1. SWOT and External Environment Analysis: A SWOT analysis is used to examine the strategic position of an organisation from inside (strengths and weaknesses) and outside (opportunities and threats). The OT part of the analysis is supported by examining the macro (or broad) external environment, which is made up of the political, economic, legal, technological, social and physical environments, as well as the sport industry environment, which is made up of media, finance, staff and members, commercial, government and leagues, and public groups.

Direct and indirect competitors

Although direct and indirect competitors are external factors, their assessment is so important that it is typically undertaken as a separate activity. Competition occurs when numerous sport organisations attempt to meet the needs of the same group of consumers. An example of a sport sector which is extremely competitive is the sporting shoe sector, where there are a large number of manufacturers and sellers trying to attract the same consumers to buy their product.

It is important for a sport organisation to understand its competition for several reasons. First, competitors may have weaknesses to be exploited. Second, competitors may have strengths that could represent a threat, or alternatively provide helpful lessons. It is also important to realise that competitors change over time. By analysing the competition, a sport organisation is forced to consider some of the opportunities and threats that it needs to manage.

There is a difference between direct and indirect competition. Direct (or immediate) competition can be defined as the competition that occurs between sellers who produce similar products and services. The example of sporting shoe manufacturers provides a good illustration. Direct competition can also exist between two products which consumers consider substitutable. Instead of purchasing Nike shoes, a sport consumer might choose to buy adidas instead. These products have differences to one another, but they are similar enough that the consumer could substitute (replace) one for the other. Secondary competition occurs when sellers produce substitute products that

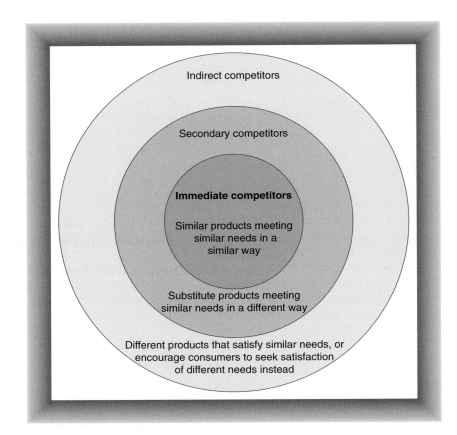

Figure 4.5 Types of Competitors.

meet consumer needs in a different way, like going to a basketball game instead of a rugby match. Here, the consumer need is entertainment rather than the experience of watching a particular sport.

Indirect competition occurs between sellers who produce *different* products and services that either satisfy similar consumer needs or encourage consumers to seek the satisfaction of different needs. In the case of sport, other forms of entertainment are a strong source of indirect competition. For example, movie theatres, music concerts, cafés, shopping centres, restaurants and even television are alternative ways that consumers could choose to spend their leisure time. Figure 4.5 illustrates the levels of direct and indirect competition.

Competitor analysis

Because competitors can have a large impact on the strategy a sport organisation develops, it is important to analyse competitors in a careful and systematic manner. In conducting a competitor analysis, it is critical to assess competitors' strategies, strengths, vulnerabilities and resources, as well as their forthcoming actions. The recommended aspects of a competitor analysis are reproduced in Table 4.2.

Five forces analysis

In addition to conducting a competitor analysis, it is advisable to conduct a *Five Forces Analysis*. This analysis was originally developed by Porter (1980), and has been adapted to the sport industry. It is the most commonly used tool for describing the competitive environment. As can be seen from

Table 4.2 Dimensions of a Competitor Analysis

Dimension	Description
Geographic scope	What region or location they operate in with emphasis on overlap.
Mission and vision	Do they intend to maintain their current market position, or do they have a vision to change their situation? What are their ambitions for the future?
Objectives	What are their short- to medium-term goals.
Market share and position	Are they a small player, a medium player or a virtual monopolist?
Strategy	What methods they are using to gain an advantage over their competition.
Resources	What are the amount and availability of resources.
Target market	To whom do they market their products and services?
Marketing mix approach	What products and services do they offer. What promotions, pricing and distribution strategies do they use.

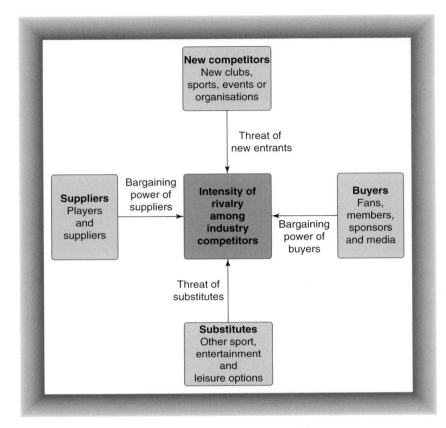

Figure 4.6 Five Forces Driving Sport Industry Competition.

Figure 4.6, this analysis focuses on five forces which drive competition in the sport industry. Understanding the competitive situation in a sport sector is a particularly helpful way of determining whether it is an attractive one in which to conduct business, and whether there is scope for existing or new products to be developed. In other words, it may help to identify future opportunities and threats. Although businesses would consider a lower level of competition better than a higher one, the situation is often not as straightforward for sport organisations. Sport organisations rely on close on-field competition to keep consumers interested. Competitive threats, however, may come in many forms, such as new leagues or sports entering the market, substitute products available to consumers, and the potential for buyers and suppliers to exert their bargaining power.

Intensity of rivalry among industry competitors

In general, greater rivalry will be present where there are more sport organisations offering similar products and services. The rivalry between Nike and adidas is an excellent example of extreme rivalry. College football teams in the

United States are another example, as would be different soccer clubs in any one country's professional soccer league. While one club is unlikely to be able to 'steal' supporters from the other, there would be significant competition between them for media exposure, corporate sponsorship, players and coaches/managers. Intensity of rivalry is placed at the centre of the diagram not only because it is so significant, but because the other four forces can all contribute to its magnitude. Typically, the outcome of a five forces analysis is represented in terms of the intensity of rivalry among industry competitors.

The threat of new entrants

Every sport organisation is faced with the possibility that at any time new competitors can enter their industry sector and offer substitute products. Of course, in some forms of professional sport, it is unlikely that new clubs or teams could enter the competition. There are typically regulations which dictate how many teams are allowed in the competition, and it may be difficult to generate a supporter base if fans hold strongly to the history and traditions of the competition. However, in other segments of the sport industry, there are often new organisations entering the marketplace, such as new sport facilities, leisure and recreational centres, events, sport apparel companies and new equipment manufacturers. In general, the greater the threat of new entrants, the higher the intensity of rivalry among industry competitors.

The bargaining power of buyers

Buyers of sport products and services include individuals, groups and organisations. Fans, sport club members, corporate sponsors and the media are all examples of parties who purchase sporting goods and services. The nature of competition in the environment will be affected by the strength of the bargaining power of buyers. The term 'bargaining power' is another way of referring to the influence that buyers have to exert pressure on suppliers in order to reduce their prices. For example, judging by the high ticket prices of some professional leagues, fans have little bargaining power. When the bargaining power is low for media broadcasters, they may have to pay extravagant sums of money to secure the rights to broadcast an event. In contrast, when bargaining power is higher, the costs of rights will be lower. For most sport organisations, however, the main buyers are fans, and since fans do not usually work together to increase their bargaining power, it remains limited. In general, the greater the bargaining power of buyers, the higher the intensity of rivalry among industry competitors.

The bargaining power of suppliers

Like buyers, suppliers may also be able to use bargaining power to force sport organisations to pay more for the inputs they require. When suppliers of raw materials threaten to raise prices or withdraw their products or services, they are attempting to improve their bargaining power. For example, suppliers of

65

inputs to sport organisations include equipment and materials manufacturers. The most significant example of suppliers using bargaining power in sport has come about in relation to players, who can be thought of as suppliers of sport talent. As some professional player groups have become unionised, they have tried to put pressure on leagues and clubs to raise their salaries and salary caps. This has been successful in some instances where the player groups have been well organised. In 2002 in the United States, for example, players in Major League Baseball threatened to strike if their salary demands were not met, which forced the league into negotiations. In contrast, a similar dispute led the US National Hockey League to cancel the entire 2004–2005 season. In general, the greater the bargaining power of suppliers, the higher the intensity of rivalry among industry competitors.

The threat of substitute products and services

Some competitors may not provide exactly the same product, but may offer alternatives or substitutes. As the sport industry expands, it is more common for different sports to compete with one another to meet similar needs of sport consumers. Other forms of leisure and entertainment also threaten to attract sport consumers' time. In general, the greater the threat of substitute products and services, the higher the intensity of rivalry among industry competitors.

Chapter Tool 4.2. Competitor and Five Forces Analyses: In order to conduct a competitor analysis it is important to be mindful of the three different categories of competitors: immediate/direct competitors, secondary competitors and indirect competitors. When considering the *what* and *how* of competitors, it is important to consider their geographic scope; vision, mission and objectives; market share and position; strategy; resources; target market; and marketing approach. It is also advisable to conduct a second type of competitor analysis: the *Five Forces Analysis* which comprises: (1) the intensity of rivalry among industry competitors, (2) the threat of new entrants into the marketplace (for example new clubs or leagues), (3) the threat of substitute products in the marketplace (such as other forms of entertainment), (4) the bargaining power of buyers (such as the media, sponsors and spectators) and (5) the bargaining power of suppliers (including players/athletes).

Analyse the organisation

The second stage in identifying sport marketing opportunities is to analyse the organisation. In order to do this, it is necessary to understand the purpose, aims and goals of an organisation in addition to the needs of an organisation's stakeholders. There are four tools which help to analyse the organisation. They are: Mission Statement; Vision Statement; Organisational Objectives; and Stakeholder Analysis.

An analysis of the organisation will provide important information about the strategic direction it intends to pursue. It is important, for example, to understand the mission, vision and objectives of an organisation, which indicate why an organisation exists, and what it is aiming to achieve. After all, the marketing efforts of an organisation are designed to fulfil its mission and achieve its objectives. It is possible that the information acquired during the organisational analysis may be considered useful to the internal (SW) analysis that contributes to the SWOT evaluation. This is one of the reasons why the three parts of stage 1 should be conducted at around the same time.

Chapter Principle 4.3: The second step in identifying sport marketing opportunities is to conduct an analysis of the organisation. This requires four tools: Mission Statement; Vision Statement; Organisational Objectives; and Stakeholder Analysis.

Mission statements

A mission statement identifies the purpose of an organisation. It should describe why an organisation was set up, what services and products it provides, and to whom they are provided. If a mission statement is not documented in writing, it can be easy for organisational members to be confused about the purpose of the organisation, or to have different ideas about what it should be. It is not uncommon for players, members, spectators, staff, coaches, media, sponsors and government representatives to have different ideas about what the purpose of a sport organisation should be. When it is recorded as a single, short statement (preferably a single sentence), this mission is a powerful declaration of the intentions of the organisation. When developing a marketing plan, this statement offers fundamental guidance in the development of a strategy, as it should be consistent with the stated purpose of the organisation. For example, imagine that a community sport organisation states that its mission is to provide access to physical activities for people with an intellectual disability in a given area. This basic guidance would be a useful starting point in developing a marketing plan. Many sport

---

Chapter Tool 4.3. Mission Statement: The sport organisation's mission statement should be reviewed in order to guide the identification of sport marketing opportunities. The mission statement reveals the purpose of an organisation: why it was created, what services and products it provides, and to whom they are provided.

organisations possess mission statements, so their consideration is a simple task within an organisational analysis.

Vision statements

Having a vision for the future is an important part of an effective sport organisation. A vision for the future is like a clear mental image of how a sport organisation would like to see itself in approximately three to five years time. A vision statement is a written record of this future image, usually no longer than a sentence. It states the medium- to long-term goals of a sport organisation, or in simple terms, what it wants to achieve in a given time. The vision is, of course, essential information before a marketing strategy can be devised. For example, if a sporting apparel manufacturer has the vision 'to be the number one brand of quality sporting clothes to the luxury market', it would be inappropriate to develop a marketing plan which involved providing budget goods and discount prices.

> *Chapter Tool 4.4. Vision Statement*: The sport organisation's vision statement should be reviewed in order to guide the identification of sport marketing opportunities. A vision statement is a written record of the desired achievements of an organisation in the future.

Organisational objectives

If a vision statement shows the medium- to long-term ambitions of an organisation, organisational objectives are the stepping stones along the way to this destination. They are the targets that must be reached in order to make the vision a reality. For example, imagine that a hockey club sits at the bottom of the championship ladder but has a vision to finish in the top three. As might be expected, achieving this vision within one season is unrealistic. Therefore, an objective might be set to improve by three places in the following season, as a stepping stone to the ultimate goal. It is essential that these objectives are measurable, which means that they must be specific enough to be able to determine with certainty that they have been achieved. For example, the objective 'to be the best team' is not measurable, as this goal does not clearly state what being the best means. Does it mean the team which wins the most games, the team with the greatest number of new players joining, or the team with the most amount of money in the bank? In sporting clubs, objectives are normally set in each of the major operational areas, such as on-field performance, youth development, finances, facilities, marketing and human resources. Just as with mission and vision statements, the objectives of an organisation help sport marketers to know where exactly to target their efforts so that they align with the broader goals of the organisation. In fact, they should provide marketers with more specific information about how to apply the mission and vision to the marketing plan.

> *Chapter Tool 4.5. Organisational Objectives*: A sport organisation's objectives should be reviewed in order to guide the identification of sport marketing opportunities. Organisational objectives are targets that must be reached in order to make the vision a reality.

Stakeholder analysis

Before an analysis of the organisation is complete, its stakeholders need to be considered. Stakeholders are all the individuals, groups and organisations that have an interest in a sport organisation. These stakeholders might include employees, players, members, the league, association or governing body, government, community, facility owners, sponsors, broadcasters and fans. The obvious question this list raises is: Who is the sport marketer going to try to make happy? The needs of different stakeholders will vary, and each will lead to corresponding implications for a marketing strategy. An interesting example is the case of some professional sport clubs, such as football clubs, which tend to focus on winning to the exclusion of all other priorities, including sensible financial management. While this may make members and fans happy in the short term, other stakeholders may not be happy, such as governing bodies, leagues and employees, who are more likely to be interested in the financial sustainability of the organisation. In a stakeholder analysis, it is necessary to consider the bargaining power of the different stakeholders. Some stakeholders, such as sponsors and government departments, may withdraw their funding if their needs are not met.

A careful analysis of the goals and objectives of each stakeholder in their affiliation with the sport organisation must therefore be completed before a strategic direction can be set. A marketing strategy can be strongly influenced by the beliefs, values and expectations of powerful stakeholders. It should be noted that sport consumers may be considered stakeholders of sport organisations. However, an analysis of customer needs is part of market research, which is outlined in the forthcoming section.

> *Chapter Tool 4.6. Stakeholder Analysis*: A stakeholder analysis involves assessing the diverse agendas of all individuals, groups and organisations that have an interest in a sport organisation.

Analyse market and consumers

The third step in identifying sport marketing opportunities refers to gathering information about the market and the consumers it contains. Market research is the process of learning about the marketplace and what consumers

69

want, assessing their desires and expectations, and determining how to entice consumers to use a sport product. Market research is also used to ascertain whether sport consumers have reacted to a marketing plan as expected. In other words, market research is a way of evaluating the success of a marketing program.

Market research is concerned with answering a number of general questions about the market, such as:

● Who are the sport organisation's customers?
● What do these customers need and want?
● In what manner and how often should customers be contacted?
● Which marketing strategies elicit the most favourable responses from customers?
● What responses will each type of marketing strategy elicit?
● What mistakes have been made?

These questions are only a starting point because market research can have quite specific uses. Figure 4.7 highlights the potential applications of market research.

As Figure 4.7 indicates, there are five applications of market research. The first is to determine specific information about the market: who are customers, and what they want? The other four areas represent what is known as the *marketing mix* (product, price, promotion, place). Market research cannot only help to identify the best strategies in these areas, but also to evaluate how successful they have been once implemented.

The more detailed the information obtained from market research, the easier it is to design an effective marketing program. However, the more the detail, the greater the cost of the market research. Thus, the difficulty facing small and resource-challenged sport organisations is that market research is expensive, time-consuming and expertise intensive. For these organisations,

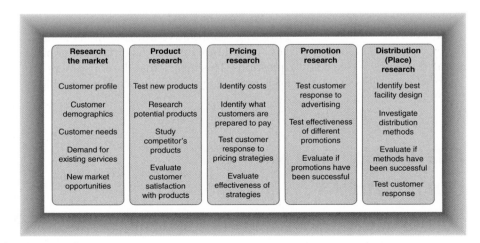

Research the market	Product research	Pricing research	Promotion research	Distribution (Place) research
Customer profile	Test new products	Identify costs	Test customer response to advertising	Identify best facility design
Customer demographics	Research potential products	Identify what customers are prepared to pay	Test effectiveness of different promotions	Investigate distribution methods
Customer needs	Study competitor's products	Test customer response to pricing strategies	Evaluate if promotions have been successful	Evaluate if methods have been successful
Demand for existing services	Evaluate customer satisfaction with products	Evaluate effectiveness of strategies		Test customer response
New market opportunities				

Figure 4.7 Applications of Market Research.

the answer is to find a rapid and inexpensive approach, while avoiding the pitfalls of poor research, which include:

- Using an unrepresentative sample
- Asking irrelevant questions
- Ignoring selected answers
- 'Stacking' questions so that they force certain types of responses that are 'leading' and include biases
- Failing to accept criticism

Different types of market research

There are two types of market research: *quantitative* and *qualitative*. Quantitative research involves numerical information; this information is superficial and usually gathered from a diverse and large sample of people. Qualitative research involves non-numerical information (such as words from an interview of a consumer). Qualitative information is in-depth, and is usually gathered from a narrow and relatively small sample of consumers. In order to better understand the differences between quantitative and qualitative research, it is helpful to consider some examples of each.

Chapter Principle 4.4: The third step in identifying sport marketing opportunities involves acquiring information about the sport market and consumers. Market research is the process of collecting information in order to learn about the marketplace and what consumers in general, and a sport organisation's customers specifically, want. It involves two kinds of information: quantitative or numerical and qualitative or non-numerical.

Quantitative research

The most common method of gathering quantitative information is to use a survey or questionnaire. A survey/questionnaire may use multiple choices or scaled responses (see below) questions. This means that the consumers can give brief responses to set questions regarding specific topics. It is possible to survey a large group of consumers this way, and to analyse the results with the help of a computer spreadsheet. Questionnaires may be conducted via mail outs, one-on-one interviews or over the phone or Internet.

An example of a scaled response survey question
Question: How would you rate the seating quality at this venue?
(please circle the number that best represents your response)

1	2	3	4	5	6	7
Poor			Average			Outstanding

Quantitative research should be used when a sport organisation already knows something about its customers and would like to refine this knowledge with greater precision. For example, if a sport organisation already knows that there are four main reasons why their customers employ their services, then they can use questionnaires to establish the relative importance of each. In addition, questionnaires can help to estimate how many customers actually share each of these reasons for using the service. Quantitative research can also be used to evaluate how satisfied customers are with the product, pricing, promotion and distribution strategies of a sport organisation. Furthermore, quantitative research techniques are valuable for constructing demographic profiles of customers (e.g. gender, age, marital status, education, etc.) or of a general segment of consumers.

There are obviously situations in which quantitative research is not a useful method. If a sport organisation does not know anything about its customers, it is not advisable to give them a survey with inflexible questions to try to get to know them. This is because the set questions and topics on a survey may miss the mark altogether, and may not give customers the opportunity to share their unique perspectives. Also, it is often desirable to find out about complex issues, such as the motivations behind customers' consumption behaviour, which cannot be revealed using the relatively superficial information that a survey elicits. Circling a number or ticking a box on a questionnaire will not help a sport marketer get to the heart of consumer opinion and behaviour. For example, a survey may show that a netball club has a married, middle-aged female player with three children who plays because she enjoys the game and wants the exercise, and is relatively happy with the quality of service. However, it is unlikely to tell us that she is thinking about taking up basketball because her kids play, it is less stressful on her knees, that she will not play next season because a business commitment will take her overseas for several months, that her sister is an expert in marketing and specialises in non-profit organisations, that she would like to try coaching a junior netball team, that she finds it annoying that the showers in the changing rooms constantly leak, and that weekends are not a very convenient time to play games after all. While some of these questions can be answered by questionnaires and surveys, designing a survey that is so comprehensive would be impractical. For these reasons, a sport organisation may choose to undertake a qualitative approach as a first step in its market research process.

Chapter Tool 4.7. Quantitative Market Research: Quantitative research involves the collection of numerical information through a survey or questionnaire and should be used when a sport organisation already knows something about its customers and would like to refine this knowledge with greater precision.

Qualitative research

Qualitative research is a method of acquiring information that is non-statistical but in-depth. Because qualitative information is more detailed, complicated and time-consuming to collect, it is usually gathered from a narrow and relatively small sample of sport consumers. The results obtained through qualitative research can also be used later to help construct a quantitative survey, if required. There are a number of effective and inexpensive approaches to qualitative market research that can provide rich and detailed information about the market and its consumers. They include:

1. Interviews and focus groups
2. Suggestion boxes
3. Complaint analysis

Interviews and focus groups

One of the fundamental tools of qualitative market research is the interview, which can be conducted in a one-to-one situation or with numerous respondents at the same time. One efficient method is known as the focus group where a group of customers from the group being studied are gathered in an informal setting, and encouraged to talk about specific issues. To be successful, the focus group should be conducted by an interviewer who has the skills to coordinate the group without inhibiting, intimidating or leading the respondents, so that ideas can free-flow and all opinions are expressed. Sessions should be always audio-recorded so that they can be evaluated for important themes after the event.

Suggestion boxes

A suggestion box is a simple tool that can work if taken seriously. It is important to both the research process and good relationships with customers that the suggestions are read regularly and acted upon. It is usually best to document all suggestions (anonymously) and responses in a prominent place within the organisation where readily accessible to all customers, members and staff. It is also best not to make excuses if there is a genuine problem, and the actions taken to improve the situation should also be identified. Nothing is worse than a suggestion box with a rusty lock, so there is no point in pursuing this form of customer feedback without the commitment to deal with the suggestions promptly and systematically.

Complaint analysis

This method is cheap and relatively easy to implement. Customer complaints can provide an insight into the elements of the product or service that are not meeting customer needs. With this information, it is possible to consider how to change and improve the situation, hopefully leading to improved customer satisfaction. Complaint analysis involves encouraging customers to contact employees directly if they have a problem or a complaint. It is advisable to respond to every complaint with a personal and formal letter or e-mail which thanks customers for highlighting the problem and gives them information about how the problem will be resolved.

> *Chapter Tool 4.8. Qualitative Market Research*: Qualitative research involves the collection of non-statistical, but in-depth information through interviews and focus groups, suggestion boxes or complaint analysis.

Sport market opportunities

The information that was obtained in stage 1 of the sport marketing framework, and its subsequent analysis, should highlight potential market opportunities. A market opportunity is a situation where a new or modified product or service can be introduced that meets an unfulfilled sport consumer need. However, it is first necessary to establish whether the opportunity is worth capitalising upon. Once that is decided, the target consumer group can be identified, along with a solid idea of where the sport product or service can be placed within the context of a marketplace that already contains sport products and services.

> *Chapter Principle 4.5*: A market opportunity is a situation where a new or modified product or service can be introduced that meets an unfulfilled sport consumer need.

A useful tool for examining the marketing opportunities available is the Product-Market Expansion Grid. The grid provides a summary of the opportunities available for 'selling' a particular product or service. The Product-Market Expansion Grid is shown in Table 4.3.

Market penetration is the first possible type of market opportunity. It is an opportunity to increase 'sales' by attracting more consumers without sacrificing the old. An example of a market penetration opportunity in the horse-racing industry would be to attract even more males over the age of 50 to attend race meetings. It is therefore a 'more of the same' approach.

Market development is similar to market penetration in that the product remains the same. However, with market development the aim is to expand the target market to reach a wider range of consumers. A market development approach therefore promotes the product or service to existing markets

Table 4.3 Product-Market Expansion Grid

	Existing Product	*New Product*
Existing markets	Market penetration	Product development
New markets	Market development	Diversification

as well as to a wider range of consumers. In the horse-racing example, a market development opportunity could be to attract more of the existing customers (males over the age of 50) as well as wider range of consumers (such as women over 50 as well).

The third category, *product development*, involves marketing to the same consumers with a new version of the product or service. This new or modified product is 'sold' to the same target market as the existing product, like Twenty20 Cricket and beach volleyball.

The final category, *diversification*, involves marketing a new product to a new target market. It is an attempt 'start-over'. Examples of diversification include indoor cricket, mixed netball and modified rules versions of sport for children.

The Product-Market Expansion Grid provides alternatives to consider when going through the process of setting a strategic market direction, which is examined in the next chapter.

Chapter Tool 4.9. Product-Market Expansion Grid: The Product-Market Expansion Grid provides a summary of the opportunities available for 'selling' a particular product or service. It highlights four possibilities: (1) *market penetration* is an opportunity to increase 'sales' by attracting more consumers without sacrificing the old; (2) *market development* is an opportunity where the product remains the same but seeks to expand the target market to reach a wider range of consumers; (3) *product development* is an opportunity involving marketing to the same consumers with a new version of the product or service; and (4) *diversification* is an opportunity involving marketing a new product to a new target market.

Case Study—Nike: Turning Adversity into Opportunity

by Sharyn McDonald

Seizing opportunities are part of innovative advancement in most sport equipment manufacturing companies, but there is more to it than just releasing the latest design. Sport consumers seeking the latest fashion and equipment readily accepted Nike's mass-produced sporting products until 1997 when negative media attention highlighted the conditions imposed upon offshore factory workers. Subjected to boycotts, protests and a declining share value, Nike responded to the poor reputation the negative publicity had generated and now proactively assumes responsibility for its manufacturing methods.

Realising the power of a good reputation, Nike sought to make significant changes to their social and environmental impact. From the buildings they operate in to the materials they use, Nike introduced sustainable design principles. 'Reuse-a-shoe' is one successful initiative which illustrates Nike's ability to turn an environmental problem into a strategic opportunity. In 1993, Nike developed a recycling program to 'close the loop'. Instead of athletic shoes sent to landfill, consumers can deposit worn out athletic shoes, regardless of the brand, at any Nike factory around the world. The shoes are recycled into a granulated rubber sports surface material. This initiative takes place in Canada, the United Kingdom, the Netherlands, Germany, Australia, Japan and the United States, where shoes are processed. Since its inception, Nike has recycled more than 20 million pairs of shoes and contributed to over 250 sport surfaces, including running tracks, basketball courts and playgrounds.

Surface donations are just one aspect of Nike's social contribution towards communities in need. There are a range of social issues Nike is involved with, including combating obesity and poverty. 'NikeGO' is a successful initiative targeting inactive youths from age eight upwards to motivate them to become involved in physical activity while having fun. They facilitate this through accessible programs both inside and outside of schools. Nike has worked cooperatively with non-government organisations to address the poor conditions in its associated offshore localities. In 2007, continued efforts to address working conditions in offshore factories saw Nike resume soccer ball manufacturing in Pakistan. Strict standards mean that the manufacturing plant vendor must offer fair wages and social benefits for workers. Nike seeks to empower the workers and improve conditions; in turn the Nike brand is enhanced.

While ensuring it has considered social and environmental needs, Nike continues to pursue innovative ideas in response to strategic opportunities. In 2002, Nike partnered with Lego developing a 'BIONICLE' shoe. The shoes have interchangeable toe caps designed to emulate the masks of Lego BIONICLE characters. Targeting children's imaginations, Nike saw this as an opportunity to further encourage children to become active. Nike's innovation has also led them to a partnership with Apple iPod. In 2006, Nike released the design of the Nike+ shoes which allows the wearer to embed an iPod transmitter within the sole. As participants walk or run, the senor relays information to their iPod nano, logging their time, distance, pace and calories burned. Despite the negative publicity surrounding their manufacturing policies, Nike have continually sought potential opportunities in the environment.

For further information see:

Apple Store (2007). Nike+ iPod Sport Kit. Available at:
http://store.apple.com/1-800-MY-APPLE/WebObjects/AppleStore?
productLearnMore=MA365LL/B

Beaverton, O. (2003). NikeGO Wraps Up Year One. Available at:
http://www.nike.com/nikebiz/news/pressrelease.jhtml?year=2003&mo
nth=08&letter=f

Beaverton, O. (2007). Nike Resumes Soccer Ball Production in
Pakistan. Available at:
http://www.nike.com/nikebiz/news/pressrelease.jhtml?year=2007&mo
nth=05&letter=h

Enfield, C. (2002). LEGO Company and Nike Launch BIONICLE™ Shoe
Partnership. Available at:
http://www.nike.com/nikebiz/news/pressrelease.jhtml?year=2002&mo
nth=11&letter=a

Nikebiz.com (2007). Reuse-a-shoe, Worn Out. Play On. Available at:
http://www.nike.com/nikebiz/nikebiz.jhtml?page=27&cat=reuseashoe

NikeGO (2007).
http://www.nike.com/nikebiz/nikego/index.jsp

Principles summary

- Chapter Principle 4.1: The Sport Marketing Framework describes the four stages of sport marketing: identifying sport marketing opportunities, developing a sport marketing strategy, planning the sport marketing mix, and implementing and controlling the sport marketing strategy.
- Chapter Principle 4.2: The first step in identifying sport marketing opportunities is to analyse the internal and external environment using the tools of SWOT analysis (with external environment analysis) and competitor analysis (with the Five Forces analysis).
- Chapter Principle 4.3: The second step in identifying sport marketing opportunities is to conduct an analysis of the organisation. This requires four tools: the Mission Statement; Vision Statement; Organisational Objectives; and Stakeholder Analysis.
- Chapter Principle 4.4: The third step in identifying sport marketing opportunities involves acquiring information about the sport market and consumers. Market research is the process of collecting information in order to learn about the marketplace and what consumers in general, and a sport organisation's customers specifically, want. It involves two kinds of information: quantitative or numerical, and qualitative or non-numerical.

● Chapter Principle 4.5: A market opportunity is a situation where a new or modified product or service can be introduced that meets an unfulfilled sport consumer need.

Tools summary

● Chapter Tool 4.1. SWOT and External Environment Analysis
● Chapter Tool 4.2. Competitor and Five Forces Analyses
● Chapter Tool 4.3. Mission Statement
● Chapter Tool 4.4. Vision Statement
● Chapter Tool 4.5. Organisational Objectives
● Chapter Tool 4.6. Stakeholder Analysis
● Chapter Tool 4.7. Quantitative Market Research
● Chapter Tool 4.8. Qualitative Market Research
● Chapter Tool 4.9. Product-Market Expansion Grid

Review questions

1. Differentiate between the four stages of the Sport Marketing Framework.
2. Identify the three parts of identifying sport marketing opportunities. Provide a general explanation of their respective functions.
3. For a sport organisation you know well, write a brief mission statement and vision statement.
4. What are the different kinds of sport marketing objectives?
5. Under what circumstances would it be advisable to use a qualitative approach to collecting market research information?
6. Devise an original example for each category in the Product-Market Expansion Grid.

Relevant websites

http://news.bbc.co.uk/sport (BBC Sport homepage)

http://www.pch.gc.ca (The Department of Canadian Heritage website, including Sport Canada)

http://www.skidubai.com (Ski Dubai website)

http://www.visit-dubai-city.com (Dubai City website)

Further reading

Mason, D., Andrews, D. & Silk, M. (eds.) (2005). *Qualitative Methods for Sports Studies*, Berg, Oxford.

Veal, A. J. (2006). *Research Methods for Leisure and Tourism*. (3rd ed.). Pearson Education, London.

Reference

Porter, M. (1980). *Competitive Strategy*, The Free Press, New York.

5

Sport marketing strategy

Overview

This chapter explains stage 2 of the Sport Marketing Framework which comprises two parts: (a) develop strategic marketing direction and (b) develop sport marketing positioning. The chapter includes guidance on the process of setting marketing objectives and performance measures, developing a sport marketing strategy, determining market positioning and market segmentation strategies, and preparing to devise the marketing mix.

By the end of this chapter, readers should be able to:

- Discuss the process of determining a strategic marketing direction.
- Identify the main considerations when developing strategic marketing objectives.
- Outline the factors critical to setting performance measures.
- Describe the importance of determining a core marketing strategy.
- Define the terms market positioning and market segmentation.
- Discuss the importance of market segmentation.
- Identify the main approaches to market segmentation.
- Describe the process and importance of market positioning.
- Outline the major elements of the marketing mix.

Stage 2: Develop a strategic marketing strategy

The second stage of the Sport Marketing Framework is to 'develop a sport marketing strategy', and is highlighted in Figure 5.1. The first step of stage 2 requires the development of a strategic marketing direction by identifying marketing objectives and performance measures.

> *Chapter Principle 5.1*: The second stage of the Sport Marketing Framework is to develop a sport marketing strategy. This requires two steps: (a) to develop a strategic marketing direction, and (b) to develop a sport marketing position.

Develop a strategic marketing direction

There are two steps involved in developing a strategic marketing direction. First, marketing objectives need to be developed. Second, performance measures need to be assigned to these objectives. Both are outlined in the following section.

> *Chapter Principle 5.2*: Developing a strategic marketing direction involves constructing marketing objectives and setting performance measures.

Marketing objectives

The word objective means an aim or goal. A marketing objective is a goal that a sport organisation may realistically achieve as the result of its marketing strategy. It is typically summarised in the form of a short sentence, which describes what will be achieved as a result of marketing activities. Marketing objectives represent a guide through all of the coming stages of the marketing framework. They should offer a clear direction to follow when it comes to conceiving the rest of the marketing plan. This means that the importance of marketing objectives cannot be underestimated. It is critical to think about marketing objectives carefully, and to document them clearly. They should provide everyone in a sport organisation with a clear direction so that all marketing activities are carried out in line with predetermined goals. As recorded in Table 5.1, there are four broad categories of marketing objectives

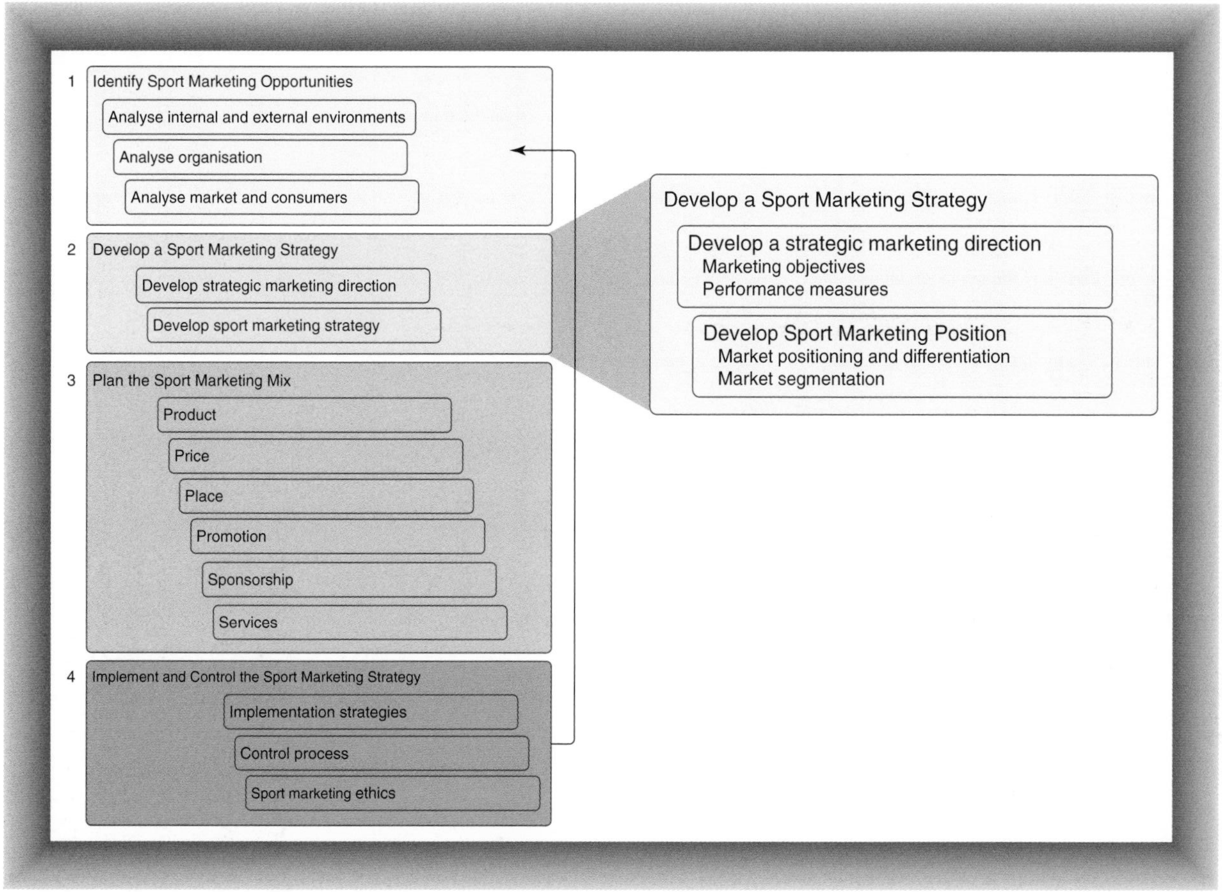

Develop a Sport Marketing Strategy

Develop a strategic marketing direction
Marketing objectives
Performance measures

Develop Sport Marketing Position
Market positioning and differentiation
Market segmentation

1 Identify Sport Marketing Opportunities

Analyse internal and external environments

Analyse organisation

Analyse market and consumers

2 Develop a Sport Marketing Strategy

Develop strategic marketing direction

Develop sport marketing strategy

3 Plan the Sport Marketing Mix

Product

Price

Place

Promotion

Sponsorship

Services

4 Implement and Control the Sport Marketing Strategy

Implementation strategies

Control process

Sport marketing ethics

Figure 5.1 Develop a Sport Marketing Strategy.

83

Table 5.1 The Four Main Categories of Sport Marketing Objectives

Category	Examples of Marketing Objectives
Participation	• To increase the number of members in a club • To increase the number of clubs in a sport or competition • To increase the number of consumers using a service • To improve spectator levels at a competition or event • To expand the number of club administrators or officials • To expand the number of volunteers involved • To increase the volume or frequency of consumer use of the product or service
Performance	• To increase market share • To increase the range of products or services on offer to consumers • To improve customer satisfaction and service quality
Promotion	• To promote a health and well-being message • To improve the public 'image' of the organisation • To increase customer awareness of the product/service
Profit	• To increase product or service sales • To increase profit margins • To acquire new sponsorships or grants • To increase annual profit or surplus (or decrease expenses or deficit) • To increase the amount that sales revenue exceeds costs • To improve the ratio of cost to revenue

that sport organisations may pursue: participation, performance, promotion and profit.

Privately owned sport facilities like gymnasiums and recreation centres will have *profit* as their main objective. This would also be the main aim for sport equipment and apparel manufacturers such as FILA, and professional sport clubs that operate in franchises like in North America, and as public companies. In fact, the corporate or professional sector of sport is interested primarily in profits. Any other objectives that these organisations might develop would remain subservient, or a means to achieving a greater profit. In theory, a privately owned professional club may want to sign up more club members, but only so that they can make more money. However, most business managers understand that the fastest route to profit in professional sport is to win.

On the other hand, many sport organisations will not have profit as their main objective. For example, sport clubs and community-based clubs will have *performance* and *participation* objectives. National sport associations and government sport agencies may also be interested in *promoting* messages about healthy lifestyles. Generally speaking, sport organisations that are member-based are set up as non-profit organisations and therefore will not set profit as their main objective. It is still important for them to make sure they are earning enough money to cover their costs, or perhaps a little more to spend on developing new services or buying new equipment. However, for them, profit should be a means to an end, not their primary objective. Some recommendations when it comes to writing good sport marketing objectives follow.

Writing good marketing objectives

1. *Marketing objectives should match organisational objectives*. Marketing objectives should help the sport organisation to achieve its overarching organisation objectives. In fact, marketing objectives should be stepping stones along the way that will help the organisation to realise its overall vision.
2. *Objectives should be realistic*. Marketing objectives should be plausible and within reach, especially considering the resources available to a sport organisation.
3. *Marketing objectives should focus on action*. Marketing objectives should say what is going to be done. This is why the examples in Table 5.1 begin with the word 'To'.
4. *Marketing objectives should be narrowed down to the most important*. By narrowing objectives down to as few as possible, the sport organisation will be better at focusing its energy on what really matters. Five or less is a good ambition.
5. *Marketing objectives should be prioritised and ranked from the most important to the least important*. An organisation should know which objectives are the most important. To do this it will need to discuss and consult within the marketing department, and with the other managers of the sport organisation.
6. *Marketing objectives should be documented*. There should be a record to review at any time in order to ensure focus remains on the objectives and so that they can be evaluated at a later stage of the sport marketing framework.
7. *Marketing objectives should be clear, specific and measurable*. If objectives are not clear, it becomes difficult to know exactly what is wanted. For example, the objectives in Table 5.1 are clear, such as the aim 'to increase membership levels'. But, if it was 'to improve participation', then this would not be clear, as the kind of participation desired is left unsaid (membership numbers, spectator levels, number of volunteers etc.). An unclear objective also makes it difficult to determine if an organisation has achieved what it wanted. As a result, all marketing objectives need to be measurable.
8. *Marketing objectives should be time-focused*. Without a time focus it is impossible to determine when further marketing activities should be undertaken.

> *Chapter Tool 5.1. Marketing Objectives*: A marketing objective is a goal that a sport organisation wants to achieve as the result of its marketing strategy. There are four different categories of marketing objectives that sport organisations may pursue: participation, performance, promotion and profit. All marketing objectives should be consistent with organisational objectives, realistic, action-oriented, narrowed down and ranked in order of importance, documented, clear, specific and measurable, and time-focused.

Performance measures

Once objectives have been set, it is important to add performance measures. The word measure refers to a way of estimating, calculating or assessing whether an objective has been achieved. It usually involves finding a way to quantify or put a number to an objective. For example, imagine that one organisational objective is 'to increase profit'. A possible performance measure would nominate the amount of the increase and the time period in which it is to be accomplished, say $10 000 in one year. This performance measure has added a quantity to the objective, and has also made it easy to determine whether it has been reached or not. Some further examples appear in Table 5.2.

> *Chapter Tool 5.2. Performance Measures*: Performance measures quantify or put numbers to objectives in terms of magnitude and time so that their specific achievement is transparent.

Table 5.2 Examples of Performance Measures

Common Examples of Marketing Objectives	*Possible Performance Measures*
To increase club membership	To increase membership from 70 to 100 members by January 2010
To increase the number of people who use our service	To increase the number of people who use our service to 50 customers per month by July 2009
To improve spectator levels at a competition	To increase spectator levels to an average of 25 000 spectators per game, by December 2009, as measured by ticket sales
To increase customer satisfaction levels	To increase customer satisfaction levels to 7/10 as rated by them on an annual customer satisfaction survey
To increase profit	To increase profit to $120 000, calculated at the end of the 2009 financial year
To increase awareness of our sport product	To increase the number of people who have heard of our product in the India to 100 000, as measured by market research

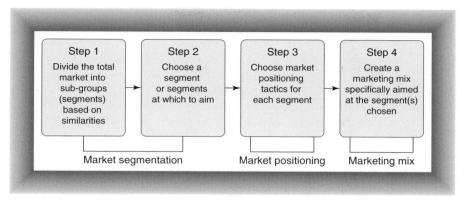

Figure 5.2 Develop Sport Marketing Positioning.

Developing sport marketing positioning

The process of constructing a sport marketing position involves four steps. Steps 1 and 2 involve market segmentation, step 3 introduces a market positioning strategy and step 4 leads to a marketing mix. This section overviews these steps, including a detailed explanation of market segmentation and market positioning. The development of the marketing mix is examined in detail over the six forthcoming chapters. Figure 5.2 illustrates the four steps of developing sport marketing positioning.

> *Chapter Principle 5.3*: Developing a sport marketing position involves four steps: market segmentation (1, 2), market positioning tactics (3) and devising the marketing mix (4).

Interactive case

Log on to the following websites and consider the examples of Formula 1 motor racing and synchronised swimming, and think about what kinds of consumers might be motivated to attend each of these kinds of events.

http://www.formula1.com
http://www.usasynchro.org

By completing the activity above, it will become apparent that there are many ways in which the consumers of Formula 1 are likely to be different to the consumers of synchronised swimming. Formula 1 attracts a significant proportion of male consumers, many of whom would be 18–35 years of age. These consumers are probably motivated by the drama and spectacle of racing, and the sensory stimulation of burning rubber and revving engines!

They may value the 'masculine' and 'macho' appeal of this type of sport, and have a keen interest in the technical features of high performance cars. In contrast, consumers who attend a synchronised swimming event are more likely to be females and will cover a wider age group beginning with pre-teens. These consumers are more likely to be attracted to the visual appeal of the sport, and value the performance skills of the athletes.

It is worth noting that just because a group of consumers is attracted to an event right now, it does not always have to remain that way. In fact, this is where marketing comes in! It is possible for a marketing program to try to attract new and different types of consumers. Formula 1, for example, might try to attract more female spectators by including new elements into their event, such as 'Fashion-On-The-Track' (this is something that many horse-racing events have successfully introduced). Grouping consumers together based on a similarity that they share is the basis of market segmentation.

Market segmentation

Not all sport consumers are the same. Different people are motivated to consume sport for different reasons. It is also true to say that different sports or events will attract different kinds of consumers; Formula 1 motor racing appeals to a different crowd than synchronised swimming. This means that sport marketers must have an understanding of the kind of consumers that are currently attracted to their products and services, as well as the kind of consumers they might like to attract in the future.

Market segmentation is the process of categorising groups of consumers together, based on their similar needs or wants. A market is the total group of potential consumers for a product, and can include retailers, businesses, government, media and individuals. Market segmentation involves breaking down this total group into smaller groups based on something that the consumers have in common, such as their age, gender, interests or needs. Market segmentation recognises that it is not possible for a sport organisation to be all things to all consumers. Once a sport organisation has selected a particular segment or segments of the market, it can customise its product and marketing strategies to meet their specific needs. By breaking down sport consumers into different segments (or sections), it is possible for a sport organisation to use its limited marketing resources more effectively.

Imagine the marketing situation of a large fitness and recreation centre with swimming facilities. A forthcoming Olympic Games might provide an opportunity for them to market their facility at a time when many people are watching and thinking about sport and fitness. One non-segmented (mass marketing) approach would involve advertising the facility on television, thereby reaching a large but diverse group of people. However, television advertising is extremely expensive and may not be the best use of money. Another disadvantage of this idea is that many people who will see the promotion will not be interested in the facility's services because they live some distance away. The advertisement is wasted on these consumers. The alternative approach would be to target a specific segment (or a couple of

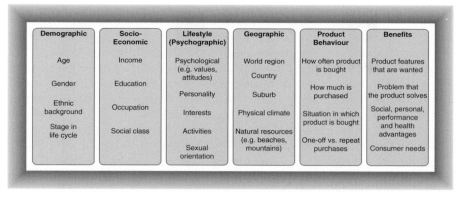

Figure 5.3 Categories for Segmenting Sport Consumers.

segments). For example, some research undertaken by the facility might reveal that stay-at-home mothers with young children who live within 20 kilometres of the facility have a strong interest in getting fit and meeting other mothers. A marketing program could be tailored to these consumers by offering a special off-peak rate during the day, creating a space for coffee and socialising, and advertising the facility through all the kindergartens in a 20 kilometre radius. Depending on the facility's resources, it may also be possible to consider developing childcare facilities or negotiating an agreement for casual childcare to be provided by a local business.

The process of segmentation

Market segmentation involves two parts. First, the market must be divided into sub-groups based on a common feature. This can be done with the help of market research, as discussed earlier in the chapter. Second, the target segment needs to be determined because the segment(s) chosen need(s) to be substantial enough to justify all the efforts associated with developing and implementing the marketing strategy. It is equally important that the segment identified is different from the general market. If the needs of all the consumers in the total market are very similar, it might not be necessary or profitable to try to break them down any further.

Ways of segmenting sport consumers

There are six ways of grouping consumers together for segmentation, and are illustrated in Figure 5.3. Consumers are often grouped together into the following categories: demographic, socio-economic, lifestyle (psychographic), geographic, product behaviour and benefits. Each is described in the following paragraphs.

Demographic segmentation

Demographic segmentation is the most conventional and common in sport marketing. Demographic variables include age, gender, ethnic background and what stage of their working 'life cycle' a consumer occupies. Sporting apparel, for example, is often targeted towards consumers based on their gender and age. A popular age demographic that has been recently recognised is known as the 'Tweenies': young people aged between 10 and 12 who are not yet teenagers, but are no longer children. Many fashion and music products in particular have been marketed specifically to this high growth consumer segment.

The life cycle category is less obvious than age and gender. Traditionally, life cycle refers to the conventional stages of life from being single, married with children, 'empty-nesters' (couples with adult children who have left the family home), retired and the elderly. In addition to these traditional stages, sport marketers also recognise relatively new categories such as: married without children, same-sex couples, single parents, blended families and the separated or divorced. The life cycle stage of a consumer will naturally make a difference to how, when and why they spend money on sport products. A single, working adult may have more income to spend on expensive tickets to high-profile sport events, whereas a parent of young children may prefer to buy a membership to the local club so that their daughter can participate in sport every week.

A consumer's ethnic background refers to their race, nationality or religion. It is important for sport marketers not to think of the ethnic background of different groups in stereotypical ways, but to try to understand their unique behaviours. The major national soccer leagues in Australia and the United States possess a strong ethnic fan base. Both of these countries have large numbers of immigrant populations, with Melbourne's Italian community the largest outside Italy itself. For a person who immigrates to a new country, the sport that they enjoyed in their country of origin can become an important link for them. It connects them not only to their personal history, but also to a new community, which may share similar experiences of settling in a new country.

Socio-economic segmentation

Socio-economic segmentation refers to aspects of a consumer's social or economic circumstances, such as their income, the highest level of education they have achieved and their occupation. These kinds of factors are often grouped together under demographic segmentation. However, they have been separated out here for clarity.

Income is a popular way to segment markets. How much money a consumer earns (and their disposable income) is likely to have an influence on their purchasing behaviour. A family living on a tight budget is unlikely to buy box seats to a football match. The sport apparel industry is another example: discount department stores offer lower income customers easy access and budget products. On the other hand, there are higher priced specialty stores, which offer middle-income customers brand names with the latest imported fashion colours and designs.

Table 5.3 Segmentation Examples

Opinions (about)	Interests	Activities	Personality
Politics	Family and children	Work	Values
Education	Home	Leisure and entertainment	Attitudes
Environment	Career	Self-care	Beliefs
The future	Art and culture	Holidays	Hopes
Religion	Sport and leisure	Hobbies	Habits
Social issues	Achievements	Home tasks	Expectations
Money	Travel and languages	Volunteering	Temperament
Morality	Community support	Social events	Reactions to situations
War	Charity	Community activities	Ways of thinking

A person's education, income and occupation are often strongly related. The higher the level of education a person achieves, the more likely they are to earn more and work in jobs with higher status. It can also be true that the higher a consumer or their family's wealth, the more likely they are to be able to afford an education which can lead to more prestigious employment. Some sports have been associated with certain social class segments. For example, football has traditionally been seen as a working class game, golf and tennis as middle class activities and polo and yachting are perceived as sports of the rich. Of course, the popularity and accessibility of these sports can shift and change over time. In Western countries the average income is significantly higher than in developing countries, and many consumers spend significant sums of money on the technologies necessary to access sport and entertainment.

Lifestyle (psychographic) segmentation

Lifestyle factors refer to consumers' day-to-day routines and their general way of life. These can be influenced by a consumer's personality, their interests, activities and their opinions. For example, a consumer's activities include what they do for leisure, socialising, sport, hobbies and holidaying; their interests may include family, home, recreation, fashion and/or a desire to achieve. It is possible to segment consumers based on lifestyle factors as Table 5.3 demonstrates.

Geographic segmentation

Sport consumers can be segmented according to their geographical residence. Geographical segments might include local (like a suburb or state/county/province), national and international regions. A local baseball club, for example, might target their services to consumers who live in a 5–10 kilometre radius. The environment, climate and natural resources in a region can also provide the basis for segmentation. For example, the high mountains in Switzerland mean that there is a large variety of snow sports available to residents (and tourists of course), while the beaches in Thailand provide plenty of opportunity for warm water sports.

Product behaviour segmentation

It is possible to segment sport consumers on the basis of their buying behaviour. For example, consumers may display similarities in how much and how often they purchase certain sport products, the situations in which they buy sport products and how loyal they are to certain sport brands (such as whether they repeat purchase, or just buy once-off). Sport consumers who have a strong emotional connection to a brand or team, and who see it as an extension of themselves, are more likely to be loyal. This means that they are more likely to repeatedly buy tickets to games and purchase memberships and memorabilia, even if the team is performing poorly. Other consumers may be more interested in sport as a form of entertainment or socialising. These consumers will probably engage with sport in situations where their friends are involved, where special events and promotions are offered and where additional entertainment options are available. Another example of behaviour segmentation in sport may be found in the consumers who buy life-memberships or season tickets, compared with those who attend games casually. Consumers who sign up for season tickets are buying sport on a 'heavy usage' basis. Those who rarely attend are light users in comparison. Chapter 3 provides a detailed set of sport fan categories based on sport consumption behaviour.

Benefits segmentation

A final way that sport consumers can be segmented is based on the similar benefits that they seek from using a sport product or service. For example, a particular sport shoe brand might have shock-absorbing qualities that are appealing to one group of consumers, while another group of consumers may be more interested in the colours and fashion appeal of a different brand. Different sport products offer different advantages, such as social, personal, performance or health advantages. Some of the consumers that are interested in one aspect of a brand's features or benefits can be grouped together, sometimes on the basis of the underlying needs that are being met, such as fitness, entertainment or belonging.

Approaches to using segmentation

In addition to the six kinds of segmentation, there are three main ways of using segmentation. In step 2 of the segmentation process, it is possible to choose one or more than one segment. It is also possible not to choose any at

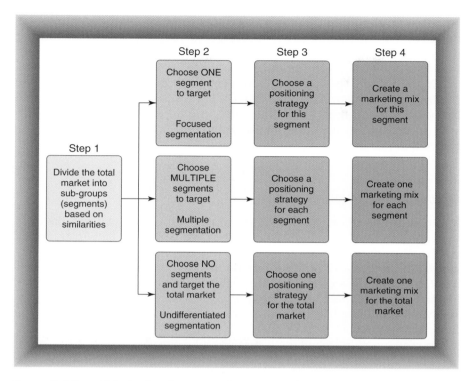

Figure 5.4 Sport Marketing Segmentation Approaches.

all! The three ways of using segmentation are: focused segmentation, multiple segmentation and undifferentiated segmentation. Focused segmentation occurs when only one segment is chosen with one corresponding marketing mix. Multiple segmentation involves the selection of more than one segment, with a unique marketing mix for each. Finally, undifferentiated segmentation occurs when a sport organisation decides not to choose a segment at all, but rather considers the total market as a single and unvarying consumer group. Figure 5.4 highlights where these three approaches fit within the four-step process of developing marketing positioning. Each is explained in further detail next.

Focused segmentation

Focused segmentation involves selecting only one of the market segments that has been identified and developing just one marketing mix with which to communicate to that segment. The result is that all of an organisation's focus is on one segment, and is sometimes called niche marketing, or concentrated segmentation. For example, a government agency might focus their efforts on a single segment of the market, such as encouraging smokers to quit.

There are some advantages to focused segmentation. By choosing one segment to emphasise it is possible to develop a highly specialised marketing mix perfectly tailored to meet the segment's needs. It also means that a sport organisation can focus all of its resources on the single market segment, making it more cost effective. However, there are also disadvantages to focused segmentation. There are dangers if the market segment turns out to be too small, or it shrinks over time. Also, another sport organisation might start to market to the same focused segment, but with more resources. Focused segmentation is powerful but risky.

Multiple segmentation

Multiple segmentation means choosing more than one segment, and developing a separate and unique marketing mix for each one. However, not all the elements of the marketing mix need to be changed for each market segment. For example, different promotions may be employed for each segment, but the same product, price and distribution options may remain. Multiple segmentation can help to spread the risk in the event that one of the segments is too small, shrinks in size over time, or was a poor choice in the first place. However, there are also disadvantages to using multiple segmentation. The main disadvantage is that it can be expensive. This is because it takes money, time and resources to create a new marketing mix for each segment. For example, it might mean that a sport organisation has to develop new products, invest in a number of different promotional programs, distribute its products in different ways and research different pricing strategies. It is often wise to limit the number of segments chosen, particularly for smaller sport organisations with constrained resources. With the exception of large national or multinational organisations, it is probably imprudent to choose more than two or three segments.

Undifferentiated segmentation

Undifferentiated segmentation reflects the decision not to choose a segment at all, but rather to consider the total market as a group of potential consumers. A sport organisation employing this strategy would develop one marketing mix for all consumers. Sometimes this approach is called mass marketing. It may seem uneconomical to follow the three steps of the segmentation process if only to decide not to proceed with any segmentation. However, one of the benefits of the segmentation process is that it reveals important information about consumers. Regardless of which segment is selected, or even none at all, it is always helpful to know as much about the market as possible. Another reason to follow the segmentation process is that it will help to decide whether choosing one, more than one or no segment at all will be most advantageous. For example, if a sport marketer discovered that there is little difference between segments in the market, it might be best to use undifferentiated segmentation.

As with the previous two approaches to segmentation, undifferentiated segmentation has advantages and disadvantages. Like focused marketing, it can be more resource effective because it requires an investment in the development of only one marketing mix. One of the disadvantages of undifferentiated segmentation is that it is harder to stand out from competitors.

Target market

Target marketing is a term sometimes used in sport marketing in reference to the way an organisation chooses one or more segments in which to target or aim its marketing mix. The segment(s) selected are like the numbers on a dartboard, where marketers take aim with a marketing mix. When the segmentation process is complete, a target market (or segment) should be the outcome.

Chapter Tool 5.3. Market Segmentation: Market segmentation describes the process of categorising groups or segments of consumers together, based on similar needs or wants. There are several important elements to the effective use of segmentation as a marketing sport tool. First, the segment(s) chosen need(s) to be big enough to justify the effort of developing and implementing a marketing mix. Second, the segment chosen should be different enough from the other segments in the market to justify the effort and resources. If they are not different enough (and all the consumers in the total market are very similar already), then it may be more advisable to use an undifferentiated approach. In addition to these suggestions, there are four relevant issues to consider when choosing a segmentation approach:

1. It is important to estimate how easy it will be to reach the chosen segment. Is there a way to communicate with them? Can it be done via the media, Internet, newspapers or another means? Is there a way of getting the sport product to them? If they cannot be reached, or there is no way to distribute the sport product to them, then they are not the right segment to choose.
2. A sport organisation must consider the resources it can apply to the marketing process. Multiple segmentation can be expensive and time consuming, and it therefore may not be the best approach for a small and/or new organisation to employ.
3. The segmentation approach should also reflect how much a sport organisation knows about consumers. If it is a new enterprise, and/or offering a new product, it may not know much about its consumers yet, and its potential consumers may not yet be aware of the sport organisation and its products. Such circumstances would make it difficult to follow a multiple segmentation approach, which would demand considerable information about consumers.
4. The level of competition a sport organisation has in the market is likely to influence the choice of segmentation approach. If there is

---

little competition, an undifferentiated approach might be satisfactory and, of course, cost less. However, in a market with fierce competition, multiple segmentation or concentrated segmentation would be helpful. This is not the only way to deal with competition. The way a product is positioned in the market helps to separate it from competitors.

Market positioning and differentiation

After the target market has been identified, a positioning strategy must be devised for use with each segment. Market positioning refers to how a sport brand is perceived by consumers relative to its competitors. For example, do consumers consider a sport brand as a luxury and high-quality product, or as a basic and value-for-money product? Do they see it as conservative and reliable, or exciting and dynamic? Positioning takes into account the fact that consumers will compare a product with others in the market. It assumes that they will put each product into a position in their minds; they will find a place where it fits compared to others.

The outcome of successful market positioning is a *differentiated* sport brand or product. If a sport brand or product has been differentiated it means that each target market segment attributes a specific value or set of features to it that are unique and special compared to competitors. In short, a differentiated sport brand or product stands out from the rest.

As reproduced in Table 5.4, there are numerous different positioning tactics that a sport organisation can choose from in order to best appeal to the target segment. Each positioning strategy will create a different perception in the minds of consumers. A positioning strategy is strongly connected with the concept of branding, where it is reinforced, amplified and extended. Sport branding is considered in Chapter 6.

Chapter Tool 5.4. Market Positioning: Market positioning is the process of attributing a sport brand or product a distinctive value or set of features for each target market segment compared to its competitors. The outcome of market positioning should be a differentiated sport brand or product. There are eight tactics of market positioning that a sport marketer might consider:
1. Product features
2. Product benefits
3. Specific product use
4. Product user
5. Price and quality
6. Against competitor
7. Product class
8. Hybrid positioning

Table 5.4 Positioning Tactics

Positioning Tactics	Method	Examples
Product features	Focus on the unique features of the product	Unique features of sport shoes could include a comfortable fit, shock-absorption qualities or a cutting-edge fashion design
		Most sport codes have unique features in the way a game is played, such as soccer, cricket, tennis and football
Product benefits	Tell customers what they will get out of the product or service	Health, fitness, social contact, fun, entertainment
Specific product use	How can consumers use or apply the product?	Consumers could go to a game in order to socialise with friends
	What does the product do in specific situations?	
Product user	Focus on the personality of the user	Show women enjoying the catwalk fashion at a horse-racing event to encourage more women to attend
	Show how the product can be used by people whom the user relates to	
Price and quality	High price may reinforce quality, and low price may reinforce value	Making sport accessible for families or appealing to those with high disposable income because it is exclusive
Against competitor	Show consumers how the product or service is better than its competitors	Position the product or service as a market leader, an innovator; emphasise a superior product or better price
Product class (associate or disassociate)	Position the product as belonging to a particular class or category of products. Tell consumers it is associated or connected to this category. Or, highlight the product as being being revolutionary or innovative, and in a class of its own. It is incomparable with other products	Promoting a sport event as a once-off experience
Hybrid positioning	Using a number of elements of different types of positioning	High-quality and innovative product; a unique experience

Table 5.5 Marketing Mix Composition

Product	Price	Promotion	Place
Service/product/facility	Level	Advertising	Location
Quality	Concessions	Sponsorship	Distribution
Features and options	Special offers	Event signage	Availability
Design and packaging	Season tickets	Exhibitions	Sport facilities
Benefits	Payment methods	Sales promotions	Accessibility
Ideas and intangibles	Social costs	Personal selling	Public transport
Licensing/merchandise	Customer time	Publicity	Parking
Brand name	Market sensitivity	Direct marketing	Media distribution
Product image	Legal constraints	Promotional licensing	Internet distribution
Resource management	Pricing objectives	Branding	Manufacturers/ wholesalers/ retailers
Staff	Break-even analysis	Public relations	Ticket distribution

Introduction to the marketing mix

The final part of this chapter is a brief introduction to the marketing mix, which is explained in detail in the six subsequent chapters. After a sport organisation has divided the total market into sub-groups (step 1), chosen a segment(s) (step 2) and identified a positioning strategy for that segment (step 3), they must then develop a marketing mix for each segment. The marketing mix is a set of strategies and activities that cover product, price, promotion and place (distribution). These are commonly referred to as 'The Four Ps'. The fact that these four elements are grouped into a set, or a 'mix', is important, because they should be coordinated together in an integrated fashion. In this text, further to the four Ps, services and sponsorship each receive a chapter of their own. This is because sport services and sponsorship demand quite unique marketing strategies. In the sport marketing mix Table 5.5 illustrates the marketing mix and their composition.

Product

It is easy to think of the word *product* as referring to a physical, manufactured item. For example, Wilson produces sport equipment. However, the term product can also refer to services, ideas and the benefits that a sport organisation offers consumers. Many sport organisations offer a service, such as a form of physical activity, entertainment or an experience. There is often no physical product to take away, but a sport organisation might offer some intangible benefits such as a lifestyle, a social group or even a belief system. The product can also include design, packaging and merchandise. Marketing the sport product is explained in detail in Chapter 6, and is heavily associated with branding. Sport services are considered exclusively in Chapter 11.

Price

The price refers to the cost that a consumer must pay to receive a product or service. This is usually thought of as the literal cost in monetary terms. In order to develop a pricing strategy it is important to consider pricing goals and match them to pricing techniques. Devising a pricing approach is considered in Chapter 7.

Place

Place is concerned with where consumers access the sport product or service. It is another word for distribution. Place is therefore about the way a product is made available to consumers; how it gets from the place where it is produced to the place where the consumer buys and consumes it. For physical, concrete products, place is concerned with the practical issues of getting a product from producers to consumers, along with any other stops along the way such as wholesalers and retailers. In recent years the Internet has provided a new way of distributing products. With the Internet or other forms of mail order, there does not necessarily need to be a retail outlet or shop, as consumers can buy directly from wholesalers, manufacturers or even just individual people (such as on eBay).

When it comes to services, sport may be delivered to people via pay, cable or satellite television, free-to-air television or other media. It may also be delivered in person by a sport organisation, such as local competitions and sports health practitioners. Place also includes different ways of getting tickets for a game or event, and decisions about where to locate sport facilities. Perhaps the most important aspect of place marketing is the way the sporting venue is used to augment the sport consumption experience. Place is considered in Chapter 8.

Promotion

Promotion is about communicating with consumers, getting a message across to the marketplace. Promotion therefore includes advertising, sponsorship, signage, exhibitions, sales promotions, personal selling and publicity. These are examined in Chapter 9. Chapter 10 examines sport sponsorship as part of a promotional strategy.

Case Study—Positioning Sport Through Commercialised Grass Roots Initiatives

by Sharyn McDonald

In 2006, an Australian survey revealed a participation rate of only 28 per cent in organised activities, the most popular organised sports being tennis, soccer, cricket, netball and Australian football. However, none of the sports attracted more than five per cent of the active population. Sport organisations are therefore faced with the dual challenge of competing with each other to attract a time poor population, and generating interest in organised sport. The result is that sport organisations are compelled to adopt marketing strategies focused on attracting new participants in their respective codes, while maintaining participants who currently participate in their sport. A popular strategy adopted by the five most prominent sports in Australian is to collaborate with corporations in order to jointly present grass roots initiatives for young children. Regular physical activity not only bolsters health, but it encourages the formation of positive exercise habits. In addition, when sport organisations are able to engage young participants, they have a better chance of retaining them into adulthood.

The question remains as to how sport organisations can attract young consumers in such a competitive market. The answer is that sport-corporation alliances allow a unique blend of expertise and resources to deliver tailored programmes that meet both youth physiological needs and consumer (children and parents) desires. Sport marketers must carefully consider the physical and mental abilities of children entering sport. Children will withdraw if the skills are too hard, and if the environment is too competitive, they may feel threatened or intimidated. As a result, program designers ensure they include fun games with embedded basic skills which can be adjusted and modified as the participants get older. From a consumer marketing perspective, the initiative needs to attract the interest of the child and remain affordable and practical for parents.

In Australia, Nestlé has built a formidable reputation for their cost-effective grass roots initiatives. It has formed alliances with soccer, cricket and snow skiing, and is able to offer children the opportunity to participate in a range of modified activities. Nestlé's soccer and cricket initiatives are widely available and are usually offered in conjunction with a local club. This not only provides the opportunity to participate regardless of locality, but also allows for the transition into modified, junior and adult competitions.

The Nestlé 'MILO Have-A-Go' program in conjunction with Cricket Australia is offered to children aged between five and eight in a 6- to 12-week block. The program allows 'the opportunity to develop cricket skills, physical fitness, social skills, sportsmanship and understanding of the game of cricket' (MILO Have-A-Go, Cricket Australia, 2007). Once children have developed their basic skills, they can move into the MILO Have-A-Go program which is offered to children up to 12 years old. To gain the attention of children and their peers, brightly branded promotional items are issued upon registration, which include a 'cricket bat, cricket ball, carry bag, T-shirt, bucket hat and more' (MILO Have-A-Go, Cricket Australia, 2007). The program is inexpensive and encourages parents to join in the activities.

Nestlé has sponsored grass roots cricket for 14 years. To be in a partnership with a prominent sport organisation for this length of time highlights the successful nature of the program. Cricket Australia has had the opportunity to promote the game of cricket to more than 10 million children since 1983, when it began to implement junior development programs. With the potential to convert this many children into cricketers, grass roots programs represent an excellent positioning initiative.

For more information see:

ABS (2007). *4177.0—Participation in Sports and Physical Recreation, Australia, 2005–06.* Available at:
http://www.abs.gov.au

MILO Have-A-Go, Cricket Australia (2007). *Welcome to MILO Have-A-Go and MILO Have-A-Game.* Available at:
http://www.cricket.com.au/default.aspx?s=milohaveago

Sutherland, J. (2007). *A Message from Cricket Australia CEO, James Sutherland.* Available at:
http://www.cricket.com.au/default.aspx?s=milohaveagoparents

Principles summary

- Chapter Principle 5.1: The second stage of the Sport Marketing Framework is to develop a sport marketing strategy. This requires two steps: (a) to develop a strategic marketing direction, and (b) to develop a sport marketing position.
- Chapter Principle 5.2: Developing a strategic marketing direction involves constructing marketing objectives and setting performance measures.
- Chapter Principle 5.3: Developing a sport marketing position involves four steps: market segmentation (1,2), market positioning tactics (3) and devising the marketing mix (4).

Tools summary

- Chapter Tool 5.1. Marketing Objectives
- Chapter Tool 5.2. Performance Measures
- Chapter Tool 5.3. Market Segmentation
- Chapter Tool 5.4. Market Positioning

Review questions

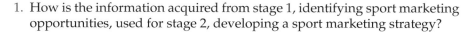

1. How is the information acquired from stage 1, identifying sport marketing opportunities, used for stage 2, developing a sport marketing strategy?

2. Identify the key criteria in devising a good sport marketing objective.
3. What is the relationship between sport marketing objectives and performance measures?
4. What are the different kinds of market segmentation options?
5. When should each kind of market segmentation be used?
6. What is the purpose of market positioning?
7. How does market positioning influence the marketing mix?

Relevant websites

http://www.formula1.com (Formula 1)

http://www.usasynchro.org (United States Synchronised Swimming)

Further reading

Ferrand, A. & Pages, M. (1999). Image management in sport organizations: the creation of value, *European Journal of Marketing*, 33(3/4): 387–401.

Gladden, J.M. & Funk, D.C. (2002). Developing an understanding of brand associations in team sport: empirical evidence from consumers of professional sport, *Journal of Sport Management*, 5(16): 54–81.

6  Sport products

Overview

The purpose of this chapter is to explore the first of the six elements of the marketing mix: the sport product. It will introduce the key components of the sport product and will outline product strategies that can be used within the marketing mix, including product augmentation, new product development and sport branding.

At the end of this chapter, readers should be able to:

- Define the term sport product.
- Outline the key characteristics of sport products.
- Explain the sport product continuum.
- Define the term product augmentation, and describe augmentation strategies.
- Identify the process of new product development.
- Explain the concept of the product life cycle.
- Describe the process of building a sport brand.

Stage 3: Plan the marketing mix

Sport product: Goods and services

Chapters 4 and 5 explained the first two stages of the Sport Marketing Framework. This chapter concentrates on the first of six elements in stage 3, Plan the Sport Marketing Mix: the concept of the sport product, and product strategies that can be used in sport marketing. The additional elements of stage 3 are presented in the forthcoming five chapters. Figure 6.1 highlights stage 3 and its major components within the Sport Marketing Framework.

What is a sport product?

A product is usually conceived as a physical good that has been manufactured; something that can be held and touched, like a sporting shoe, football or baseball cap. However, the term product can also refer to services and ideas. In fact, the word product is used in sport marketing in several ways including (1) a good (physical item), (2) a service, (3) an idea and/or (4) a combination of these. Each is explained next.

Sporting goods

In the sport industry, examples of physical products include sport shoes, tennis rackets, memorabilia, golf balls and skateboards. There are also goods that are not only used exclusively for sport, but can be used along with sport or as part of the sport experience. These include sunglasses, caps, T-shirts, watches, iPods, gym-bags, sporting apparel and sunscreen. These items are all tangible, which means that they can be experienced physically by the senses of sight, touch, taste, smell and hearing.

Sporting services

Sport services, on the other hand, are not tangible. Patrons of sport services receive benefits in the form of an intangible experience. For example, services are offered in the form of fitness and recreation opportunities, entertainment through live or televised matches, physiotherapy or coaching. These services are not physical objects that can be purchased and removed. Sport organisations cannot make extra services and store them away for consumers who may wish to buy them later. There are four important differences between sport goods and services that are highly relevant to sport marketing. These are tangibility, consistency, perishability and separability.

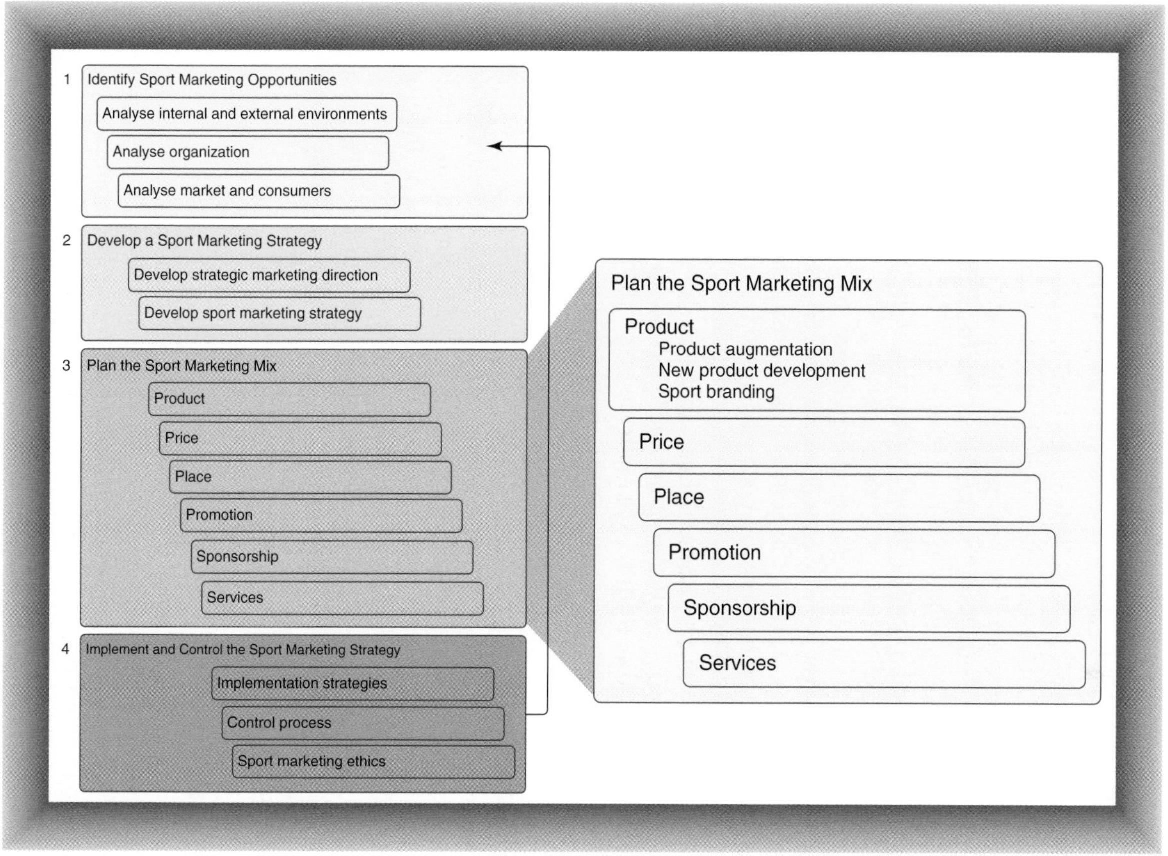

Figure 6.1 Plan the Marketing Mix.

1 Identify Sport Marketing Opportunities
- Analyse internal and external environments
- Analyse organization
- Analyse market and consumers

2 Develop a Sport Marketing Strategy
- Develop strategic marketing direction
- Develop sport marketing strategy

3 Plan the Sport Marketing Mix
- Product
- Price
- Place
- Promotion
- Sponsorship
- Services

4 Implement and Control the Sport Marketing Strategy
- Implementation strategies
- Control process
- Sport marketing ethics

Plan the Sport Marketing Mix
- Product
  - Product augmentation
  - New product development
  - Sport branding
- Price
- Place
- Promotion
- Sponsorship
- Services

Tangibility

Sporting goods are tangible when they are physical and are experienced by the senses. From a practical viewpoint, sport product tangibility means that a consumer can take the product away with them for use later, and most often, for repeated use. Services are intangible because they are not physical and cannot be taken home to keep. Services are experienced for a period rather than owned.

Consistency

Consistency is another way by which sport goods and services can be separated. Consistency refers to how reliable the quality of the product is from one time that it is purchased and used to the next. Sporting goods usually have a high degree of reliability. There is not much change in the quality of a sporting shoe or a football of the same brand and model from one version to the next. On the other hand, sport services are likely to have more variable quality. The service quality of a sport experience may change depending on who is providing the service as well as the special conditions of its offering (e.g. weather). The fact that the quality of a sporting match will change from one time to the next has already been addressed in Chapter 2. Of course, an athlete may perform brilliantly in one competition or game, then fail miserably at the next. When this issue of variability in the sport product was discussed, it was emphasised that sport marketers should focus their attention on the quality of those parts of the service or product that they have some control over, like service quality, prices, food and beverages, and the venue.

Perishability

Perishability refers to whether a sport product can be stored and used at another time. Sporting goods (like clothing and equipment) are not perishable. Basketballs, cricket bats and bicycles can be stored if they are not bought by a consumer without any damage to the product. Services cannot be stored. For example, it is not possible to hold onto unsold tickets to a sport contest to sell them at another time. Once the game has been played any seats that were not filled are lost forever.

Separability

Separability is a term that is used to describe whether the creation or manufacture of a sport product happens at the same time as when it is consumed. Naturally, sporting goods are made prior to their use. For example, a hockey stick is made, delivered to a wholesaler and/or retailer, placed on the shelf or online and ultimately bought by a consumer. The quality of the good (the hockey stick) is separated from the quality of service at the sport store where it is bought. It is also possible to separate the item from the person selling it, although sometimes one can affect the other. Sport services, in contrast, are made and consumed at the same time. At a live sport event, the entertainment benefits are created at the same time that it is consumed by fans. It is also more difficult to separate the service from the person providing the service.

> *Chapter Principle 6.1*: Sport goods may be differentiated from services on the basis of four factors: tangibility, consistency, perishability and separability.

Ideas

Although it might sound strange, ideas can form the core of some sport products. One example is when a consumer buys a gymnasium membership with the idea of being thinner or more muscular. Another example is the power of sport in providing a sense of identity and vicarious achievement for fans. From this viewpoint, sport stimulates consumers to feel (emotional response) and to believe certain things (thinking response). At sport events it is not just goods and services that are offered to consumers. There may also be ideas that are sold to consumers, such as those relating to belonging and success.

A combination of goods, services and ideas

In practice, most sport products and services are a mixture of tangible and intangible elements. Many physical products have a service or idea element. In fact, goods are frequently bought by sport consumers because of the intangible benefits they deliver. Equally, many services are sold together with something tangible to take away. For example, a membership to a football club may come with a package including club stickers, badges and regular newsletters. In many instances, a sport consumer buys a mixture of goods, services, benefits and ideas. There are also examples of sport services being transformed into sport products, like live games that have been recorded on DVD for later sale. In sport marketing it is common to combine products and services, and the tangible and intangible, to provide a more flexible, textured and appealing set of materials to sell to sport consumers.

> *Chapter Principle 6.2*: A sport product is the complete package of benefits presented to a sport consumer in the form of physical goods, services and ideas, or a combination of these to produce a sport experience.

The sport product continuum

Although sport products may feature a mixture of tangible and intangible elements, some sport products are mainly tangible and some are mainly intangible. The Sport Product Continuum is a useful tool to help show that products can be defined along a continuum (or a scale) with *mainly tangible* products on one end, *mainly intangible* products on the other end and a mixture of the two in the middle.

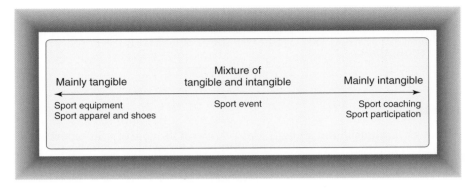

Figure 6.2 The Sport Product Continuum.

As Figure 6.2 demonstrates, some products are mainly tangible like tennis balls and fitness equipment. Although they might provide intangible benefits that consumers want, these products depend on their tangible or physical elements. Take away the physical object and the product is essentially gone as well. In contrast, a suburban tennis competition or surfing lessons are examples of products that are mainly intangible. Even if there is a physical good supplied as part of the service (such as a racquet or surfboard), the product depends on its intangible service element. Take away the service, such as all the volunteers and administrators and the product is untenable. Finally, a sport event provides a good example of a product that is a mixture of tangible and intangible elements. The intangible elements of a baseball game include what happens on the diamond, while the tangible elements include the food, beverages and merchandise that are offered as part of the experience. Fans are usually looking for all these elements in a sport event, not just one or another. For sport marketers, it is a useful exercise to locate all their products on the sport product continuum.

Mainly tangible and mainly intangible products

Products that sit exclusively at either end of the continuum can present sport marketers with unique challenges. Imagine, for example the difficulties associated with marketing a tennis ball. There is little to make one brand of tennis ball stand out from others. One common approach is to use pricing to form a point of differentiation, which can make the product more appealing for economic reasons, but it is also easy for competitors to copy this tactic. As a result, sport marketers try hard to add intangible value to their tangible products, such as the use of a famous tennis player to endorse a brand of tennis balls, or by emphasising that the product has a unique feature or quality.

Similarly, mainly intangible products are challenging to market. Consider, for example, golf lessons. When the consumer has nothing tangible to take away with them, there is no definitive reminder of what they have bought. It may be difficult for them to judge or remember what the quality of the lesson was because the advice given was essentially intangible and easily forgotten. One way to overcome these difficulties is to include some tangible elements like brochures on certain golf skills or rules, or even bonus golf balls with the service name or logo. One pivotal tactic in sport marketing is to try to move products away from either of the extremes of the continuum, and to create a mixture of tangible and intangible elements. Sport events, for example may emphasise the physical qualities of the venue, as well as opportunities to purchase memorabilia and merchandise. Many sport events make more profit from these tangible value add-ons than they do from the core entertainment product of the game itself. For example, it is common at sport events for consumers to spend more money on merchandise and food and beverages than they do on the actual ticket.

> *Chapter Tool 6.1. Sport Product Continuum*: The Sport Product Continuum is a useful tool to help show that products can be defined along a continuum (or a scale) with mainly tangible products on one end, mainly intangible products on the other end and a mixture of the two in the middle.

Product augmentation

Key variables of the sport product

Sport products possess a range a benefits as well as tangible and intangible elements. In addition, if the sport product is lacking in either tangible or intangible elements, it can be more difficult to market. It is therefore important to think of the sport product as being a complete package or a 'bundle' of elements, consisting of core benefits, product features and the augmented product, as illustrated in Figure 6.3.

Core benefit

The core benefit represents the principal advantage that the consumer receives from buying and using a product. For example, if a consumer buys a sports car, the main benefit is transportation. If a consumer buys a T-shirt, the main benefit is a covering for the body. If a consumer buys a ticket to a sport event, the main benefit is the entertainment value or experience the consumer receives as a consequence of attendance. Finally, if the consumer buys a service, like a sport physiotherapy session or a sport skills lesson, the core benefits are physical treatment of an injury, or instruction on how to play a sport, respectively.

It is easy to underestimate the importance of the core benefit of a product, and focus on the other variables like features (actual product) or add-ons (augmented product). But the core benefit is the most *fundamental* benefit of the product; if it does not meet the needs of sport customers, then it is unlikely to be successful. It is always important to understand the main need that the consumer has, or the primary benefit that they get from using the product. It is no use adding frills to a product if it does not meet the basic needs of consumers in the first place.

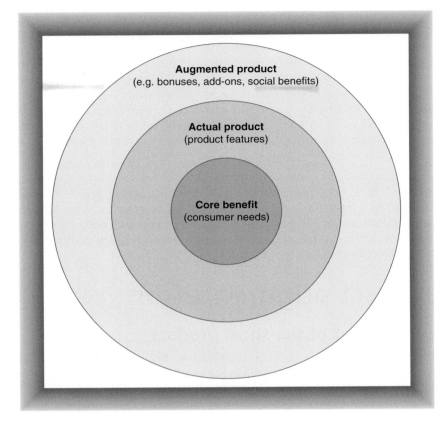

Figure 6.3 Key Variables of the Sport Product.

Actual product

The actual product refers to the features of the product. The features of a merchandised sport T-shirt, for example could include the colour, sizing, fabric and pattern. The product features of a sport event could include the venue, facilities, the participating athletes or players and the scoreboard. The features of a sport physiotherapy service could include the length of time of the appointment, and where the treatment is performed (e.g. at home or at a clinic). Paying attention to the features of the product can be one way of making it stand out against competition. As long as the core benefit of the product is something that people want, then developing the right features can help amplify a product's effects or allow it to be better moulded to the specific needs of consumers.

Augmented product

The word augmented means improved or increased. When a product is augmented, it is made better in some way. The augmented product refers to any extras or extensions that are added to the actual features of the product. These may be additional benefits, bonus extras or even the image of a product.

A sport T-shirt may be augmented by adding a bonus cap (an extra or add-on); it may also be improved in the eye of the consumer by being a particular brand that they think is fashionable. A sport event could offer extras such as merchandise, programs, fanzines, posters, DVDs and autograph signing opportunities. A sport lesson could include special guest appearances by well-known players or the bonus of a free lesson after every ten. Finally, in the case of the sport physiotherapy session, the therapist could offer information brochures, or provide a reminder call the day before the appointment. It is important to remember that aspects like the status, image or social appeal of a product are all examples of augmentation.

Understanding how sport products can be augmented is particularly useful in markets where there is substantial competition, or where different products have similar core benefits and product features. The market for sports shoes provides a prominent example. The core benefit of shoes (a covering protection for feet) is the same no matter who makes them. Different manufacturers try to create different product features, such colour schemes, air pockets for shock absorption or Velcro straps. However, these features are often quickly copied by competitors. One of the most effective ways of making sport shoes stand out is through the image of the product. Many manufacturers like Nike and adidas use athlete sponsorship to give the product an association with success, exclusivity or style.

It is not as easy as it might appear to differentiate between the three variables of the sport product. Sport consumers might have different motivations for their consumption decisions. For example, although the core benefit of a sports car is transportation, it is probably reasonable to conclude that it is not actually the benefit of transport that is compelling in such a purchase. Rather, the features of a sports car make its transportation benefit much more appealing. In addition, augmented product add-ons such as belonging to a sports car club might provide a further set of advantages that add to the satisfaction of a consumer.

Chapter Principle 6.3: Sport products should be seen as a bundle of benefits comprising the core benefits, actual product features and the augmented product. These three variables of the product are interrelated and should be manipulated as a group.

Interactive case

Reebok sponsors a range of athletes and sports, including a strong presence in the United States through official endorsements with the National Football League and Major League Baseball. Examine the Reebok website and consider what the sponsored athletes and sports have in common, and what effect this has on the way that the Reebok product is perceived.

http://www.rbk.com/

New product development

Sport marketers may consider the possibility of new product development. Developing a new product can be expensive and risky. Every year there is a proliferation of new sport products introduced to the market, but only a small fraction of these are successful. If a new product is a failure, the sport organisation has lost time and money, and perhaps even some of their reputation. But what does it mean to develop a new product? A new product does not have to mean a brand new product. In sport marketing, a new product can take many forms, such as the improved performance of an existing product, new functions added to an existing product, a new way to use an existing product, combining existing products, or a new look or design for a product.

> *Chapter Principle 6.4*: In sport marketing, a new product can take many forms such as the improved performance of an existing product, new functions added to an existing product, a new way to use an existing product, combining existing products, or a new look or design for a product.

The process of new product development is usually coordinated by high-level managers in large sport organisations. However, irrespective of the level, it is important for sport marketers to understand the process to which they are expected to contribute. The process of new product development has five stages, which are shown in Figure 6.4.

Consider new product opportunities

This first step of product development involves creating and collecting new product possibilities and ideas. There are many different approaches to acquiring new ideas for products. Some of the more common ways of collecting ideas are through market research, examining what competitors are doing, studying what is being done overseas, and consulting with other staff

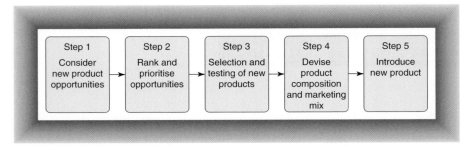

Figure 6.4 Steps of New Product Development.

and current customers. Some new product options are likely to have emerged in stage 1 of the Sport Marketing Framework.

Rank and priorities opportunities

The second step in new product development involves sifting through all the ideas that have been collected and only keeping the ones that fit with the marketing objectives of the sport organisation. It is also helpful to consider how well the new product ideas fit with existing products, and how they relate to current trends. This is not the stage to be concerned about financial realism, but by the end of this step the new product opportunities should have been ranked according to priorities determined by marketing objectives.

Selection and testing of new products

Step three of the process involves a more careful assessment of the ideas that were retained following step two. In fact, the highest ranking options should be identified and piloted to determine their potential in the market. This is the time to check feasibility by undertaking cost and financial estimates, and to conduct additional market research, or concept testing. Concept testing involves giving potential customers a description of the new product, and asking them if they would be likely to buy it. It may also mean providing a prototype of the new product for customers to try.

Devise product composition and marketing mix

With the results of the new product's feasibility and market testing available, it is time to make a final decision about how to proceed. It is possible that the best decision is not to proceed and to choose the next highest ranked new product opportunity to investigate. If the feasibility and testing results are promising, the final product composition should be determined. This involves specifying the core product benefits, actual product features and augmented product composition. The other elements of the marketing mix will also need to be determined to provide the appropriate positioning strategy.

Introduce new product

Finally, if a sport product has successfully made it through all these stages, it is ready to be released onto the market. With this decision, an implementation plan will need to be created to support the deployment of all the variables in the marketing mix. The details of implementation are provided in Chapter 13.

Chapter Tool 6.2. New Product Development: The process of new product development involves five stages: (1) Consider New Product Opportunities, (2) Rank and Prioritise Opportunities, (3) Selection and Testing of New Products, (4) Devise Product Composition and Marketing Mix and (5) Introduce New Product.

Product life cycle

Sport products come and go. At first they seem like the latest fashion, then consumers lose interest and a new product takes its place. After a product has been on the market for a while, sometimes sport organisations change it in some way, creating a 'new and improved' version. These changes reflect that fact that every product has a life cycle. A product is 'born', introduced to the market, people learn about it and buy it, then they lose interest and the product may 'die' or be changed or upgraded. The term *product life cycle* refers to the stages that a product goes through from first being introduced onto the market to its decline. There are four stages of the product life cycle as depicted in Figure 6.5: introduction, growth, maturity and decline.

> *Chapter Principle 6.5*: The term *product life cycle* refers to the stages that a product goes through from first being introduced onto the market to its decline. There are four stages of the product life cycle: introduction, growth, maturity and decline.

Introduction

The introduction phase refers to the period when a product first enters the market. Many sport products fail at this stage, and/or they are changed as problems become apparent. Sales and usage usually increase slowly, and there may not actually be a profit for the organisation once the costs of product development and marketing are taken into account. Marketing costs are

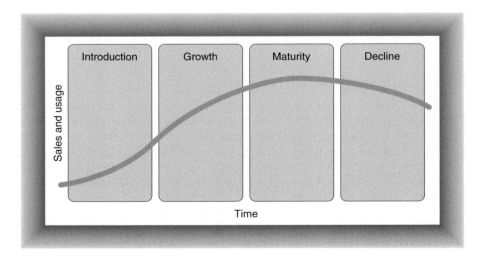

Figure 6.5 Product Life Cycle Stages.

usually high because of advertising needs (the need to inform consumers about the new product and its benefits), the need to give consumers incentives to try the product and the need to encourage distributors to sell the product by giving them attractive profit margins. The length of time that a sport product stays in this stage will vary greatly. For example, there may be a long introduction time if there are already plenty of other substitute products on the market.

Growth

Growth is the stage when the product has already attracted the awareness of the target consumers, and there is a rush or increase in sales. Profits usually rise quickly at this stage, however, so does the amount of competition.

Maturity

Once the product has been on the market for a long period it is in the maturity phase. There are likely to be more competitors in the marketplace for the product and the producer may be forced to make some changes. This is normally the longest stage of the product life cycle. Gradually, profits or usage will decrease during this stage.

Decline

A product is in the decline stage when it experiences a drop in sales or usage as an enduring trend; how quickly sales drop will be different for every product and every situation. Eventually the product may be substantially changed or taken off the market.

Understanding the product life cycle is pivotal in sport marketing because different marketing strategies should be used during different stages of the cycle. Some examples are reproduced in Table 6.1.

Chapter Tool 6.3. Product Life Cycle Stages: Different marketing strategies should be employed at each stage of a product's life cycle using variations to the mix including price, promotions, sponsorship, distribution and services.

Sport branding

The idea of branding is closely linked with positioning. A brand is like an identifying badge, often reinforced by a name or a logo that helps consumers recognise a product or an organisation. A brand becomes linked with consumers' opinions and perceptions of a sport product and organisation.

Table 6.1 Marketing Strategies at Each Stage of the Product Life Cycle

| Marketing Mix | Stage of the Product Life Cycle | | | |
	Introduction	Growth	Maturity	Decline
Product strategies	Narrow or single product option with ongoing changes to adapt to initial market feedback	More changes to product and more options to the range and variety	Introduce new variations of product to appeal to new segments	Products which are no longer popular are removed
Pricing strategies	High prices to cover high costs or low prices and discounts to encourage people to 'try and buy'	Reduce prices, especially if there are lots of competitors	Continue to reduce prices if number of competitors has increased	Continue to reduce price, unless there is not much competition
		If a low-price strategy was used in introduction, the price may be increased once some customer loyalty has been developed	Stabilise price if there is strong customer loyalty	
Promotional strategies	Advertising to develop awareness of product and its benefits	Emphasise the difference between the product and competitor's product	Increased promotion to distributors to continue to encourage them to sell product	Reduce or eliminate promotion and the costs associated with it

	Personal selling to distributors Incentives to encourage people to 'try and buy', like offering samples	Promote to new market segments		
Sponsorship strategies	High-profile athlete or team sponsorship for new product	Increase the range of sponsorship categories covered by introducing a greater range of endorsements	Reduce endorsements	No sponsorships
Distribution strategies	Offer good profit margins to distributors to encourage them to try selling the product, or use a short supply chain strategy such as the Internet	Build long-term relationships with distributors Increase number of distributors and/or different methods of distribution	May reduce the profit margins that are given to distributors May give incentives to distributors to encourage them to keep stocking product	Stop using unprofitable distribution outlets and/or methods
Services strategies	Introductory offers to build regular users	Heavy focus on service processes, quality and customer satisfaction	Develop new aspects of services to renew point of differentiation	Re-train service deliverers to prepare for end of service delivery

A brand serves to remind consumers of its positioning compared to other products. Because branding and positioning are associated, it is important to keep branding, segmentation and positioning strategies closely related. It is no use having a branding concept that emphasises luxury and quality, choosing a segment that is interested in value for money and positioning the product as belonging to the 'x-treme' class of sports. In this example, the branding, segmentation and positioning strategies do not match or complement one another. The result would be confusing and off-putting to consumers.

In a competitive industry like sport, product sales can be affected by how easily a consumer can tell different products apart. Branding is one of the key strategies that sport marketers use to help their product stand out from the crowd. The way a consumer thinks about a product becomes a powerful form of reinforcement. Branding is therefore a way of augmenting a product by helping to create associated ideas that make it different. The added value that a product possesses because of its brand name and identity is called brand equity.

Brands can help consumers to remember products, and can set off images in their minds. A powerful brand is one that has both a high level of recognition in the market, and strong associated imagery. Manchester United, Ferrari, Dallas Cowboys, Los Angeles Lakers, IOC, FIFA and Nike are all examples of very powerful sport brands.

> *Chapter Principle 6.6*: A sport brand is the symbolic representation of everything that a sport organisation seeks to stand for, leading to expectations about its value and performance. A brand can be portrayed as an identifying badge which triggers consumers to remember a product or an organisation. It can be a name, a design, a symbol (or logo), an image or a combination of these things. Branding is one of the key strategies that marketers use to help their product to stand out from the crowd by positioning it through associated ideas and concepts.

Interactive case

Visit both the Manchester United and the Dallas Cowboys' websites. Create a list of brand attributes (those aspects of the brand that are defining, unique and special to each organisation). Compare the lists and see whether there are some commonalities between these two powerful sport brands.

http://www.manutd.com/

http://www.dallascowboys.com/

Brand names and logos

To recap, a brand can be many things, including a name, a design, a symbol, an image or even a combination of these. A brand name and a brand mark (or logo) are two of the most common representations of a brand. A brand name is a word, a written label or even group of letters and/or numbers; it is usually something that can be verbalised rather than merely an image. The choice of brand name will put across (or symbolise) a unique idea. For example, some brand names might suggest strength and confidence, like the All Blacks New Zealand Rugby Union team, while others might suggest boldness, like Nike. If you do not agree with these connotations it means that you hold a different brand identity in your mind.

There are a number of issues to keep in mind when choosing a brand name. It is important that it communicates ideas that an organisation would like its consumers to possess. It should be related to the kinds of benefits that consumers will get from the product. It is also useful if it is memorable and unique enough to be registered and trademarked. A brand name should be easy to say, and easily translatable into another language. The Olympic rings and the Ferrari prancing horse are two well-known logos associated with sport. Some suggestions for a good brand name follow.

What makes a good brand name?

- Short
- Positive
- Easy to remember
- Easy to say
- Easy to recognise
- Unique
- Describes the product/product use/benefits
- Able to be registered or trademarked
- Translates into other languages

Interactive case

Go to Interbrand's website and look at their rankings of the world's most valuable brands. See if you can recognise which ones have a strong involvement in sport via sponsorship.

http://www.interbrand.com/best_brands_2006.asp

Building a sport brand

Sport branding is more than choosing a memorable name, or having an appealing logo designed. A brand has to be sold to consumers if it is going to elicit the desired reaction. Brands have to be built. There are four steps to brand building as outlined in Figure 6.6.

Chapter Principle 6.7: Building a brand is a process made up of four steps including (1) establish brand awareness, (2) develop and manage a brand image, (3) develop brand equity and (4) develop brand loyalty.

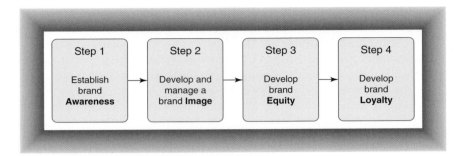

Figure 6.6 Building a Sport Brand.

Table 6.2 Image Variables and the Marketing Mix

Image Variables	*Relationship to Marketing Mix*
Brand name	Product and promotion
Product features	Product
Product quality or performance	Product
Packaging	Product
Price point	Price
Advertising	Promotion
Promotion	Promotion
Sponsorship associations	Sponsorship (promotion)
Customer service	Place and services
Distribution channels	Place

Step 1: Establish brand awareness

Brand awareness refers to the extent to which consumers recognise and remember a brand name. It is the first step of building a sport brand because consumers must be aware of a brand to understand its identity or image. The process of improving consumer awareness of a brand is one of the key roles of promotion, which is addressed in Chapter 9.

Step 2: Develop and manage a brand image

A brand's image is the way it is represented in the minds of consumers. For example, do consumers believe that it stands for reliability, luxury, adventure or excitement? Once consumers are aware of a brand, it is essential to mould and manage their perceptions of it. Managing a brand also means that continual effort needs to be made to remind consumers of the brand image. There are numerous variables which can be manipulated to affect consumers' perceptions of brand image. These are summarised in Table 6.2 along with the corresponding aspect of the marketing mix needed to introduce an effect.

120

Interactive case

Olympic Marketing: Visit the IOC's website and examine their approach to marketing. See if you can determine what their basic branding approach is.
http://www.olympic.org/uk/organization/index_uk.asp

Step 3: Develop brand equity

Brand equity is the added value that a sport product holds because of its brand name. Consumers are more likely to be loyal to a product if it develops high levels of brand equity. Brand equity can be influenced by several factors including consumer awareness, price, concepts and ideas that consumers connect to the brand, the prominence of competitor's brands and their respective images, the nature of the products offered under the brand, and consumer loyalty. However, the most influential factor is perceived quality. This means that the most productive avenue to develop brand equity is by increasing awareness while controlling the quality of the products offered. Because of the differences between goods and services, there are additional issues to consider when it comes to service quality compared to goods quality. In fact, there are five areas that are commonly used to describe the specific aspects of service quality. These five areas were originally developed by Parasuraman et al. (1985). They are reliability, assurance, empathy, responsiveness and tangibles. Each is briefly described in Table 6.3 and explained in detail in Chapter 11.

Table 6.3 Five Elements of Sport Service Quality

Service Quality Element	Explanation
Reliability	The ability to provide a service in a consistent and dependable way
	How reliable a customer believes a service is depends on how strongly they believe their expectations of the service will be met every time
Responsiveness	The willingness to help customers and to provide them with the service on time
Assurance	The level of confidence and trust that a customer has in the service
Empathy	The ability to get to know customers and their needs, and to deliver a personalised service
Tangibles	Physical features of the service (e.g. information booklets, equipment, appearance of staff, facilities, sport venue)

Table 6.4 Eight Elements of Sporting Goods Quality

Service Quality Element	Explanation
Conformity to specifications	Whether the goods meet the design standards of the manufacturer
Features	Whether the features of the product are high quality
Performance	How well the product carries out its main function (core product)
Reliability	How consistently the product performs
Durability	How long the product will last
Serviceability	How quickly and conveniently the product can be serviced if there are problems
Aesthetic design	Whether the design of the product looks to be of high quality
Product warranty	The guarantee of support if something goes wrong with the product

There are also several important considerations when it comes to the quality of goods in comparison to services. There are eight elements of quality when it comes to physical goods (Garvin, 1987). These are features, performance, reliability, conformity to specifications, durability, serviceability, aesthetic design and product warranties. Each is summarised in Table 6.4.

Chapter Principle 6.8: Brand equity increases when consumers rate products as high quality. There are different elements of product quality for goods compared to services. There are five elements of *service* quality: (1) reliability, (2) assurance, (3) empathy, (4) responsiveness and (5) tangibles. There are eight elements of *goods* quality, these are (1) features, (2) performance, (3) reliability, (4) conformity to specifications, (5) durability, (6) serviceability, (7) aesthetic design and (8) product warranty.

Step 4: Develop brand loyalty

When a customer is loyal to a brand it means that they will choose it repeatedly in preference over alternatives offered by competitors. As explained in the previous section, the quality of a sport good or service will play a role in encouraging loyalty, and it therefore needs to be continually addressed. It is also useful to look at how easy it is for consumers to buy the product on an ongoing basis. For example, is the product distributed in a way that is convenient for consumers to access? Sport organisations sometimes try to encourage loyalty by offering rewards to consumers for buying their product more than once.

Branding and licensing

Licensing is an arrangement where a sport organisation allows another party to use their brand for a fee. The organisation which purchases the right to use the brand (called the licensee) will then produce a good, service or promotion, and will give a percentage of the money they make, or pay a fixed fee to the real owner of the brand (called the licensor).

Licensing is particularly common in the area of sporting merchandise and apparel. Sport merchandise can include toys, collectible cards, board games, school supplies, videos, DVDs, magazines, and computer and console games. Sport clubs and leagues do not have the resources to make all of these kinds of products by themselves. Instead, they may make an agreement with another company to make the merchandise for them, and of course they will want their sport brand or logo to be used. As a result, sport brands offer specific companies the right to use their brand. Also, both organisations will want to make money out of the agreement, so each of them will agree on a percentage of profits that they will receive.

Licensing is a very common product strategy in sport, and each year it generates billions of dollars in sales internationally. As with all strategies there are opportunities and risks associated with licensing for both parties. These are outlined in Table 6.5.

Table 6.5 Licensing Sport Brands

	Opportunities	*Risks*
For the licensee	● An association with a prominent sport brand with an automatic level of brand awareness and equity	● Reliant on the continued (sporting) performance of the brand ● After heavy investment, the licensor can terminate the agreement
For the licensor	● New markets become accessible through broader distribution network ● More volume of the product can be made available ● Increase brand awareness and equity through greater exposure of the brand to new consumers ● No capital investment	● Out of control of the way their brand is portrayed and marketed ● More difficult to manage quality of the product

Case Study—Brand Beckham

By Sharyn McDonald

'David Beckham' is a sport brand. He is acknowledged as one of the best football (soccer) players in the world, captaining England for six years and twice runner up for FIFA player of the year. He is also a Goodwill Ambassador for UNICEF with a special focus on their 'Sports for Development Program'. The popularity and strength of his name allowed Beckham to create his own 'David Beckham Academy', which provides young players with the opportunity to fulfil their athletic potential. His high profile has led to numerous commercial ventures including the 'David Beckham Instinct' fragrance for men, and he has prominent and lucrative sponsorship endorsements with adidas, Pepsi and Motorola, making his one of the most recognised names in the world of sport. This provides a massive promotional platform for Beckham who is faced with injecting new life into the US soccer league.

When Beckham moved from Manchester United Football Club in the United Kingdom to Real Madrid in Spain, he brought with him a sizeable fan base. The exclusivity of signing Beckham brought immediate value to Real Madrid. In the first six months of playing for the club, Beckham's brand power increased merchandising profits by 137 per cent.

In January 2007, Los Angeles Galaxy Soccer team announced that they had signed Beckham in what was the most substantial athlete contract ever. The global branding associated with Beckham's name has projected LA Galaxy into the spotlight. LA Galaxy are successfully utilising this new brand power to influence the US market. Contracted for five years, within the first six months, LA Galaxy attracted a shirt sponsor injecting $20 million over five years, a further $6 million from other investors and increased ticket revenue by $4 million.

There is more at stake than just profits, however. Will David Beckham be able help improve and maintain the popularity of soccer in the United States? Soccer is popular with children in the United States, but Beckham's presence has the opportunity to take the game to a higher level and a new market. With similar media attention in the 1970s, Brazilian superstar Pele helped raise the profile of soccer, motivating children to become involved in the game. Some sport marketers believe that the multidimensional Beckham brand is powerful enough to radically expand soccer's influence in the United States. Of course, the very nature of sport including the ongoing potential for injury means that Beckham remains a big risk for the LA Galaxy.

For more information see:

Isidore, C. (2007). *Brand It Like Beckham. David Beckham's Economic Impact on Long-Suffering U.S. Soccer League Is Being Felt, Even Before His First Game Here*. Available at: http://money.cnn.com/2007/07/05/commentary/sportsbiz/index.htm (CNNMoney.com, web page).

Principles summary

- Chapter Principle 6.1: Sport goods may be differentiated from services on the basis of four factors: tangibility, consistency, perishability and separability.
- Chapter Principle 6.2: A sport product is the complete package of benefits presented to a sport consumer in the form of physical goods, services and ideas, or a combination of these to produce a sport experience.
- Chapter Principle 6.3: Sport products should be seen as a bundle of benefits comprising the core benefits, features of the product and augmented product. These three variables of the product are interrelated and should be manipulated as a group.
- Chapter Principle 6.4: In sport marketing, a new product can take many forms such as the improved performance of an existing product, new functions added to an existing product, a new way to use an existing product, combining existing products or a new look or design for a product.
- Chapter Principle 6.5: The term product life cycle refers to the stages that a product goes through from first being introduced onto the market to its decline. There are four stages of the product life cycle: introduction, growth, maturity and decline.
- Chapter Principle 6.6: A sport brand is the symbolic representation of everything that a sport organisation seeks to stand for, leading to expectations about its value and performance. A brand can be portrayed as an identifying badge which triggers consumers to remember a product or an organisation. It can be a name, a design, a symbol (or logo), an image or a combination of these things. Branding is one of the key strategies that marketers use to help their product to stand out from the crowd by positioning it through associated ideas and concepts.
- Chapter Principle 6.7: Building a brand is a process made up of four steps, including (1) establish brand awareness, (2) develop and manage a brand image, (3) develop brand equity and (4) develop brand loyalty.
- Chapter Principle 6.8: Brand equity increases when consumers rate products as high quality. There are different elements of product quality for goods compared with services. There are five elements of service quality: (1) reliability, (2) assurance, (3) empathy, (4) responsiveness and (5) tangibles. There are eight elements of goods quality, these are (1) features, (2) performance, (3) reliability, (4) conformity to specifications, (5) durability, (6) serviceability, (7) aesthetic design and (8) product warranty.

Tools summary

1. Chapter Tool 6.1. Sport Product Continuum
2. Chapter Tool 6.2. New Product Development
3. Chapter Tool 6.3. Product Life cycle Stages

Review questions

1. What is the difference between a sport product and a sport service?
2. Provide a simple definition of a sport product.
3. Sport products can provide both tangible and intangible benefits. Why does this present challenges for sport marketers?
4. What are the three variables of a sport product and provide an example of each for a sport product of your choice?
5. Identify the four stages of the product life cycle. Provide a brief description of the best marketing strategy to employ at each stage.
6. What is the relationship between branding and positioning?

Relevant websites

http://www.rbk.com (Reebok)

http://www.manutd.com (Manchester United)

http://www.dallascowboys.com (Dallas Cowboys)

http://www.interbrand.com (Interbrand)

http://www.olympic.org (The International Olympic Committee)

Further reading

Duffy, N. (2003). *Passion Branding*, Wiley, West Sussex, England.
Rein, I., Kotler, P. & Shields, B. (2006). *The Elusive Fan: Reinventing Sports in a Crowded Marketplace*, McGraw-Hill, New York.

References

Garvin, D.A. (1987). Competing on the eight dimensions of quality, *Harvard Business Review*, Nov-Dec: 101–109.
Parasuraman, A., Zeithamal, V. & Berry, L. (1985). A conceptual model of service quality and its implications for future research, *Journal of Marketing*, 49: 41–50.

7 Sport pricing

Overview

The purpose of this chapter is to explore the second of the six elements in the marketing mix—price. The chapter is structured around a step-by-step pricing process. Steps 1 and 2 provide guidance on setting pricing goals and analysing market sensitivity. The remaining steps involve a break-even analysis, considering other variables that affect pricing, and choosing a pricing strategy.

At the end of this chapter, readers should be able to:

- Describe the strategic pricing process.
- Outline the most common pricing goals.
- Outline the factors that influence price sensitivity.
- Explain what a break-even analysis is, and how to perform it.
- Discuss other factors that influence pricing.
- Outline the common pricing strategies used in the sport industry.

Introduction

Chapter 6 explained the first element of the marketing mix—the product—and this chapter expands the discussion to consider the second element of the marketing mix—price. Price and its components can be located in Figure 7.1

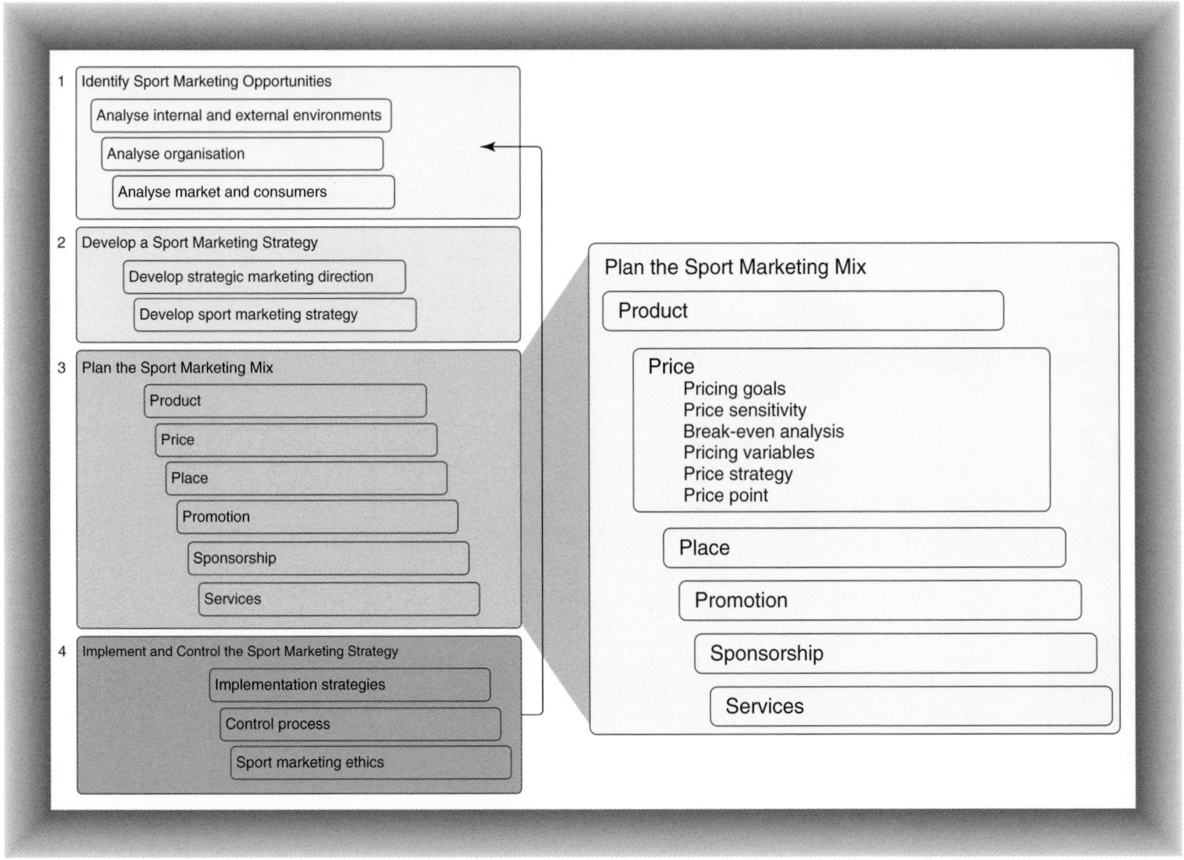

Plan the Sport Marketing Mix

Product

Price
Pricing goals
Price sensitivity
Break-even analysis
Pricing variables
Price strategy
Price point

Place

Promotion

Sponsorship

Services

---

1 Identify Sport Marketing Opportunities
- Analyse internal and external environments
- Analyse organisation
- Analyse market and consumers

2 Develop a Sport Marketing Strategy
- Develop strategic marketing direction
- Develop sport marketing strategy

3 Plan the Sport Marketing Mix
- Product
- Price
- Place
- Promotion
- Sponsorship
- Services

4 Implement and Control the Sport Marketing Strategy
- Implementation strategies
- Control process
- Sport marketing ethics

Figure 7.1 The Sport Marketing Framework.

within the Sport Marketing Framework. In order to set the groundwork, there are four important terms to understand: price, value, revenue, and profit, which are reviewed in the following sub-sections.

It is easy to imagine that pricing a product simply involves working out what it costs to produce it, then adding on a margin for profit. However, pricing sport products is a far more complicated process. In fact, the way that a sport product is priced will have a dramatic influence on the way that consumers perceive it. In addition, pricing tends to change continually, depending on a range of variables including a product's position in its life cycle.

Pricing not only influences a sport product's profitability, it communicates a powerful message to consumers about the brand. A simple example can be found in the contrasting prices of general admission tickets versus corporate box tickets to sport events. The prices of these two types of tickets will immediately communicate quite different messages about the sort of experience that a consumer might expect. The higher the cost of the corporate box tickets, the more a consumer would expect quality, indulgence, business networking opportunities, great seating, weather (and spectator) protection, and quality food and alcohol. On the other hand, the cheaper general admission tickets might lead a consumer to expect average seating, exposure to the weather, and the possibility of mixing with unruly fans. The difference in price is one of the key symbols representing what a consumer should expect. When there is little difference in price, consumers expect little difference in the quality of the product.

> *Chapter Principle 7.1*: Pricing communicates an important symbolic positioning message to consumers about a sport product.

Price

The price of a product represents what a consumer relinquishes in exchange for a sporting good or service. A price should also reflect the value of a product. Generally, price is thought of in financial terms, but may include other things that a customer has to give up in order to obtain the product, such as time (e.g. waiting in a queue) or social costs (e.g. being in an aerobics class with others instead of a one-on-one instruction). This chapter will focus on monetary pricing, but it is worth remembering that the other sacrifices a consumer makes to acquire a product may also have an influence on whether they buy it.

Value

A useful way to think about pricing decisions is to consider them in terms of value. In sport marketing, the value of a product is a factor of how its price relates to the benefits that consumers believe they will receive in exchange. Value is expressed in terms of the following equation.

$$\text{Value} = \frac{\text{Benefits a consumer thinks they will receive from the sport product}}{\text{Price of the sport product}}$$

129

Chapter Principle 7.2: The value of a sport product is the relationship between its price and the benefits a consumer believes they will receive from it.

The benefits of a product are what it offers the consumer, as described in Chapter 6. Consumers will feel that a product is of good value if the benefits received from it are equal or greater than the price paid. With sport products, this can be a highly variable and individual assessment. Sport memorabilia provides an example. Consider a sport uniform that has been signed by all the current players of a prominent team. Although it would be possible to buy a new uniform for $200, it would be reasonable to assume that a fan of the team would pay considerably more for the same uniform with signatures on it. Given the popularity of sport memorabilia, it is likely that some fans would pay as much as several thousand dollars. Many sport consumers believe that owning an unusual item connected to sport is worth a high price. However, someone who is not a sport fan would probably be unwilling to buy the uniform at any price, and would perhaps consider it of less use than ordinary clothing. Both value and the perceived benefits of sport products vary considerably.

Chapter Principle 7.3: The price of a product is the amount of money a consumer must give up in exchange for a good or service. However, price also represents the value of a product. Although price is usually seen as an amount of money, it may also include other consumer sacrifices in order to acquire a sport product, such as time or social cost.

Revenue and profit

Two further relevant pricing terms are revenue and profit. Revenue is the price that consumers pay for a product, multiplied by the number of product units product sold. For example, if a sport venue sells tickets to an event for $38.50 each, and 45799 tickets are sold, then revenue is $38.50 × 15799 = $608261.50. When costs are removed from this revenue, the remainder is considered profit. In other words, profit equals revenue minus expenses.

On the surface, it may seem logical to assume that the higher the price, the more revenue earned, and the larger the resulting profit. However, in order to make a profit, the price of a product must be set appropriately, in a way aligned with its positioning strategy. It is therefore important that the price is not higher than the perceived value consumers hold of the product. It is also important that the reverse does not occur because this can undermine the perceived quality that a sport brand holds in consumers' perceptions. For example, if a motor racing event increased its prices by 200 per cent, many consumers would probably decide that the price is not worth it. On the other hand, if the price is set too low it may not cover costs, or consumers may get the idea that the product is old, out of fashion, of poor quality, or not exclusive enough.

> *Chapter Principle 7.4*: *Revenue* is the price that consumers pay for a product, multiplied by the number of units sold. *Profit* is revenue minus the costs of producing and selling the product.

Strategic pricing process

By calling the pricing process 'strategic', it is meant that setting a product's price should be planned with careful analysis and a consistent aim. The steps of the strategic pricing process are outlined in Figure 7.2. The remainder of the chapter will examine each of these steps in turn.

> *Chapter Principle 7.5*: The strategic pricing process provides a structure for setting price. The process involves: (1) setting a pricing goal, (2) determining price sensitivity, (3) conducting a break-even analysis, (4) assessing pricing variables, (5) selecting price tactics and (6) setting a price point.

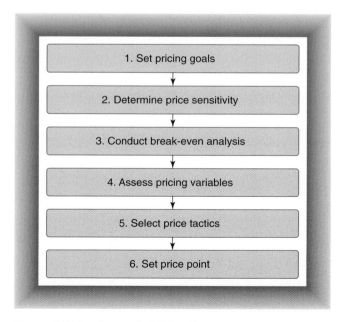

131

Figure 7.2 The Strategic Pricing Process.

Pricing goals

Because different pricing strategies will achieve different outcomes, it is important to begin by determining what goals are being sought. It is essential to remember that pricing goals should support a broader product and brand positioning strategy, which in turn should underpin marketing objectives and the achievement of organisational objectives.

There are two main types of pricing goals: (1) profit-based pricing goals, and (2) sales-based pricing goals. Profit-based goals are focused on how much money a sport organisation earns after it has paid all of its costs. Sales-based pricing goals are focused on the amount of sales an organisation makes. Both of these goals have a number of sub-goals, which are described next.

Interactive case

Choose one brand of athletic footwear like Nike, Reebok, FILA or adidas. See if you can create a list of shoe products from the least expensive to the most expensive. Examine how wide the range of pricing is and consider whether there is a positioning strategy behind the approach. How many distinctive price 'points' are there? In other words, at what levels are the prices set? (e.g. $80, $100, $120, etc.)

http://www.rbk.com	Reebok website
http://www.nike.com	Nike website
http://www.fila.com	FILA website
http://www.adidas.com	adidas website

Profit-based pricing goals

Profit maximisation means setting a price that will maximise the margin or difference between revenue and expenses. It does not automatically mean that prices should be set as high as possible. It is unwise for an organisation to set a price above the *perceived value* of the product. One of the potential problems with a profit maximisation goal is that it can encourage sport organisations to think in the short-term rather than the long-term. For example, it could encourage a sport organisation to cut costs and wages as much as possible, and as a result lead to a lower quality product delivered by unhappy staff.

Satisfactory profit means a reasonable or realistic profit. What is reasonable and realistic will vary for different organisations and different product markets. It can be difficult to set a specific goal corresponding to how much profit is reasonable because it requires research into the market and competitors.

Target return on investment is the most common profit-based pricing goal. In principle, target return on investment means an earnings target for a pre-defined target market. Using this approach, a sport organisation would consider the amount of money it intends to make from selling a product, taking into account the amount they had to invest to develop and bring it to the market. Based on this calculation, a price can be determined. Naturally, a higher return on investment is better, but of course, many sport organisations are not profit seeking and therefore choose a price that is sustainable rather than profitable.

Sales-based pricing goals

Market share is a measure of the percentage one product or brand has acquired of the total sales in a sector or part of the sport industry. Market share can be calculated in terms of dollars, or in terms of how many units of the product that are sold. It is not automatic that sport organisations with the largest market share make the biggest profits. While it is true that increasing market share can increase profit, some organisations with a low market share can survive and do very well. Market share tends to be a better measure for the sporting goods sector as sport teams and sport organising bodies are not oriented towards profit. Indeed, sport organisations participating in competitions will never hold the allegiance of all fans, and were they to, it would mean the end of the competition. However, it is reasonable that sport organisations oriented towards participation may find market share useful to gauge whether they are attracting more or fewer participants.

Sales maximisation refers to the goal of acquiring as many sales as possible. Sport organisations that pursue this goal are less concerned with profit, and are more focused on increasing the number of sales. For profit-oriented sport organisations, this goal is generally not a good long-term goal because it does not pay enough attention to whether the organisation is earning enough money to survive. It can be a short-term goal, however, if an organisation needs to generate some quick cash, or if it wants to sell off some old stock to make way for new products. For participant-based sport, sales can translate into participant numbers. For these organisations, as long as they can cover their costs, participation represents success.

Chapter Tool 7.1. Pricing Goals:

- Profit maximisation: Setting a price that maximises profit, but that is not above the *perceived value* of the product.
- Satisfactory profits: A reasonable or realistic profit.
- Return on investment: A mathematical sum where net profit is considered in light of the investment in the product.
- Market share: How many sales or how much money an organisation makes as a percentage of the total sales/revenue in the market or a segment of the market.
- Sales maximisation: Trying to achieve as many sales as possible.

Price sensitivity

The second step of the strategic pricing process involves determining how sensitive consumers are to the price of the product. Price sensitivity is sometimes called *market sensitivity* because it refers to how sensitive consumers are (in other words how sensitive the market is) to changes in the price of a product. For example, if prices for a product rise, will customers be very sensitive and stop buying it, or will they ignore the price rise and keep spending their money? Price sensitivity is influenced by demand, supply, price elasticity and the perceived value of the product.

Demand

Demand represents how many units of a sport product will be wanted by the market (the sum total of consumers) at a certain price. Usually the higher the price for a product, the fewer goods or services consumers will want. Equally, the lower the price, the more goods and services customers will want. This relationship is shown in Figure 7.3.

Product demand is also influenced by product *substitutes* and *complements*. Product substitutes are products that can be used in place of another product.

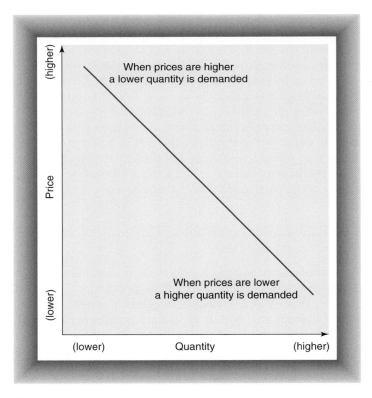

Figure 7.3 Demand for a Product.

For example, if the price of a family ticket to the tennis increased dramatically, other products like movie or theme-park tickets could be used as a substitute for a cheaper family outing. Product complements are those that are used together. For example, membership to a rock-climbing gymnasium and sales of climbing harnesses are complementary products. If the cost of a membership rises, the quantity of both products (memberships and harnesses) demanded by consumers would likely fall.

Supply

Supply represents the quantity of a product that is available in the market at a certain price. In principle, the higher the price of a product, the greater the returns. Consequently, the more resources an organisation has in order to produce more of the product. Also, when the price is higher, other organisations may become interested in trying to produce and sell a similar product themselves. In other words, a higher product price usually leads to a greater amount of the product being supplied to the market. This is illustrated in Figure 7.4.

The volume of a product supplied to the market will also be influenced by other factors, such as the prices of raw materials and resources, the number of competitors, and consumers' expectations about future prices and technology. For example, if the cost of cotton (a raw material) to make a sport

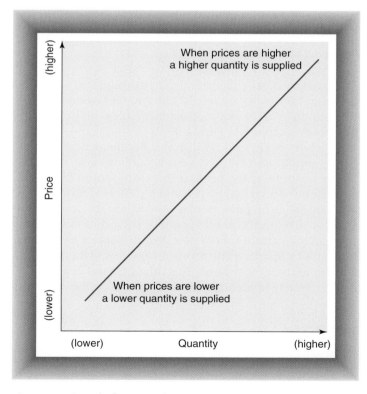

Figure 7.4 Supply for a Product.

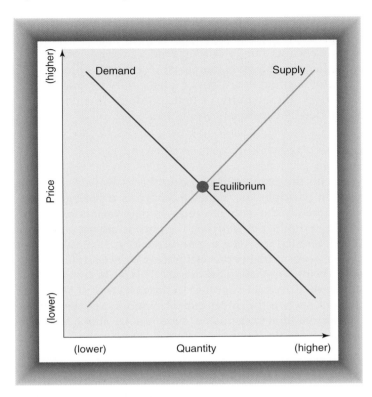

Figure 7.5 Market Equilibrium.

branded T-shirt dramatically increased, then the number of T-shirts supplied in the sporting apparel industry would fall. Another example is that the volume supplied to the market of a product increases with growth in the number of competitors (suppliers) offering it.

The graph shown in Figure 7.5 illustrates the theoretical conditions when demand equals supply, also known as market equilibrium. At market equilibrium price, the quantity of the product that is produced by suppliers is the same as the quantity demanded by consumers. There is no excess product left unsold, and there are no consumers who want to buy the product but miss out. Of course, this is merely a theoretical possibility which is almost impossible to predict or achieve in practice. However, the concept of market equilibrium helps to explain why sport organisations review the relationship between the volume of their product or service offerings and demand. Equally, sport organisations can deliberately influence demand by changing their pricing structure.

Price elasticity

Price elasticity refers to how easily consumer demand for a product changes when there is a change in price. There are two different types of price elasticity: inelastic demand and elastic demand. In most competitive sport, inelastic demand is more prominent. This means that it is difficult to substitute (or replace) one sport league, team or competition for another. Many sport fans are fiercely loyal to their team or their sport. Even if the price of tickets to a game changes, loyal fans are unlikely to stop buying them.

The opposite is elastic demand, which means that demand for the product will change in response to changes in price. In this case, if the price of a product increases, consumers will buy less of it, but if the price falls, a higher quantity will be demanded. Demand for the product is like an elastic band (therefore the term elastic demand), which stretches or shrinks depending on the price. The more substitutes available for a sport product, the easier it is for consumers to replace it with another if the price rises.

Perceived value

The level of demand and supply, and the price elasticity of a sport product are not the only variables that influence how sensitive consumers are to changes in price. Consumer sensitivity to price change is also affected by the perceived value of the product. If consumers believe that a sport product has substantial benefits, or provides them with social status, then they may be willing to pay a price that is higher than the market average. Furthermore, if sport marketers can increase the perceived value of a sport product, then consumers may be willing to pay more for it, and the sport organisation may receive more revenue. Equally, some consumers will be willing to go without some product benefits in exchange for a cheaper price. For example, consumers may be willing to buy a T-shirt without a fashionable logo for the benefit of paying less. This means that the T-shirt producer can spend less money on marketing their logo, and sell the product for less.

Chapter Tool 7.2. Price Sensitivity Analysis: Price sensitivity refers to how sensitive consumers are to changes in the price of a product. Consumers are considered price sensitive if they do not buy a product when the price is high, or when they buy more of a product when the price is low. The more sensitive consumers are, the more they will change their buying habits when the price changes. The process involves:

1. Examining how much of the same or a similar product is supplied and demanded at each price level. This may provide a guide in order to determine a realistic price that consumers are willing to pay. This is an assessment of supply and demand.
2. Considering how many product substitutes exist in the market. The more product substitutes, the more sensitive consumers will be to higher prices. This is an assessment of price elasticity.
3. Determining if there are any product complements. It can be revealing to discover that sales of complementary products change corresponding to price changes of a sport product. This is an assessment of the price elasticity of the product.
4. Assessing the degree of perceived product value held by consumers. This is undertaken through market research.

Break-Even analysis

The third step of the pricing process requires a break-even analysis to be conducted. Break-even analysis is used to determine how many product sales are needed in order to ensure that revenue is equal to the costs of producing the product. When a product reaches break-even point, its revenue is equal to its costs; there is no extra money left over (this would be a profit), and costs are not greater than revenue (this would be a loss).

The costs of producing a product are usually divided into fixed costs and variable costs. Fixed costs are the expenses an organisation incurs in producing and delivering a product that will not change, no matter how much of the product is sold. For example, the cost of rent, equipment and insurance are often constant for a sport organisation, no matter how many products are made or services delivered.

Variable costs are the expenses that change (either up or down) depending on how much of the product or service is made or delivered. For example, the cost of fabric for a sport apparel producer would increase if they had to buy more fabric to make additional T-shirts. Another example is the cost of staff in a service business; more staff is needed to deliver more services, which in turn costs the sport organisation more. Usually, an organisation will calculate how much it spends on variable costs per unit. For example, a sport shoe company might calculate that for every pair of shoes they make (one unit each), they spend $15 on variable costs (such as leather and shoelaces). Similar calculations can be performed as extra participants are added to sport events.

To calculate a break-even point, the following formula can be used:

$$\text{Break-even point} = \frac{\text{Total fixed costs}}{\text{Price per unit} - \text{variable costs per unit}}$$

For example, imagine the situation of a company that produces collectible sports cards. Its fixed costs (such as factory rental, printing equipment and insurance) equal $450 000. The variable cost for each packet of cards (such as paper, ink and packaging) is $1.50. It sells each packet for $10.00.

Step 1: Put the amounts for total fixed costs, price per unit and variable costs per unit into the formula.

$$\text{Break-even point} = \frac{450\,000}{\$10 - \$1.50 \text{ per unit}}$$

Step 2: Take the variable costs per unit away from the price per unit ($10.00 minus $1.50 equals $8.50)

$$\text{Break-even point} = \frac{450\,000}{\$8.50 \text{ per unit}}$$

Step 3: Divide the total costs by the figure on the bottom (remember, the figure on the bottom is the price per unit minus the variable costs per unit).

$$\text{Break-even point} = \frac{450\,000}{\$8.50 \text{ per unit}}$$

Step 4: The outcome represents the number of units needed to break-even.

$$\text{Break-even point} = 52\,941 \text{ units}$$

The company in the example needs to sell 52 941 packets of sports collector cards in order to break-even. Determining the break-even point is advantageous in setting a price for a product because it means that the financial implications of various alternative pricing strategies can be explored. When these are considered in light of other factors that influence pricing, then a final price can be set.

Chapter Tool 7.3. Break-even Analysis: A *break-even analysis* calculates the quantity of sales needed to ensure that revenue earned is equal to the costs of producing the product or service. At *break-even*, revenue is equal to costs.

The costs of producing a product are divided into *fixed* costs and *variable* costs. Fixed costs are the expenses an organisation has that do not change no matter how much they sell of their product. Variable costs are the expenses that change (either up or down) depending on how much of the product is made.

Break even = Total fixed costs/Price per unit − Variable costs per unit.

Pricing variables

Armed with an appreciation of a price point required in order to break-even, the next stage is to consider any other variables that could affect the price set. These other factors include the pricing strategies of competitors, any legal or technical boundaries that may be relevant to the pricing of the product and the impact of choices associated with other marketing mix variables.

Competitors' pricing

The price that competitors charge for the same or similar products will offer an insight into consumer expectations. When considering the pricing approach of competitors, it is important to keep positioning and quality in mind. For example, some competitors will offer a product or service at the upper end of the quality scale, and will position the product with supportive marketing accordingly. It is helpful to determine which competitors' pricing strategies are most successful. In some cases, competitors' pricing levels will be unsustainable to match and an alternative positioning approach will be essential in order to compete with a higher price.

Legal and technical boundaries

A pricing boundary is an encumbrance that restricts or limits the price that can be set. One prominent boundary placed upon pricing comes in the form of laws or regulations established by government or governing sport bodies that restrict or modulate the price that can be set. For example, clubs in a sport league may be told by the league what prices they can charge for tickets. Alternatively, a local council may control the range of fees that a club passes on to its customers for using council facilities (such as a council-owned gymnasium or tennis court). In addition, in most countries there are laws that affect the way price can be structured. For example, price fixing (agreeing with competitors to each charge the same price) is illegal in many industries, although as noted in Chapter 2, many sport leagues are allowed to collude on prices. There are frequently laws which prevent prices being set so low that they drive competitors out of business. This practice is known as predatory pricing. Further boundaries can be technical in nature, such as production methods, which limit supply, and environmental sustainability, which adds to costs.

Marketing mix

All of the marketing mix variables should reflect the positioning strategy a sport brand selects. As a result, it is important to consider how the other marketing mix variables influence price setting. The approaches chosen with the other variables (product, promotion, place, sponsorship and services) will have an effect on the choice of best pricing strategy. For example, the way that a product is distributed to consumers may affect the price that they are willing to pay. If a product is convenient to buy, consumers may be willing to pay a little more than normal for it. This is why food, beverages and merchandise always cost more at a sporting venue than they do in other outlets. Also, sport services can be priced higher if they are accompanied by a tangible product, like a junior football program that comes with a backpack, stickers and a football. Finally, if a product is positioned at the top end of the market, it is advantageous to bolster the brand with a prominent sponsorship.

Chapter Tool 7.4. Assess Pricing Variables: Several environmental factors can influence the price set for a product, including the pricing strategies of competitors, any legal or technical boundaries, and the impact of the other marketing mix variables in the marketing plan.

Interactive case

Visit the websites given below for the Wimbledon All England Tennis Championships and the Indianapolis 500. Compare the two pricing approaches.

http://www.wimbledon.org/
http://www.indy500.com/

Pricing tactics

The fifth step in setting a price is to select a pricing tactic. The pricing tactic should be directly related to the positioning strategy that is chosen for the product. As a reminder, market positioning refers to how consumers think and feel about a brand or product when they compare it with others. It is the image or perception of a sport brand or product. For example, consumers might perceive a brand or product as luxury and high quality, or as basic and value-for-money. Consumers might see a brand or product as conservative and reliable or exciting and changeable. Positioning takes into account the fact that consumers will place a brand or product into a position in their minds that is relative to others. The positioning strategy that is chosen will have an influence on the best choice of pricing strategy. For example, if a sport organisation has decided to position one of its products as high quality, it would be appropriate to set a premium price goal. A high price can help to give consumers the idea that the quality of the product is correspondingly high. There are a number of common pricing strategies that sport marketers should consider, which are outlined in the following sub-sections.

Prestige pricing

In some situations the quality or benefits of a product may be more important to consumers than price. The product may be so excellent, fashionable or even essential that the price is not important. In the sport industry, examples of prestige pricing include exclusive memberships, special events, prestige seating, celebrity seating or special services. Because price is not the most important variable in the decision to purchase a product, prestige pricing involves setting a high price. It must be remembered that by setting a high price, a product appears to be exclusive and of high quality. Sometimes it can be effective to produce only a limited number of goods or provide a limited service in order to enhance the image of a product or service. For example, a gymnasium may decide to offer only premium-priced memberships, and give consumers higher quality service, state-of-the-art equipment and less crowding than competitors. One of the drawbacks of prestige pricing is that it will only appeal to a relatively small number of consumers. The power of prestige pricing is that it confers a psychological benefit by encouraging consumers to believe they are special because they have access to such an exclusive product. This is why a variation of prestige pricing is called psychological pricing, which emphasises the intangible quality of a special product.

Status quo pricing

Maintaining the status quo means keeping things the way they are. Status quo pricing aims to either keep prices at the same level or to meet competitors' prices. One advantage of this strategy is that it does not require much planning. It can be a useful approach against a competitor that is an established price leader. However, it is also worth noting that offering a lower price (and therefore better value) and a higher price (for a better product) is two ways of setting a product apart from competitors.

Price skimming

Price skimming involves setting the highest price possible that consumers will pay for a new product. This can help an organisation to quickly cover the costs of product development and promotion. Price skimming will not work in all situations or for all products. It is best used when new equipment or technology is introduced, such as a brand-new golf club or a new exclusive service. Because price skimming is likely to reduce the total number of consumers who buy the product, it is not suitable for all products. Some sport products need a large volume of consumers in order to be successful (like ticket sales to a sport event). However, there are examples in sport where demand is so high for a prestige event that price skimming can be combined profitably with high volume. Good examples are the finals of major sport competitions and hallmark events, like the Olympic Games opening and closing ceremonies.

Penetration pricing

Penetration pricing is the opposite of price skimming because it involves setting a low introductory price for the product in the hopes of encouraging people to give it a first try. The word penetration is used to mean entry or access to the market. Penetration pricing can be effective in parts of the sport industry where there is a high level of competition, or where consumers already have strong loyalties to products. It is one way of developing some interest in a new product, or trying to increase its market share. After a certain amount of time, penetration pricing is usually replaced with a more standard price that can be realistically maintained. It is hoped that by this time sufficient numbers of consumers will continue to use the product.

Cost-plus pricing

The cost-plus pricing method is common in the sport industry. Using this method, the price is set by calculating the costs of the product, then adding a flat fee or a percentage (e.g. cost plus 10 per cent). If this method is selected, it is essential to have accurate information about fixed and variable costs.

Break-even pricing

A break-even price is one that generates just enough money to cover the costs of the product. This may be a pricing tactic that is useful to non-profit or community sport organisations. It has the advantage of being a simple, consumer-friendly strategy. However, the danger is that consumers will become used to the 'cheap' price, leaving the organisation with little opportunity to change prices in the future, even if costs rise unexpectedly.

Competition pricing

This means setting prices that copy those of competitors. In a highly competitive market, this may prove a useful strategy. It has the advantage of reducing the possibility of being undercut, but it does require a reactive rather than proactive approach. As such it is best employed selectively.

Market demand pricing

Market demand pricing involves setting a price according to the level consumers are willing to pay at a given time. It has the potential of generating high profits for a sport organisation, but it may need to be changed over time because the price consumers are willing to pay changes. It is possible that consumers could feel exploited if they believe they are being charged high prices just because they will pay it. It may also leave an organisation vulnerable to the penetration pricing of competitors.

Discount pricing

Discounting involves reducing or cutting a price in special situations. In the sport industry, discounts may be offered for long-term memberships, group or family concessions, frequent use or bulk purchases. It is used as a way of encouraging consumers to buy more than they otherwise would. Discount pricing can increase overall sales, and by selling more, an organisation can still earn a good profit even though the price per product is reduced. Of course, discounts can only be used occasionally if they are to be successful. Variations of discount pricing include sales and two-for-one offers.

Seasonal pricing

Sometimes it is possible to price a product based on changes in demand that occur over a time period. In competitive sport, leagues often charge different prices at different times in the playing season; they may have different prices for off-season, pre-season, regular season and finals. This is one way that sport leagues can stimulate sales when they are not in the main playing season. Seasonal pricing can cause difficulty if the price needs to be set below cost to stimulate demand.

Off-peak pricing

Like seasonal pricing, off-peak pricing involves setting different prices for different periods. Where seasonal pricing takes advantage of changes over the course of a year, off-peak pricing focuses on changes over the course of one day. Off-peak pricing is commonly employed in sport services where demand is centred on a particular period. For example, gymnasiums and leisure centres often provide discounted memberships for consumers prepared to use the facilities at low-demand times. One of the problems with this kind of pricing is that it can be difficult to control and manage.

Price bundling

A more sophisticated but common pricing tactic is known as bundling, where numerous product benefits are included in one price. Bundling has been popularised through television advertising which promises 'steak knives' and other extras when a product is ordered. In a sport context, bundling may include free merchandise with a product purchase, such as a sports watch with a sporting magazine subscription. Bundling is most common in memberships where consumers are offered a range of services and products in one package, such as access to a pool, social club, gymnasium, spa and sauna for one price in a health club. Bundling is effective because it gives consumers the experience of receiving something extra for nothing. For sport marketers, bundling is popular because the extras offered are rarely expensive to include.

Discriminatory pricing

Sometimes known as differential pricing, discriminatory pricing involves making changes to prices according to the category or segment of consumer to whom it is offered. As a result, this tactic is particularly useful for sport organisations that deal with a range of target segments. For example, a sport organisation might offer a less expensive membership to students, pensioners or the unemployed even though the service and benefits are the same.

Exchange pricing

Exchange pricing is a form of reciprocal trade where exchanges are made, such as corporate boxes, signage, tickets to events, and access to players and athletes, for 'everyday' items, including furniture and paper, as well as other necessities such as travel, accommodation and advertising. This is a useful tactic for sport organisations because exchange pricing is effectively bartering,

Table 7.1 Summary of Pricing Tactics

Tactic	Summary
1. Prestige (psychological)	Setting a high price for a product that has a high perceived value.
	Pricing where quality is more important than price because of 'special' circumstances.
2. Status quo	Keeping the price the way it is, or following competitors' prices.
3. Skimming	Setting the highest price possible that consumers will pay.
4. Penetration	Setting a low, introductory price for a product. The opposite of skimming is to introduce the product at such a low price that it will attract a large market share.
5. Cost plus	Pricing calculated by adding the costs of delivering the product, then adding a flat fee or percentage (e.g. cost + 10 per cent).
6. Break-even	Pricing products at 'cost'.
7. Competition	Pricing copies competitors.
8. Market demand	Setting pricing according to market demand at the time, taking into account elasticity and growth/shrinkage rates.
9. Discount	Decreasing the price of a service or a product in special circumstances.
10. Seasonal	Pricing according to seasonal demand.
	Useful for extra stock or downturns due to the season (e.g. winter competitions).
11. Off-peak	Pricing according to daily demand.
	Useful for maintaining turnover during normally lower daily usage times.
12. Bundling	Offering additional products, services or benefits at the same price.
13. Discriminatory (differential)	Prices change according to categories of customers.
14. Exchange	Reciprocal trade where exchanges are made.

allowing asset-rich, cash-poor sporting organisations to 'save' their liquid finances. It is worth noting that in most countries, while legal, exchange pricing does incur tax. Table 7.1 provides a summary of pricing tactics.

> *Chapter Tool 7.5. Select Pricing Tactics*: A pricing strategy should be related to the positioning strategy that an organisation selects for its product. There are at least 14 types of pricing strategies that sport organisations might employ: prestige pricing, status quo pricing, price skimming, penetration pricing, cost-plus pricing, break-even pricing, competition pricing, market demand pricing, discount pricing, seasonal pricing, off-peak pricing, price bundling, discriminatory pricing and exchange pricing.

Price point

The final step of the pricing process is to set the final price point for each product. A price point is a deliberately selected level of price that reflects the positioning approach underpinning the product's marketing strategy. In general, it is advisable to select a final price point that makes positioning as clear as possible. For example, if the positioning strategy calls for differentiation from a competitor's product, then it is critical to set a price that is distinctly different from that of competitors. If one were to study the price points of most major sport products, it would become clear that pricing tends to operate at different levels. An obvious example is that it is easy to find tennis racquets and cricket bats at around $150, $250 and $400 for each of the dominant brands. Consumers will tend to select between products that cost approximately the same. This is not the end of the work, however, as pricing strategies need to be reviewed and their success evaluated. Like all stages of the Sport Marketing Framework, pricing requires research and should be managed and controlled over time.

> *Chapter Tool 7.6. Select Price Point*: A price point is a deliberately selected level of price that reflects the positioning approach underpinning the product's marketing strategy.

Case Study—Transport Ticketing in Major Sporting Events

by Sharyn McDonald

The successful hosting of a major sporting event such as the Olympic or Commonwealth Games can bring enormous infrastructure, economy and tourism benefits. With global media attention, it is important for the host city to look its best and for all operations and services to run smoothly. Past host cities of mega sport events have received negative publicity about empty stadiums, displacement of local residents, crowding, congestion and failure to meet environmental targets. For example, the world looked on as Atlanta struggled to cope with the increase in visitation to the Centennial Olympic Games in 1996. The resultant bad press highlighted transport chaos as one of the central problems.

Although there are many uncertainties in hosting mega events, organisers should be able to foresee the potential problems of transport delays and empty venues. Organisers of the Sydney 2000 Olympic Games ensured that Sydney's transportation would not under-perform in the same way as Atlanta. Sydney's approach to the Games was to showcase a sustainable transport system which would ensure smooth organisation and deflect negative publicity. To ensure spectators used the public transport system, organisers incorporated free public transport into the price of the tickets, a bundling tactic that was innovative for a traditional event. The overall success of the Sydney Games has forced organisers of subsequent mega sport events to take note of the important link between transport and ticketing.

Sydney 2000 was not without criticism, however. It is important to provide an inclusive system for local residents who in the past have been excluded from attending sporting events because of ticket allocation policies or exclusive prices. Organisers of the Sydney Games had hoped their ballot system would make tickets available and prices affordable to all income levels. However, there was controversy surrounding the process, which saw many consumers disappointed. One point of difference for Athens, which hosted the Olympics in 2004, was a 34 per cent reduction in ticket prices including free public transport for ticket holders. Athens considerably upgraded their transport system, which received accolades from environmental groups.

Manchester in the United Kingdom, which hosted the 2002 Commonwealth Games, spent 125 million pounds on a transport system upgrade. To encourage spectators to use public transport, organisers warned patrons in advance of the potential traffic congestion. Although public transport was not free to travel into Manchester, travel alternatives were offered. By offering ticket holders a park and ride system and free shuttle buses around the city, Manchester boasted 80 per cent usage of their public transport system compared to the estimated 50 per cent. Notable successes of the Manchester Games included the affordability of ticket prices, which saw capacity crowds at most venues and the rejuvenation of decrepit areas within the metropolitan area.

Unfortunately, Manchester's Games failed to attract nationwide interest, which presented a potential problem for its successor city Melbourne, given Australia's geographical expanse. The Melbourne 2006 Commonwealth Games strategy was to enhance regional visitation by discounting rail fares by up to 88 per cent. Ticket holders could purchase a return regional fare for AUS$10 and subsequently enjoy free metropolitan public transport on the day of their ticketed event, a saving of approximately AUS$9 per person. Between 75 per cent and 80 per cent of spectators used public transport to visit to see the Games.

Improvements to public transport and subsequent inclusive ticketing are a logical bundling combination in mega event organisation. There is less impact on local commuters, visitors can conveniently reach the sporting event, and it is a positive initiative towards becoming carbon neutral. If a host city can provide a faultless ticket distribution process and an accessible transport system, it has two key ingredients for an economically successful and environmentally sustainable event.

For more information see:

BBC Sport (2002). *Games 'A Financial Success'*. Available at: http://news.bbc.co.uk/sport1/hi/other_sports/2289642.stm

Bovy, P. (2006). Solving outstanding mega-event transport challenges: the Olympic experience, *Public Transport International*, 6: 32–34.

Embassy of Greece (2004). *ATHENS 2004 OLYMPICS: General Fact Sheet.* Available at: http://www.greekembassy.org/Embassy/content/en/Article.aspx?office=3&folder=95&article=12033

Global Forum for Sports and Environment (2007). Mixed Results for Athens Olympics' Environmental Scorecard. Available at: http://www.g-forse.com/archive/news295_e.html

Haynes, J. (2001) *Socio-Economic Impact of the Sydney 2000 Olympic Games.* Seminar of the International Chair in Olympism. Available at: http://64.233.179.104/scholar?num=100&hl=en&lr=&q=cache:PYV4rykbbG0J:www.blues.uab.es/olympic.studies/web/pdf/od013_eng.pdf+were+events+well+attended+at+sydney+olympics+

Higham, J. (1999). Commentary—Sport as an avenue of tourism development: an analysis of the positive and negative impacts of sport tourism, *Current Issues in Tourism,* 2(1): 82–90.

Insight Economics (2006). Appendix A: Legacy Programs. PDF available at: http://www1.dvc.vic.gov.au/ocgc/News/Final_Report_Appendicies.pdf

Principles summary

- Chapter Principle 7.1: Pricing communicates an important symbolic positioning message to consumers about a sport product.
- Chapter Principle 7.2: The value of a sport product is the relationship between its price and the benefits a consumer believes they will receive from it.
- Chapter Principle 7.3: The price of a product is the amount of money a consumer must give up in exchange for a good or service. However, price also represents the value of a product. Although price is usually seen as an amount of money, it may also include other consumer sacrifices in order to acquire a sport product, such as time or social cost.
- Chapter Principle 7.4: Revenue is the price that consumers pay for a product, multiplied by the number of units sold. Profit is revenue minus the costs of producing and selling the product.
- Chapter Principle 7.5: The strategic pricing process provides a structure for setting price. The process involves: (1) setting a pricing goal, (2) determining price sensitivity, (3) conducting a break-even analysis, (4) assessing pricing variables, (5) selecting pricing tactics and (6) setting a price point.

Tools summary

- Chapter Tool 7.1. Pricing Goals
- Chapter Tool 7.2. Price Sensitivity Analysis

- Chapter Tool 7.3. Break-even Analysis
- Chapter Tool 7.4. Assess Pricing Variables
- Chapter Tool 7.5. Select Pricing Tactics
- Chapter Tool 7.6. Select Price Point

Review questions

1. What effect does pricing have on positioning? Provide an example of how price can influence a consumer's perception of a product.
2. What is the difference between value and price?
3. Outline the steps of the strategic pricing process.
4. Using examples to illustrate, describe some conditions which make sport consumers more price sensitive.
5. Why is price bundling so popular? Why do you think it works for both consumers and sport marketers?
6. Explain what a price point is and why it is so important to think of pricing in levels.

Relevant websites

http://www.rbk.com	(Reebok)
http://www.nike.com	(Nike)
http://www.fila.com	(FILA)
http://www.adidas.com	(adidas)
http://www.wimbledon.org	(Wimbledon All England Tennis Championships)
http://www.indy500.com	(Indianapolis 500)

Further reading

Daniel, K. & Johnson, L.W. (2004). Pricing a sporting club membership package, *Sport Marketing Quarterly*, 13(2): 113–116.
Stewart, B. (2006). *Sport Funding and Finance*, Elsevier, Oxford.

8 Sport distribution

Overview

The purpose of this chapter is to explore the third of the six elements of the marketing mix, place, or what is better described as sport distribution. The chapter begins by introducing the basic concepts and issues in sport distribution, and subsequently considers three central issues: distribution channels, the sport facility as 'place' and ticket distribution.

At the end of this chapter, readers should be able to:

- Understand the importance of distribution to successful sport marketing.
- Discuss the basic concepts of sport distribution.
- Identify the variations of sport distribution channels.
- Specify the importance of the sport facility as 'place'.
- Explain the main issues in ticket distribution.

Introduction

Sport distribution, or place, is concerned with how and where consumers get access to a sport product or service in order to use it. There is little use in having a great product available for a value price if consumers cannot easily acquire it. Distribution is therefore an instrumental part of the marketing mix. It is shown in Figure 8.1 within the Sport Marketing Framework.

When the term 'place' is employed in sport marketing it refers to any location or method for distributing a product. Distribution means transporting a product from the producer or sport organisation to the final consumer. For the purposes of this chapter, the words *distribution* and *place* should be considered interchangeable. There are several major ways in which sport products are distributed in the sport industry. It is a good start to keep in mind that sporting goods and services are distributed differently.

To transport sporting goods from producers to consumers, there are numerous steps along the way. For example, a sporting good like a golf ball is made by a manufacturer, gets passed on to a wholesaler, then a retailer and finally to a consumer who purchases it. In contrast, sport services tend to be distributed quite differently. For example, a professional sporting match could be 'produced' by two competing teams, filmed by a television network, and then broadcast to viewers. For a spectator watching the game live at the sport venue, the stadium itself is the 'place' where the sport product is distributed. One final example is a sports masseuse, who produces the service and delivers it directly to the customer; there are no people or organisations in the middle at all.

As can see seen from these simple examples, there are many different places where sport products are distributed. This chapter will introduce the variety of places pivotal to the distribution of sport products. First, some of the important concepts used in distribution will be introduced, at the core of which is the notion of a distribution channel. Second, the centrality of the sport facility or venue as a place where consumers buy and experience sport products will be considered, followed finally by a review of sport ticket distribution.

Distribution channels

As noted earlier, in the distribution of a sporting good such as a basketball there are several steps involved in transporting it from the producer to the sport consumer. To begin with, there is the manufacturer who physically makes the ball, but who usually does not sell it directly to the public. Often manufacturers sell their goods to a wholesaler, who in turn sells it to a retailer. Finally, the retailer sells the balls to sport consumers. In other words, there is a chain of people who are involved in getting the basketball to the consumer. It gets passed from one to the next down a path or a channel.

What if the sport product is a sporting contest on television that a sport consumer watches in a bar with friends? There is no 'manufacturer' or 'retailer' in the same way as there is for a basketball. The product is produced by the two sport clubs or teams competing. They sell this product via the league they compete in to the television network which puts the contest on air. In this example, the bar accesses the television broadcast and shows it to the consumers present. This is another example of a distribution channel

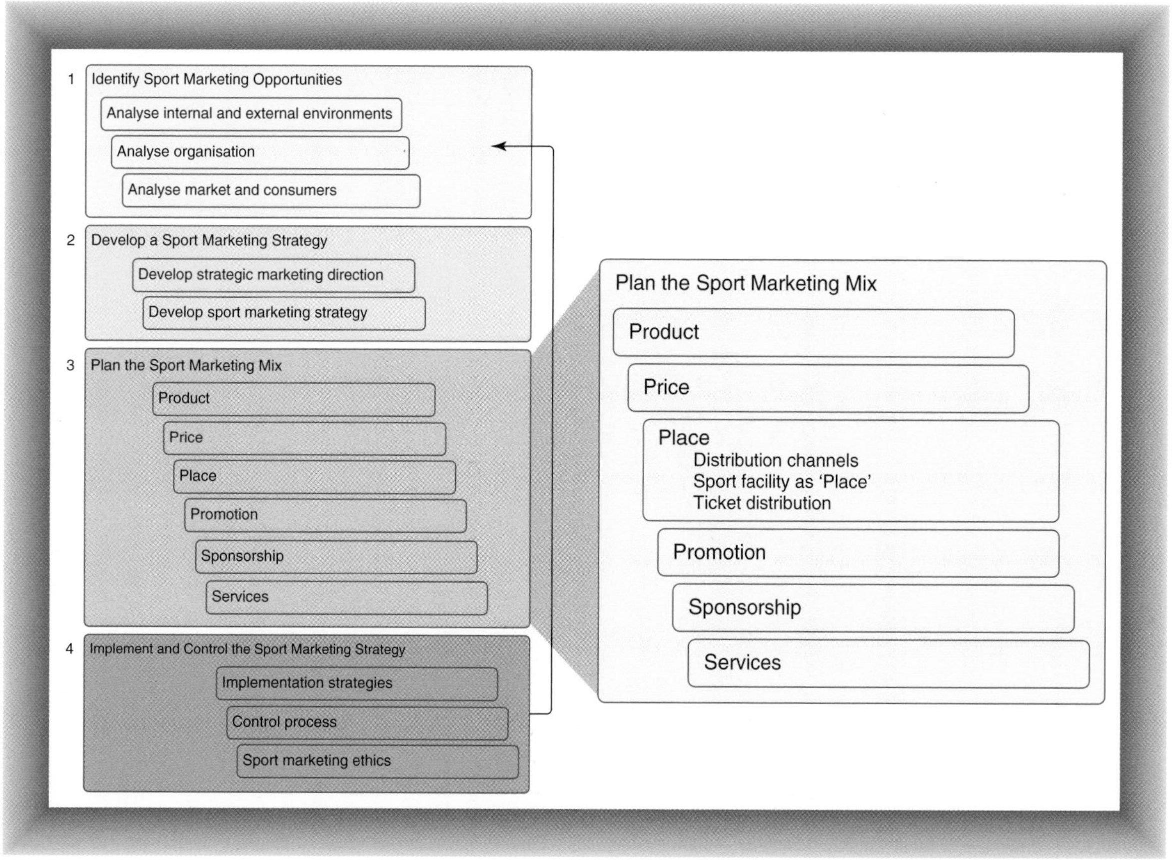

Plan the Sport Marketing Mix

- Product
- Price
- Place
  - Distribution channels
  - Sport facility as 'Place'
  - Ticket distribution
- Promotion
- Sponsorship
- Services

1 Identify Sport Marketing Opportunities
- Analyse internal and external environments
- Analyse organisation
- Analyse market and consumers

2 Develop a Sport Marketing Strategy
- Develop strategic marketing direction
- Develop sport marketing strategy

3 Plan the Sport Marketing Mix
- Product
- Price
- Place
- Promotion
- Sponsorship
- Services

4 Implement and Control the Sport Marketing Strategy
- Implementation strategies
- Control process
- Sport marketing ethics

Figure 8.1 The Sport Marketing Framework.

153

because the product has been moved from the producer (the two sport clubs) to the consumers (the people watching the game).

When considering the two examples of distribution channels just described, it is obvious that they both involve the circulation of a product from the producer to the consumer through a sequence of different steps and organisations. This sequence is known as a distribution channel.

> *Chapter Principle 8.1*: A sport distribution channel is an organised series of organisations or individuals that pass a product from the producer to the final consumer.

Distribution systems

Two different kinds of sport distribution channels have been used as examples. They both described the movement of products from producers to consumers, but they do it in different ways, or with different *sport distribution systems*. A distribution *system* is the way that a distribution channel is organised or arranged. There are different ways of structuring distribution, which are explained in the following sub-sections.

Types of distribution channels

Distribution channels have different lengths, and as a consequence they may be characterised as *direct* or *indirect*. A direct distribution channel is short where the producer sells the product directly to the consumer. For example, a sports physiotherapist produces the service and sells it directly to the consumer. Direct distribution also occurs when a sporting good producer sells products on the Internet, or by direct mail. Many manufacturers of sport products do this in addition to the use of normal retail stores. The process is illustrated in Figure 8.2.

An indirect distribution channel is long because there are a number of organisations or people involved along the way. Those in the middle are usually called *intermediaries*, because they mediate between producers and consumers. When it comes to sporting goods, wholesalers and/or retailers are added into the channel. The following diagrams show two different kinds of indirect distribution channels. Figure 8.3 shows both a retailer and a wholesaler in the channel, while Figure 8.4 excludes the wholesaler step.

> *Chapter Principle 8.2*: There are both direct and indirect distribution channels that vary in length. A direct distribution channel is short where the producer sells the product directly to the consumer. An indirect distribution channel is a long channel where there are a number of intermediaries involved along the way.

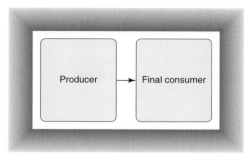

Figure 8.2 Direct Distribution Channel.

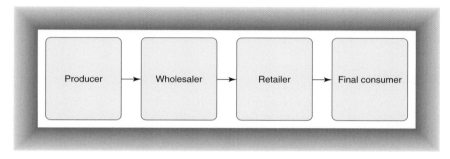

Figure 8.3 Indirect Distribution Channel A.

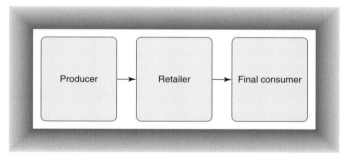

Figure 8.4 Indirect Distribution Channel B.

Channel members

A channel member is any organisation or individual involved as part of a distribution channel. When it comes to sporting goods, in addition to the producers (manufacturers), the most common channel members are wholesalers and retailers.

Wholesalers

A wholesaler is an organisation or individual acting as the middle step between a producer and a retailer. It is reasonable to ask what the point might be of having a wholesaler in the distribution channel. Why would the manufacturer not simply pass the sporting goods straight on to the retailer? However, a wholesaler can be important in helping other channel members. First, they usually buy goods in bulk from the manufacturer and then store them. When the retailer is ready to order some goods, the wholesaler transports the sporting goods to them. A wholesaler can also stock a large range of goods from a variety of different manufacturers. As a result, instead of having to contact all of these producers, the retailer only has to talk to the one wholesaler to gain access to a range of different sporting goods.

Of course wholesalers are not always involved in a distribution channel. If a retailer does not want to use a wholesaler (e.g. they many not want to pay extra for the product), then they have to undertake for themselves all the tasks performed by the wholesaler. They may have to store and transport the sporting goods, and may have to keep in contact with a diverse number of producers.

Retailers

Retailers are the organisations and individuals involved in the final sale of a sporting good or service to a consumer. There are many different kinds of retailers, and choosing the right retail outlet can be an important decision for a sport marketer. Most importantly, the retail outlet that is selected should be convenient for consumers and suitable to the kind of products that are being sold. For example, it might seem convenient to be able to buy a tennis racket from the corner store, but a specialised retail sports outlet would be more appropriate for the range and advice required to make a fitting selection.

There are several different kinds of retail outlets. To begin with there are physical locations housed in buildings like department stores and shopping centres. These retailers are sometimes called 'bricks and mortar' retailers. There are also 'virtual' stores like Internet sites, television home shopping and mail order catalogues. These retailers can be called virtual retailers. Some examples of both are provided in Table 8.1.

> *Chapter Principle 8.3*: A channel member is any organisation or individual that is involved in the sport distribution channel. Channel members may include wholesalers and retailers, as well as producers and consumers.

Distribution issues for sport products

Table 8.2 highlights the chief distribution issues that different sport products, such as sporting goods, sport-consulting services and facility-dependent sport services, are faced with. Sport-consulting services include market researchers, sport management consultants and even sport psychology experts. Facility-dependent sport services are those that need a sport facility to run, like a community netball competition, a recreation centre or a professional

Table 8.1 Types of Sport Retailers

Bricks and Mortar Retailers	Virtual Retailers
Supermarkets	Television shopping channels
Shopping centres	Mail order catalogues
Speciality sporting shops	Special merchandise during televised sport
Sport clubs	Internet sites and downloads
Recreation and leisure centres	Infomercials
Gymnasiums	Mobile or cellular phone offers
Factory direct outlets	
Sport stadiums and venues	

Table 8.2 Distribution Issues for Sporting Products

Distribution Variables	Sporting Goods	Sport-Consulting Services	Facility-Dependent Sport Services
Length of distribution channel	Long, often many channel members	Short, often just the producer (service provider) and consumer	Short, often just the producer (service provider) and consumer
Location of distribution	Many locations (potentially unlimited)	Many locations (potentially unlimited)	The sport facility
How customer accesses distribution	Consumer goes to distribution point	Service provider usually goes to consumer	Consumer goes to distribution point
Interaction between producer and customer	Indirect	Direct	Direct
Use of technology	Limited but increasing	Technology usually used for initial contact (e.g. website, e-mail contact etc.)	Heavy for the sale of tickets

league. Table 8.2 shows that sport products can have different distribution channel lengths, kinds of distribution locations, consumer interaction, dependant technology and consumer access.

> *Chapter Tool 8.1. Distribution Issues Analysis*: Sport products have different distribution issues to deal with. Sport marketers can employ various distribution channel lengths, kinds of distribution locations, consumer interaction, dependant technology and consumer access. These can be examined against the type of sporting product offered, whether sporting goods, consulting services or facility-dependent sport services.

157

Sport facility as 'place'

A sport facility is a place where sport competitions are delivered as entertainment to sport spectators and as activity to sport participants. The sport facility is the most important distribution channel for two types of sport products: (1) sport activity services and (2) professional sport events. Sport activity services are those offering participation or a personal service in sport including physical education lessons, coaching, community competitions, health and rehabilitation consultations, and local or recreational sport practice and events. Professional sport events offer a forum for elite athletes to compete, and entertainment for spectators. They include state, national or international competitions, covering all sports from football, swimming and motor-racing, to gymnastics, surfing and rock-climbing. All of these sport activities and events need a sport facility. Without a sport facility these product cannot be made, and there is nothing to market.

Designing a sport facility to fit in with the local area can help to make it an attractive distribution point, which is also useful for media attention. For example, many sport facilities possess a special design element that reflects the character of the city or country. In the 2004 Athens Olympics, a new weightlifting facility was built in a disused quarry. The facility was designed to look like an ancient Greek amphitheatre, and it commanded impressive views of the local mountains and tourists sites. This facility received substantial attention, which is relevant because weightlifting does not typically attract much media coverage. However, marketers have little control over the design of sport facilities and even less over their composition once built. This part of the chapter therefore focuses on the aspects of the sport place that can be manipulated by facility and event marketers.

For sport activity services and professional sport events, the sport facility represents the 'place' dimension of the marketing mix. A fundamental point to remember is that the sport product (the competition or activity) is both produced and consumed at the same location and at the same time. There are a range of sport facility features that a sport marketer must manage, which are considered next.

> *Chapter Principle 8.4*: The sport facility is the most important distribution channel for sport activity services and professional sport events.

Features of the sport facility

The features of a sport facility can have a powerful influence on a sport consumer's experience of an event, such as seating, layout, accessibility (how easy it is to get to, and to get around in), seating comfort, the 'look' or design of the venue, cleanliness and even the scoreboard. Naturally, when consumers perceive that a venue is of high quality, they are more likely to be satisfied and return. The sport facility is more effective as a distribution channel when its features are designed and handled carefully as part of a well-considered marketing plan.

Sport stadia and venues that have a good location, an attractive atmosphere, luxury seating, excellent eateries and other entertainment services like night clubs, bars, theatres and shopping areas, attract larger crowds. As a consequence, sport marketers are compelled to consider four main areas in which they can maximise the sport consumer experience. These pivotal marketing features of a sport facility are: (1) location and accessibility, (2) design and layout, (3) facility infrastructure and (4) customer service. Characteristics of each are provided in Table 8.3 and are discussed further in the following section.

Chapter Principle 8.5: Sport marketers must consider four main aspects of sport facilities in which they can maximise the sport consumer experience: (1) location and accessibility, (2) design and layout, (3) facility infrastructure and (4) customer service.

Interactive case

'Tailgating' is a practice where sport fans gather in the parking lot of a sport stadium or venue to have a party, barbeque and drink prior to a game. Although popularised in the United States, the practice has a rich tradition in Europe and Australia as well, particularly for motor- and horse-racing enthusiasts. Log into YouTube (http://www.youtube.com) and enter the word 'tailgating' in the search engine. See how many different sports are represented. Take note of the marketing activities that support and surround tailgaters.

Tools for facility marketing

Of the four features some are more influential than others in satisfying sport consumers. In addition, sport marketers have varying control over the features and may be able to do little to enact change because to do so would require substantial expenditure on a venue's infrastructure. However, even if sport marketers are unable to make changes, they must be aware of the impact that existing facility features have on consumer experience. In some case, it will be necessary to take action in one area to compensate for a poor feature elsewhere that cannot be modified. For example, a sport marketer can decrease the possibility of complaints by reducing the cost of seats with sight line obstructions. In the next section, the four features of facilities have been expanded into eight practical marketing tools which are particularly important in the management of distribution or place in the overall marketing mix. Customer service is omitted, but only because it is so important that it forms a central part of Chapter 11.

Table 8.3 Features and Characteristics of Sport Facilities

Location and Accessibility
Attractive location
Convenient to get to
Good signage and directions
Enough parking
Accessible by public transport
Accessible by different forms of public transport
Easy to enter and exit facility
Disabled access (ramps, lifts, washroom facilities)

Design and Layout
Fits in with local area
Attractive design (size, colour, shape and light)
Ambience and atmosphere
Easy to get from one area to another
Good direction signs
Seating arrangements with good viewing
Weather protection
Control of noise levels
Areas for non-smokers and non-drinkers
Lighting of playing area
Protection from heat and cold
Air circulation
Adequate storage
Safety issues (emergency procedures, fire detection,
standby power, emergency communication, exits)
Security (surveillance, control room, entrance security)
Spectator control (zones, safe barriers, security, police)

Facility Infrastructure
Variety of food and drink outlets
Overall seating quality
Premium seating available
Corporate boxes and special services
Toilets: number and location for convenient access
Childcare facilities
Scoreboards and screens
Message centres and sound systems
Emergency medical services
Merchandise areas
Broadcasting and media requirements

Customer Service
Queuing and waiting times
Prominent information stands/booths
Efficient, friendly and helpful staff
Sufficient security and emergency staff
Entrance staff, ushers
Services for elderly, disabled and children
Telephone enquiry service

Seating

The most important marketing aspects of seating selection include cost, look, comfort, durability and ease of maintenance. Their purpose is also relevant, such as whether the seats are to be used for a corporate box or for public access. Some sport facilities include ventilation holes and a full back support to prevent spectators from pushing their feet into the person sitting in front of them. It is also useful in most instances to have seats that can be easily removed, so that damaged seats can be replaced or new sponsorship logos attached. The most versatile seating options in recent venues are moveable seats which can be relocated in sections to different parts of the venue. This is advantageous because it allows more flexibility in the types of sport than can be played and watched at a venue. Some venues use their seating selection as part of their positioning strategy. For example, several stadia, such as the Denver Broncos National Football League home ground, have employed a material and design that increases the sound of the stomping noise spectators make during games, thereby amplifying the atmosphere for fans. In addition, seats can be used to differentiate the level of consumer spending. Most new venues use some form of personal viewing screen for corporate sections or for special kinds of memberships. From a marketing perspective this means that there is greater opportunity to enhance consumers' interaction with the sport product, other entertainment options like gaming, statistics and alternative camera angles, as well as with all marketing messages.

> *Chapter Tool 8.2. Seating*: Seating selection influences sport consumers' experience and can be used to enhance their viewing comfort as well as the marketing messages they are exposed to.

Scoreboards and signage

The scoreboard requirements of a small, recreational basketball venue will obviously be quite different to those demanded by an international multi-purpose stadium, which will need to broadcast video replays and advertisements. However, for all sport facilities the scoreboard is one of the main spaces to promote sponsors. After all, it is guaranteed that spectators will be looking at the scoreboard. Similarly, even a small facility can use signage to promote sponsors, other events or even further products that are available.

> *Chapter Tool 8.3. Scoreboards and Signage*: Scoreboards and signage are an essential method of communicating marketing messages irrespective of the size of a venue.

Lighting and sound system

Strong lighting on a sport field is ideal for both large and modest grounds. In fact, smaller-sized outdoor sport venues can attract larger crowds if they employ flood lighting. For example, local recreational and school sport fields can benefit from installing night-time illumination because but they can radically increase participation and crowds by allowing activity after working hours. This approach is extremely successful for outdoor tennis courts and athletics tracks. Lighting is also important in car parking areas for both safety and security. For a limited cost it is possible for indoor venues to install lighting and sound systems, which have a significant effect on the atmosphere of the event as well improving general communication about the activities and opportunities in the venue.

> *Chapter Tool 8.4. Lighting and Sound Systems*: Lighting and sound systems can be used to attract sport consumers at attractive times and can also improve the atmosphere of a venue and event.

Transport

It is often important for consumers to be able to easily access a sport facility by public transport or by other services offered by the venue. If a facility is easy to get to, then consumers are more likely to make return visits. Public transport is particularly important for large national or international events when thousands of people need to get to an event. The Sydney Olympics provides a good example. A new station was built at the main stadium, and special timetables were developed to allow 50 000 people to be transported per hour. More modest events and venues may consider using buses or minibuses to help move crowds from parking areas to the main doors. It is especially important to provide some transportation services to assist those with restricted mobility. These services may also be branded with marketing signage. They do not necessarily have to be complementary services either.

> *Chapter Tool 8.5. Transport*: Transport can be used to assist consumers in accessing a facility and can be marketed as a special customer service.

Media and broadcasting

Sport facilities need to consider how they can facilitate media involvement with their sport events. Most large sport and entertainment facilities have recently installed wireless technology so that media representatives can use a high-speed connection from any 'hot-spot'. Display screens for spectators and VIPs can also be important in some venues and events. For example, the Fosters British Grand Prix at Silverstone uses around 17 giant video screens, as big as 30–40 square metres. They also have special screens in the VIP and food areas. Almost every sport facility can benefit from a dedicated area for sport broadcasting and media commentary. The most recent sport stadia are built as immense television studios with the infrastructure for broadcasting embedded underground.

> *Chapter Tool 8.6. Media and Broadcasting*: Providing media facilities can encourage broadcasting and general media interest in events that occur in a sport facility.

Childcare facilities

While a suburban football ground is unlikely to need childcare, community recreational facilities, as well as large facilities need to consider the childcare needs of their staff and patrons. For example, a facility that wants to attract 30- to 40-year-old women to a fitness programme must look at how they can facilitate their potential customers' involvement. It is complex and expensive to set up a childcare centre in a sport facility, but in some cases it might be possible to work out a deal with a local childcare centre to provide casual care to the children at certain times of the day, or during particular events.

> *Chapter Tool 8.7. Childcare Facilities*: The provision of childcare facilities can be important in attracting consumers during non-peak periods or to special events.

Merchandising

The price of a ticket to a sport competition may not be the only thing that a customer is willing to spend money on at a sport event. In fact, sales from merchandise can be more profitable than gate receipts. Small community facilities can usually accommodate merchandise in the front reception, which takes up less space and staff time. Medium- to larger-sized sport facilities can sell merchandise in a number of different ways, such as having a temporary sales tent, roaming sales staff, a special merchandise shop or an online outlet.

> *Chapter Tool 8.8. Merchandise*: Selling merchandise in sport facilities is a powerful marketing tool because it provides consumers with a convenient way of spending more money on items that emphasise the sport product's brand image.

Food and beverages

The supply of food and beverages is amongst the most lucrative of all services that can be offered at a sport facility. The type of food and beverages sold should reflect consumer preferences. This means, of course, that some market research is required before food and beverage outlets are planned and built. This is especially important in regards to where the outlets are positioned within a facility. For example, if sport consumers cannot get to a food and beverage outlet within 60 seconds of leaving their seats from anywhere in a stadium, then there are probably too few outlets available. Equally, it is unsatisfying for consumers to have to stand in a queue for lengthy periods. It is critical to examine not only what consumers like to eat and drink but also when, how often and why they leave their seat to buy food or drinks. Spectators will eat and drink more or less, and at different times, depending on the sport they are watching. It is particularly annoying to spectators when they miss pivotal moments of play because they were standing in a queue. As a result, many venues are beginning to build food and beverage stands facing the field of play so that spectators can continue to watch the action.

> *Chapter Tool 8.9. Food and Beverages*: The supply of food and beverages is among the most lucrative of all services that can be offered at a sport facility, which means that they demand careful planning.

Ticket distribution

Ticket sales are still one of the most important sources of revenue for sport organisations that conduct competitions or events. It follows then that ticket distribution is an extremely important issue for sport marketers. For large sport organisations, most tickets are purchased from a ticket distributor, either in person, over the phone or on the Internet. For smaller sport organisations, tickets might be bought directly from a sporting club or event organiser. In general, like other sport products, sport tickets get passed down a distribution channel from the producer to the consumer. The ticket distributor is one of the channel members. In this model, ticket distributors do more than just provide tickets, they also show advertisements, offer sales promotions, provide customer service, conduct personal selling and physically send out the tickets to consumers.

When consumers contact a ticket distributor to purchase a ticket for a sport event, they are often looking for more than just a ticket. They want convenience, easy accessibility and a fast, user-friendly service. Some consumers may want to have questions about the event or the sport facility answered, and they certainly want a reasonable price which has not been increased too much because the ticket distributor is taking a large percentage. If a consumer becomes unhappy with the service or price they receive from a ticket distributor, they can feel dissatisfied about the sport event or club as well. It is therefore important that the sport organisation carefully discusses the features of a contract with the ticket distributor. Furthermore, sport organisations should maintain communications with the ticket distributor's customer service staff, which should include regular training and information updates.

One of the trends in ticket distribution is to sell tickets online. Ticketmaster in the United States and Ticketek in Australia are examples of online ticket distributors. These companies usually sell tickets for a wide variety of events, including music concerts, comedy, theatre and sport events. Even though they are not specialist sport ticket distributors, the general public know that they sell tickets to almost any entertainment event in their city. As a result, it is easy and convenient for consumers to remember the website and log on. One of the drawbacks is that consumers are able to easily compare the different entertainment events that are available, and could choose another activity. The use of a distribution agent also increases the cost of a ticket as they charge a percentage of the ticket price to manage the booking and distribution process.

Chapter Principle 8.6: Ticket sales are one of the most important sources of revenue for sport organisations that conduct competitions or events. The smooth distribution of tickets is essential to the satisfaction of consumers and the maximisation of sales.

Case Study—Marketing Sport Experiences Inside and Outside Stadia

By Sharyn McDonald

Sport supporters arrive at stadia parking lots in North America prepared to have pre-game and post-game parties. This involves the consumption of food and beverages from the back of their cars; a practice appropriately named 'tailgating'. There are mixed feelings about the social appropriateness of tailgating given its tendency to encourage excessive alcohol consumption. For example, tailgating was banned by the NFL at the 2007 Super Bowl. However, some sport marketers have found ways of supporting the practice. The University of Georgia designated alcohol-free, family-friendly tailgate zones where they organised interactive games, inflatable play equipment and autograph opportunities. Similarly, the Minnesota Vikings paid $45 million in 2007 to purchase areas they could designate as tailgating zones. Marketing sport experiences outside of the venue itself is proving a popular new strategy.

The NFL's New York Giants and New York Jets appear to have taken the phenomenon of external and peripheral marketing activity into consideration in the development of their new joint facility. The two teams are financing a new stadium which is expected to cost $1.3 billion. The plans include improved public transport by way of a new rail facility able to drop fans directly at the stadium, and improved access and parking for private vehicles. This will be further enhanced with the inclusion of tailgating zones that are linked to the stadium via pedestrian walkways.

External to the stadium, there are plans for a 300 000 square-foot outdoor plaza which will surround the entire stadium offering 'fancentric' pre-game entertainment and activities. There will be pre-game entertainment, interactive games, merchandise outlets, food and beverage outlets, barbeque facilities and public conveniences available: 'The outward appearance of the stadium's eight-level aluminum louvered exterior will be illuminated by the colors and iconic imagery of the team playing that day. This imagery will be projected on the spectacular Great Wall, a huge (40 × 400-foot) frieze of panels visible through the louvers as well as on 2 500 high-definition displays throughout the stadium plus, 18 000 square feet of video display and league-high, four jumbo video boards in the bowl' (The Official Site of the New York Giants, 2007).

Inside the stadium there will be further merchandise, eateries and themed activity opportunities. The new stadium will be technologically advanced with the inclusion of high-definition video displays inside the arena and in the concourse. Included are sound systems, digital boards and electronic signage as well as four immense LED video screens in each of the stadium's corners. With prudent management of both internal and external areas, sport facility managers can extend their products' influence.

For more information see:

Quigley, R.K. (2006). *UGA Sticks to Family-Friendly Plan, Alcohol-Free Tailgating Zones*. Available at: http://onlineathens.com/stories/091306/uganews_20060913045.shtml (accessed 13 September 2006).

Seifert, K. (2007). *Tailgating: This is More Like It*. Available at: http://www.startribune.com/vikings/story/1388716.html (accessed 29 August 2007).

The Official Site of the New York Giants (2007). *Giants and Jets Unveil New Stadium Design. New Facility to be the Largest Privately-Funded Stadium in US History*. Available at: http://www.giants.com/news/special_features/story.asp?story_id=2583 3 (accessed 5 September 2007).

Principles summary

- Chapter Principle 8.1: A sport distribution channel is an organised series of organisations or individuals that pass a product from the producer to the final consumer.
- Chapter Principle 8.2: There are both direct and indirect distribution channels that vary in length. A direct distribution channel is short where the producer sells the product directly to the consumer. An indirect distribution channel is a long channel where there are a number of intermediaries involved along the way.
- Chapter Principle 8.3: A channel member is any organisation or individual that is involved in the sport distribution channel. Channel members may include wholesalers and retailers, as well as producers and consumers.
- Chapter Principle 8.4: The sport facility is the most important distribution channel for sport activity services and professional sport events.

- Chapter Principle 8.5: Sport marketers must consider four main aspects of sport facilities in which they can maximise the sport consumer experience: (1) location and accessibility, (2) design and layout, (3) facility infrastructure and (4) customer service.
- Chapter Principle 8.6: Ticket sales are one of the most important sources of revenue for sport organisations that conduct competitions or events. The smooth distribution of tickets is essential to the satisfaction of consumers and the maximisation of sales.

Tools summary

Chapter Tool 1. Distribution Issues Analysis
Chapter Tool 2. Seating
Chapter Tool 3. Scoreboards and Signage
Chapter Tool 4. Lighting and Sound Systems
Chapter Tool 5. Transport
Chapter Tool 6. Media and Broadcasting
Chapter Tool 7. Childcare Facilities
Chapter Tool 8. Merchandise
Chapter Tool 9. Food and Beverages

Review questions

1. What is a sport distribution channel? Provide an example.
2. What is the difference between a direct and an indirect distribution channel?
3. What kinds of sport products might pass through wholesaler and retailer intermediaries?
4. Provide five examples of sport activity services and five examples of professional sport events.
5. Of the eight tools for marketing facility features, which three do you think are the most practical for a sport marketer to manipulate?
6. What are the advantages and disadvantages to using a ticket distributor?

Relevant websites

http://www.youtube.com   (YouTube)

http://www.giants.com   (New York Giants NFL Team)

Further reading

Miller, L.K. & Fielding, L. (1997). Ticket distribution agencies and professional sport franchises: the successful partnership, *Sport Marketing Quarterly*, 6(1): 47–55.

Wann, D.L. & Wilson, A.M. (1999). Variables associated with sport fans' enjoyment of athletic events, *Perceptual and Motor Skills*, 89: 419–422.

Westerbeek, H.M., Smith, A., Turner, P., Green, C., Emery, P. & van Leeuwen, L. (2006). *Managing Major Sport Events and Facilities*, Routledge, Oxford.

9 Sport promotion

Overview

The purpose of this chapter is to explain the role of the fourth element of the marketing mix—promotion. It begins by examining what promotion means in the context of sport marketing, as well as its range of uses. The chapter also highlights the application of four promotional tools, known as the promotions mix, which includes advertising, personal selling, sales promotions and public relations. Promotional goals are examined and the process of promotions planning is outlined.

At the end of this chapter, readers should be able to:

- Define the term promotion.
- Outline the elements of the promotions mix.
- Describe the strengths and weaknesses of each element of the promotions mix.
- Identify the three main goals of promotions.
- Explain the steps involved in planning a promotions approach.

Introduction

It is common for people to think of promotion as being nothing but advertising in the form of commercials on the television, radio, Internet and in the print media. However, other common applications of promotional activities include face-to-face personal selling, free samples, trade shows, contests and give-aways. The first step is therefore to clearly define promotion in sport marketing. Its position in the Sport Marketing Framework is shown in Figure 9.1.

Promotion

In sport marketing the word promotion covers a range of interrelated activities. All of these activities are designed to attract attention, stimulate the interest and awareness of consumers, and of course, encourage them to purchase a sport product. Promotion is about communicating with and educating consumers. For example, promotion might involve telling potential consumers about a product, reminding them of its benefits or persuading them that it is worth trying. Promotion involves all forms of communication with consumers, not just advertising. Promotion is best seen as the way that sport marketers communicate with consumers to inform, persuade and remind them about a product. The aim of promotion is to encourage consumers to develop a favourable opinion about a sport product which is aligned to a pre-determined positioning strategy, and then to stimulate consumers to try the sport product. Promotion concentrates on *selling* the product.

> *Chapter Principle 9.1*: Promotion can be defined as the way that sport marketers communicate with consumers to inform, persuade and remind them about the features and benefits described by a sport product's positioning.

The promotions mix

It is common for sport organisations to use a number of different promotional activities simultaneously, rather than to just focus on one. Because different promotional activities can be combined together, they are collectively known as the promotions mix. In other words, it is advantageous to combine a number of promotional activities together into one promotional plan or strategy. A promotional strategy is a plan that aims to use the four main elements of the promotions mix for the best results. The promotions mix elements are: (1) advertising, (2) personal selling, (3) sales promotions and (4) public relations.

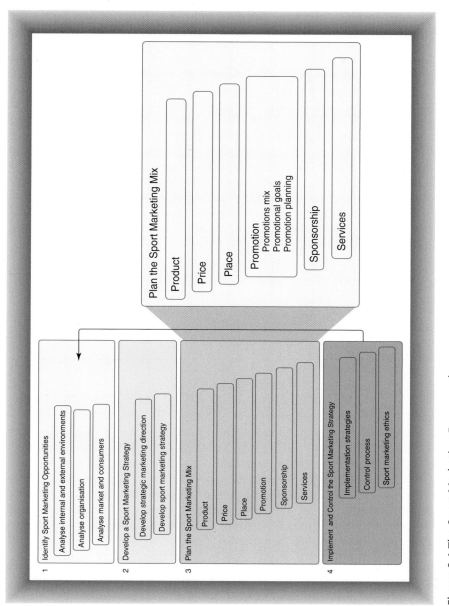

Figure 9.1 The Sport Marketing Framework.

> *Chapter Principle 9.2*: The promotions mix consists of four marketing tools: (1) advertising, (2) personal selling, (3) sales promotions and (4) public relations.

Advertising

It is easy to think of advertising examples: television commercials, magazine and newspaper advertisements, radio spots, posters, billboards, Internet pop-ups and advertisements on public transport. In all of these examples, a sport organisation would pay someone else (such as a radio station or magazine) to present the advertisement. Even though intermediaries present advertisements, they are always produced from the perspective of the organisation or brand that is paying for it. A first important point about advertising is that it is a one-way communication from marketers to consumers. Advertising is a form of one-way communication where a marketer pays someone else to have their product, brand or organisation identified. One of the advantages of advertising is that it can reach a large number of people at once. However, it is often an expensive form of promotion that few sport organisations can afford.

> *Chapter Tool 9.1. Advertising*: Advertising is a form of one-way communication where a marketer pays someone else to have their product, brand or organisation identified. Common examples include television commercials, magazine and newspaper advertisements, radio spots, posters, billboards, Internet pop-ups and advertisements on pubic transport.

Personal selling

Personal selling involves one-to-one communication between a consumer and a salesperson. Personal selling might involve talking to a consumer on the phone, talking face-to-face, communication through text messaging on a mobile cellular phone or through an Internet portal. The aim of personal selling is to build relationships with consumers in order to convince them to accept a point of view about the brand or product in question, and ultimately to convince them to take some action and try the product. Endorsements and sponsorships are two forms of personal selling that are common in the sport industry, each of which will be explained further shortly.

> *Chapter Tool 9.2. Personal Selling*: Personal selling involves one-to-one communication between a consumer and a salesperson. Common examples include talking to a consumer on the phone, talking face-to-face, communication through text messaging on a mobile cellular phone or through an Internet portal. Endorsements and sponsorships are two forms of personal selling that are common in the sport industry.

Sponsorship

Endorsements and sponsorships are two forms of personal selling that are prevalent in the sport industry. *Sport sponsorship* occurs when a sporting organisation or an individual athlete is supported by a separate company (or person). The sponsorship is designed to benefit both parties: the sport organisation (or sponsee) receives money or products, and the sponsor receives the benefits of positive associations with prominent sporting teams or athletes. It can sometimes be unclear what these other benefits are for the sponsor. For this reason, the sporting organisation is nearly always the one approaching a company for a sponsorship. Sport organisations therefore must have a clear idea of what they have to offer or 'sell' to the potential sponsor. Common benefits that are offered to sponsors include:

- Naming rights
- Signage
- Media coverage/indirect advertising
- Goodwill (reputation) for being involved with sporting heroes
- Direct advertising opportunities
- Access to a new consumer market
- Opportunity for new sales (e.g. special offers to members)
- Demonstration of products (e.g. use of product at a sporting event)
- Political benefits

Because the sporting organisation is nearly always the one asking a company for sponsorship, they must undertake substantial preparatory planning. This involves conducting some research to ensure that they are choosing the right company to approach with a formal proposal. Sponsorship is such an important part of sport marketing that Chapter 10 is exclusively dedicated to it.

Interactive case

Visit the website of the Volvo Ocean Race and its section on 'Marketing Opportunities'. Review the benefits that are offered to potential sponsors in becoming involved in the race. Create a list of these benefits and compare them to those Volvo is likely to be receiving.
http://www.volvooceanrace.org/marketing/

Endorsements

An *endorsement* occurs when a well-known celebrity or athlete uses their fame to help a company sell its products. They may also use their reputation to help enhance the image of the company, its products or brand. A celebrity athlete may appear in an advertisement or other public forum using a product, saying that they endorse it, and recommending that everyone use it.

Because sport fans can have a strong psychological connection to celebrity sport stars, endorsements can be an effective method of persuading fans to buy particular products. If the sports star is seen as trustworthy, this can help fans to believe that the product is reliable. This is why superstars like Kobe Bryant in the National Basketball League in the United States can be so effective when they endorse a product.

Sales promotions

A sales promotion is usually a short-term program that aims to stimulate an increase in sales. Examples of sales promotions include 'two-for-one' offers, prize give-aways, competitions and free trials or samples. Sales promotions can be useful supplements to other promotional activities, as they tend to draw attention thereby providing the other activities with more exposure. Typically, sales promotions provide consumers with an incentive (or a bonus) to buy the sport product.

A sport organisation may target a sales promotion towards the general public or sometimes to wholesalers and retailers. One of the advantages of sales promotions is that it is relatively easy to keep track of how many consumers were enticed to use a product because of a special deal. For example, if a 'two-for-one' coupon is part of the sales promotion, it is possible to count the number redeemed. Sales promotions can help to achieve a variety of promotional goals, such as encouraging loyal customers to buy more often, encouraging consumers to change when they buy a particular product or persuading consumers to switch to the brand being offered.

> *Chapter Tool 9.3. Sales Promotions*: A sales promotion is a short-term program that aims to stimulate an increase in sales. They offer consumers an *incentive* (or a bonus) to buy the sport product. Common examples include 'two-for-one' offers, prize give-aways, competitions and free trials or samples.

Public relations

Public relations is concerned with building a good 'image' for sport organisations. It is important for sport organisations to have a good relationship with different groups in the community, including the media, government sport departments, local councils and even fan clubs. To have a good relationship with these groups, sport organisations need to communicate with them on a regular basis. It is therefore essential that sport organisations identify what sort of information about their products public groups will be interested in. Once determined it is a matter of working out how to communicate this information in a way that will enhance the sport organisation's reputation and cultivate improved relationships.

Public relations is different to other forms of promotion in that it is free to a sport organisation. It usually involves getting some information into the mass media as a news item. For this reason, *public relations* is often called *publicity*. For example, a surfing manufacturer might provide a 'press release' about a new product in the hope that the media will want to make a story out of it. Another example could be a sport club that publishes result lists on the Internet, or submits an article about the club or a prominent player to a magazine. In these examples the sport organisation does not have to pay to have their information presented as they would with advertising. However, one problem is that they do not have control over how their organisation or product is presented; it is just as easy to get bad publicity as it is to get good publicity.

Chapter Tool 9.4. Public Relations: Public relations is concerned with building a good 'image' for a sport organisation. Public relations is different to other forms of promotion because it is free. It usually involves getting some information into the mass media as a news item, and for this reason it is often called *publicity*.

Each of the four elements of the promotions mix represents a tool that can be used to promote a sport product. Table 9.1 summarises the key strengths and weaknesses of each of the four promotion tools, and provides examples helpful to their application.

Table 9.1 Promotional Techniques

Tools	Advantages	Disadvantages	Methods
Advertising	Wide reach	High initial outlay	Press
			Radio
	Dramatic images	Impersonal	Television
			Magazines
	Reaches consumers fast	Very little feedback from consumers	Direct mail
			Ticketing agents
			Scoreboard displays
	High exposure	Delayed feedback	Bus and taxi posters
			Billboards and posters
		Unable to customise message to individual consumers	Brochures
			Ticket stubs
			Internet
			Text messages
		Difficult to tell how many consumers buy the product as a result of viewing or hearing the advertisement	Multimedia messages

(*Continued*)

Table 9.1 (Continued)

Tools	Advantages	Disadvantages	Methods
Sales promotion	Attention-grabbing Informative	Minimum reach Medium cost per exposure	In-store promotions Point of purchase sales Exhibitions
	Fast in reaching consumers	Usually impersonal	Product give-aways (stickers, shirts, admission give-aways)
	Moderate control over the communication	Unable to customise message to individual consumers	Two-for-one offers Free admission with purchase
	Relatively easy to track how many consumers buy the product because of the promotion		Prizes tied to tickets Frequent purchaser cards (loyalty cards)
			'Selling' of heroes Competitions Free trials or samples Bonus packs Trade deals
Personal selling	Direct communication	Narrow reach	Telemarketing Door-to-door sales
	Informative	Variable cost per exposure	Endorsements Referrals Party pans
	Immediate feedback from consumers	Slow to reach target customers	Sponsorship
	High control over promotional message Able to customise message to individual consumers		
Public relations	Wide reach	Variable image	Press releases Result lists
	Informative	Very little feedback from consumers	Photographs Commentary and reviews
	Low cost per exposure	Delayed feedback	Feature articles
	Fast in reaching consumers	Impersonal	

> *Chapter Principle 9.3*: Promotional elements should be combined in order to complement one another in order to achieve a promotional goal that is consistent with the overall marketing and positioning strategy.

Promotional objectives

To review, promotion is the way that sport marketers communicate with potential consumers in order to inform, persuade and remind them about a product or brand. The aim of promotion is to encourage consumers to develop a favourable opinion about a product or brand with the intention of stimulating them to try it. There are four main kinds of promotional activities that are collectively known as the promotions mix, because the different activities can be effectively combined. With this background in place, it is now time to consider the goals of promotion, or what it aims to achieve. There are three main objectives of promotion: (1) to inform, (2) to persuade and (3) to remind.

> *Chapter Principle 9.4*: There are three main objectives of promotion: (1) to inform, (2) to persuade and (3) to remind.

Informing

Until a new product is promoted, consumers are unlikely to be aware that it exists. Naturally, it is important for potential consumers to be aware of a sport product, to understand its benefits, to respond to how it is positioned in the marketplace and to know how to acquire it. Promotions that aim to *inform* consumers of these aspects of a product are usually done during the early stages of the product life cycle. Informative promotions are also helpful if the product is complex or technical, such as a range of sports equipment with sophisticated electronic components.

> *Chapter Principle 9.5*: Promotions that *inform* aim to communicate the product's existence, its benefits, its positioning and how it can be obtained. Promotions that aim to inform consumers are usually undertaken during the early stages of the product life cycle.

Persuading

Once consumers are aware of a product and its benefits, it may be necessary to persuade them to try it. *Persuading* consumers means convincing them or influencing them to buy a sport product. In order to achieve this aim, it is essential to give consumers a good reason to buy the product. It is important that sport marketers do not deceive consumers in order to persuade them to buy it. Aside from being illegal, it is counter-productive as the product will not reach expectations, leading to consumer dissatisfaction.

Persuasive promotions are more common when a product enters the growth stage of the product life cycle. By this time consumers should have a general awareness of the kind of product that is being offered, as well as the benefits that it can give them. At this point it is unnecessary for sport organisations to utilise promotional activities that inform, but it remains important to convince consumers to purchase the product on offer and not one offered by competition.

Persuasive promotions are used when the aim is to change the ideas that consumers hold about a product. For example, it might be desirable to change consumers' ideas about a product's features, or a brand's image. Persuasion is also a common strategy that sport organisations employ when they want consumers to switch from a competitor's brand to their own.

> *Chapter Principle 9.6*: Persuasive promotions are utilised when trying to give consumers good reasons to buy a sport product. Persuasive promotions are more common when a product enters the growth stage of the product life cycle.

Reminding

Reminder promotions aim to keep a product or brand name prominent in consumers' minds. Once consumers have been informed about a product and have been persuaded to buy it at least once, it is sensible to remind them to continue buying it in the future. Reminder promotions are most common during the maturity stage of the product life cycle.

> *Chapter Principle 9.7*: Reminder promotions aim to keep a product or brand name prominent in consumers' minds. Reminder promotions are most common during the maturity stage of the product life cycle.

The three types of promotional goals are summarised in Table 9.2 along with advice on their best timing and some typical examples.

Promotion planning

A common theme in excellent sport marketing is careful planning. Designing a promotional strategy is no exception. A promotions mix needs to be supported by market research and a well-structured plan in order to ensure that it remains aligned with other marketing initiatives and stays on track once it has begun. The promotions planning process is also essential to

Table 9.2 Promotional Goals

Goal of Promotion	Timing	Examples
To inform	Commonly used during the *introduction* stage of the product life cycle	Make consumers aware of a new brand Make consumers aware of new product Inform consumers of product features Inform consumers of price and where to buy Explain how a product works, especially a complex or technical one Build a positive image for the organisation Suggest new ways to use a product
To persuade	Commonly used during the *growth* stage of the product life cycle	Encourage brand switching Convince consumers to buy a product Change consumers' ideas about the product
To remind	Used in highly competitive marketplaces Commonly used during the *maturity* stage of the product life cycle	Remind consumers they need a product Remind consumers where to buy it Keep consumers aware of the product

determining whether the deployed promotional strategy has been effective. Figure 9.2 outlines the stages of the promotion planning process.

> *Chapter Principle 9.8*: A promotional strategy is a plan that aims to use the elements of the promotions mix for the best results. The promotions planning process involves five steps: (1) align with marketing objectives, (2) consider target market, (3) set promotional objectives, (4) set promotional budget and (5) develop promotional mix.

Align with marketing objectives

The first step in planning a promotional strategy is to use general marketing objectives as a guide to formulating a promotional plan. As a reminder, a marketing objective is a goal expected to be achieved as the result of a selected marketing strategy. Any choices made for the promotion plan need to align with marketing objectives and further their achievement.

> *Chapter Tool 9.5. Align with Marketing Objectives*: Any choices made for the promotion plan need to align with marketing objectives and further their achievement.

Figure 9.2 Promotion Planning Process.

Consider the target market

The second step of the promotion planning process is to examine the intended target market. The promotional strategies selected should be specific to the target market. There are two ways of promoting a sport product, depending on whether the target market is the final consumer of the product, or whether it is an intermediary (an 'in-between' company like a wholesaler). The two types are known as a push strategy and a pull strategy.

Push strategy

A push strategy involves promoting a sport product to a wholesaler with the ambition of convincing them to carry the product. If successful then the wholesaler must also push the product towards a retailer. In turn, the retailer promotes the product to the eventual consumer and may use advertising or other forms of promotion in the process. This is called a push strategy because the sport product gets *pushed*, step-by-step, down the line of distribution to the final consumer. With a push strategy it is common to rely strongly on personal selling strategies, although other promotional techniques can also be used. A push strategy is appropriate when specific wholesalers or retailers have been identified as the primary target market.

Pull strategy

A pull strategy involves promoting a sport product directly to the final consumer. A pull strategy requires that demand for the sport product must first be developed. The assumption behind the pull strategy is that as consumers become aware of the product they will ask retailers to stock it. Retailers will then have to ask wholesalers to sell them the product, and in turn these whole-salers will have to order it from the manufacturer. When using a pull strategy, it is common to use advertising, as well as sales promotion techniques like sampling, discounts and coupons. A pull strategy is appropriate when a group of final consumers has been identified as the primary target market.

Since the goals of sport organisations vary considerable, there are different ways in which a push or pull strategy can be used. For example, a large national governing sport organisation might have the objective of winning more medals at the international level. A push strategy would involve bol-stering the grassroots levels of the sport to encourage more participation with the intention that a larger participation base will push a higher range and quality of athletes to the elite level. In contrast, a pull strategy would involve offering more support directly to the elite level through coaching or training academies in order to pull the best athletes through to the highest level. It is important to realise that it is unusual for sport organi-sations to use exclusively a push strategy or a pull strategy. Rather, most use a combination. For example, sporting equipment and apparel manufacturers work hard to convince wholesalers and retailers to stock their brand (push), while also marketing heavily to consumers about the value of the brand itself (pull).

Chapter Tool 9.6. Consider the Target Market: Promotional strategies should be selected with the target market in mind. There are two strategies behind promotion depending on whether the target mar-ket is the final consumer of the product or an intermediary. The two are a push strategy and a pull strategy.

A push strategy involves promoting a sport product to a wholesaler with the ambition of convincing them to carry the product. If successful then the wholesaler must also push the product towards a retailer. In turn, the retailer promotes the product to the eventual consumer, and may use advertising or other forms of promotion in the process. A pull strategy involves promoting a sport product directly to the final consumer.

Set promotional objectives

The third step in the promotion planning process is to set promotional objectives. The three main goals of promotion—to inform, persuade and remind—have already been introduced. These represent the broad object-ives of promotion. It is therefore important to pinpoint which of these goals will be the focus of the promotion plan. However, when setting promotional objectives, it is possible to be even more specific. The ultimate promotional objective is to stimulate consumers to act. For example, it may be desirable for consumers to buy the product, volunteer their time, donate money to

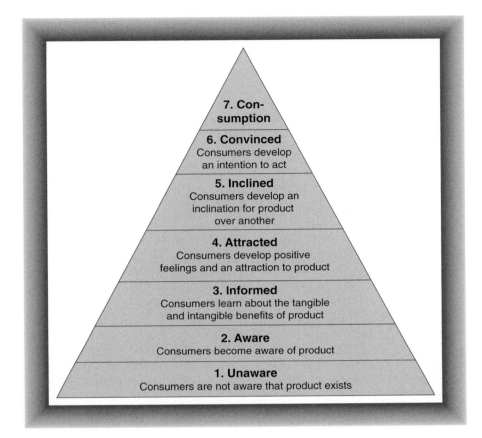

Figure 9.3 The Hierarchy of Effects.

fundraising or just attend an event. It is easy to understand how to inform, persuade or remind consumers, but it is more difficult to get them to take action. Sport marketers can encourage consumers to act by guiding them through a series of steps known as *a hierarchy of effects*. The word *hierarchy* means that there are stepped levels, and that one step builds on another to reach an ultimate goal. The hierarchy of effects is displayed in Figure 9.3.

The idea behind the hierarchy of effects is that all consumers must pass through each stage (starting at the bottom) before they consume a product. Consumers are unaware, aware, informed, attracted, inclined, and convinced before they actually consume. It is worth remembering that there are some common situations where consumers might not pass through every stage of the hierarchy. For example, when someone makes a split-second decision to buy a product (called an impulse purchase), they may not know much about the product benefits. Also, sometimes consumers purchase a product for someone else as a gift, and may not even like it themselves.

Even though the hierarchy of effects is not useful in every situation, sport marketers may employ it to give them a general guide for developing promotional goals. If a group of consumers can be located on the hierarchy, then it is easier to select a matching promotional objective.

The hierarchy of effects starts at the bottom of the pyramid when consumers are *unaware* that a product exists. At this stage the promotional objective is to make consumers *aware* of the product. When consumers are aware of the product they know it exists but may not know much else about it. Thus, consumers need to be educated about the product's tangible and intangible benefits. At this stage the central promotional objective is to give consumers product information so that they become *informed*. Just because a consumer is aware of a product and knows about its benefits does not mean that they will necessarily like it. The main promotional objective at this stage is to encourage consumers to be *attracted* to the product, and to create positive feelings towards it. Once consumers are attracted to the product it is important to convince them to prefer it, or become *inclined* towards it over all alternatives. The corresponding promotional objective is to establish that the product on offer is the best available for the target market. With consumers' interest in the product, they must next become *convinced* that the product is right for them, leading to a definitive intention to make a purchase. Therefore, the main promotional objective at this stage is to create a strong desire to act. Desire does not automatically mean that a consumer will act, as they may not have enough money or time, or new and superior alternatives may become available instead. However, desire is a powerful precursor to *consumption*. There are circumstances where consumers have become convinced about a product and do genuinely intend to purchase it, but still do not act. Dealing with this problem requires a good understanding of what is stopping consumers from buying a product when they desire it. In some cases, the obstacle might simply be price. A Ferrari is desired by many but purchased by few. In the case of sport services, availability might be an issue, such as with tickets to hallmark events or the final series of a league.

Chapter Tool 9.7. Set Promotional Objectives: The hierarchy of effects shows how consumers may pass through a number of stages before they actually consume, and represents a tool for connecting promotional objectives with the promotions mix. The stages of the hierarchy of effects are: (1) unaware, (2) aware, (3) informed, (4) attracted, (5) inclined, (6) convinced and (7) consumption. These stages illustrate how consumers first become aware of a product (from unaware to aware), learn about its benefits (informed), (3) become interested in it (attracted), (4) develop a preference for one product or brand over others (inclined), (5) experience a desire to do something about it (convinced) and (6) then act (consumption).

Set a promotional budget

The next step in a promotional plan involves setting a promotional budget. A budget determines how much money will be spent on promotion. Not only do sport organisations typically have limited resources available to spend on promotion, it is possible for them to choose different methods for deciding on how much is appropriate. Some of the common methods used for deciding on a budget include: (1) arbitrary allocation (randomly choosing an amount), (2) competitive parity (matching competitors), (3) competitive disparity (being deliberately different to competitors), (4) percentage of sales and (5) the objective and task method (the amount is determined by promotional objectives and tasks). Each is overviewed next.

Arbitrary allocation

If an amount to spend on promotion is determined *arbitrarily*, then it is done subjectively, or without an obvious reason. Often this means that the sport organisation will allocate as much money as it can afford to promotion (after all the other business costs are considered). If a sport marketer chooses this method, then they are not paying any attention to what their competitors are doing, what the economic climate is, or how effective their promotional budget was last year. In other words, this is not a very sensible or well thought out way to allocate a budget.

Competitive parity

Competitive parity (or equality) means deciding to spend a similar amount to that of competitors. Competitive parity is more common in highly competitive marketplaces, where a number of businesses are trying to attract the attention of consumers. However, this may be a difficult (and even impossible) method for some organisations if they do not have the same revenue to spend.

Competitive disparity

It is also possible to estimate what competitors are spending on promotion, and deliberately decide to spend a different amount. This is known as competitive disparity. Disparity means difference or inequality. It can be a way of standing apart from competitors, and differentiating the product or brand. Competitive disparity is also common with sporting goods that are designed with a low cost in mind and which are successful when sold in large volumes with few costs allocated to promotions.

Percentage of sales

It is possible to calculate a promotional budget as a percentage of total sales. To do this it is first essential to determine a standard percentage of sales that will be allocated to promotions. Sometimes sport organisations will choose a percentage based on what their competitors are doing, while at other times it may be an arbitrary choice. Once the standard percentage has been determined, the previous year's sales figure is used as a guide to next year's sales. From here it is possible to calculate a percentage of the predicted amount of sales. For example, if five per cent of sales is set as a guideline, and five million dollars in sales is expected in the forthcoming year (five per cent of five million), then the promotional budget is $250 000.

There are several limitations to the percentage of sales approach. First, it may be difficult to calculate what level of standard percentage should be used in the first place. Second, it may not be accurate to use last year's sales as a guide to estimating the forthcoming year. Finally, if sales are declining, it may be more important to spend additional money on promotion rather than less.

Objective and task method

The objective and task method demands that the promotional *objectives* that have been set, and the promotional *tasks* needed in order to carry out those objectives, should guide the budget that is allocated. It is simply a matter of calculating what it will cost to actually carry out the tasks. This method is logical, but it can run into difficulty if the promotional objectives and tasks that were planned were actually inappropriate, leading to substantial spending on a promotional plan that is not going to be effective.

Chapter Tool 9.8. Set Promotional Budget: Setting a promotional budget means deciding how much money to spend on promotion. Some of the common methods used for deciding on a budget are: (1) arbitrary allocation (subjectively choosing an amount), (2) competitive parity (matching competitors), (3) competitive disparity (being deliberately different to competitors), (4) percentage of sales and (5) the objective and task method (the amount is determined by promotional objectives and tasks).

Develop a promotional mix

The final step of the promotion planning process is to develop a promotions mix. To recap, the elements of the promotions mix are: (1) advertising, (2) personal selling, (3) sales promotion and (4) public relations. These elements are called a *mix* because they are combined together. Sport organisations do not just use one promotions element but rather use a mixture of some or all of them in their promotional strategy. It is important to realise that if a number of promotional elements are used, they should be designed to complement one another. In the end, a promotions strategy should be created so that the different elements of the promotions mix are combined together to work towards the promotional goals that have been set.

Chapter Tool 9.9. Develop Promotions Mix: In developing a promotions mix, sport marketers must choose which elements of the promotions mix will reach the desired promotional objectives and be achievable within the budget that has been set.

Case Study—Governments Promoting Sport

By Sharyn McDonald

Increasingly, governments wishing to reduce the health costs of inactivity are considering the benefits of promoting sport. The cost of medical care for an inactive population amounts to billions of dollars every year. With the rising risk of health disorders such as obesity, governments have begun to consider preventative measures.

Mass marketing campaigns can be used to encourage people to consider the sport and leisure opportunities that surround them. In 1978, the Australian Federal Government expanded nationally the successful Victorian state government's 'Life. Be in it.™' campaign. This campaign saw a rapid increase in awareness about leisure opportunities and increased participation levels. The campaign ran a series of television commercials and publicity materials popularising the now iconic cartoon characters, inactive Norm and his energetic sister Libby. In 1981, the federal funding was withdrawn and 'Life. Be in it.™' continued as a non-profit organisation.

Several of Australia's state governments have tried to replicate the success of the 'Life. Be in it.™' campaign by implementing state-funded promotional campaigns. They are currently utilising various forms of promotions such as the Internet, television commercials, mail outs, and promotional materials to remind people to be more active on a regular basis. From a public relations perspective, mass media campaigns have broad-reaching communication opportunities that display the government's social investment. In addition, Federal and state governments benefit economically through reduced medical costs, increased income generated through the use of government-funded facilities, and the improved use of leisure services such as playgrounds and bike trails. These benefits also have implications for government departments and health organisations that can capitalise on the success of existing campaigns or contribute as a partner to help a campaign evolve.

Partnered campaigns help organisations to meet their individual goals while collectively working towards the overarching aim of promoting healthy lifestyles. The new Victorian government campaign, 'Go for your life™', targets all age groups and life stages. Many of the campaigns target healthy living by addressing activity levels and healthy eating. Developers of the 'Go for your life' campaign have realised the importance of targeting primary aged children, and as a result have partnered with schools to strengthen their promotions. Primary schools can join the Award Program which provides resources and training for teachers, canteen managers and parents in an effort to encourage children to develop healthy habits.

The state park authorities in Australia can be considered part of the network of government departments contributing to the healthy lifestyle message. They have their own goal to improve visitation to parks and as such promote their 'Healthy Parks, Healthy People' campaigns. The advantage of pooling resources or working together to achieve similar aims extends beyond inter-governmental interaction. Organisations such as The National Heart Foundation of Australia are helping to promote the healthy lifestyle message by endorsing existing campaigns such as 'Healthy Parks, Healthy People'. In Western Australia, The National Heart Foundation of Australia has control of the 'Find thirty. It's not a big exercise™' campaign initially created by the Department of Health, Western Australia. With multiple departments and sectors working towards the same aim and sharing knowledge and resources, mass media health promotion campaigns have never been more effective.

For more information see:

Diabetes Australia at
http://www.diabetesaustralia.com.au/home/index.htm

Healthy Parks, Healthy People at
http://www.parkweb.vic.gov.au/1grants.cfm

Life. Be In It. at
http://www.lifebeinit.org/

National Heart Foundation at
http://www.heartfoundation.org.au/index.htm

New South Wales at
http://www.livelifewell.nsw.gov.au/

South Australia at
http://www.beactive.com.au/

Tasmania at
http://www.getmoving.tas.gov.au/

Victoria at
http://www.goforyourlife.vic.gov.au/

Western Australia at
http://www.findthirty.com.au/

Principles summary

- Chapter Principle 9.1: Promotion can be defined as the way that sport marketers communicate with consumers to inform, persuade and remind them about the features and benefits described by a sport product's positioning.
- Chapter Principle 9.2: The promotions mix consists of four marketing tools: (1) advertising, (2) personal selling, (3) sales promotions and (4) public relations.
- Chapter Principle 9.3: Promotional elements should be combined in order to complement one another in order to achieve a promotional goal that is consistent with the overall marketing and positioning strategy.

- Chapter Principle 9.4: There are three main objectives of promotion: (1) to inform, (2) to persuade and (3) to remind.
- Chapter Principle 9.5: Promotions that inform aim to communicate the product's existence, its benefits, its positioning, and how it can be obtained. Promotions that aim to inform consumers are usually undertaken during the early stages of the product life cycle.
- Chapter Principle 9.6: Persuasive promotions are utilised when trying to give consumers good reasons to buy a sport product. Persuasive promotions are more common when a product enters the growth stage of the product life cycle.
- Chapter Principle 9.7: Reminder promotions aim to keep a product or brand name prominent in consumers' minds. Reminder promotions are most common during the maturity stage of the product life cycle.
- Chapter Principle 9.8: A promotional strategy is a plan that aims to use the elements of the promotions mix for the best results. The promotions planning process involves five steps: (1) align with marketing objectives, (2) consider target market, (3) set promotional objectives, (4) set promotional budget and (5) develop promotional mix.

Tools summary

Chapter Tool 9.1. Advertising
Chapter Tool 9.2. Personal Selling
Chapter Tool 9.3. Sales Promotions
Chapter Tool 9.4. Public Relations
Chapter Tool 9.5. Align with Marketing Objectives
Chapter Tool 9.6. Consider the Target Market
Chapter Tool 9.7. Set Promotional Objectives
Chapter Tool 9.8. Set Promotional Budget
Chapter Tool 9.9. Develop Promotions Mix

Review questions

1. In what ways are promotions more than just advertising?
2. What are the four tools of the promotions mix? Provide an example of each.
3. Why is public relations such a useful tool for sport organisations with constrained marketing resources?
4. Describe how a sport brand like adidas uses push and pull strategies simultaneously.
5. Provide some examples illustrating when the hierarchy of effects is not an accurate description of a consumer's decision-making process.
6. Explain why the promotions mix should be integrated for best results.

Relevant website

http://www.volvooceanrace.org   (Volvo Ocean Race)

Further reading

Irwin, R.L., Sutton, W.A. & McCarthy, L. (2002). *Sport Promotion and Sales Management*, Human Kinetics, Champaign, IL.

McDonald, M. & Rascher, D.A. (2000). Does bat day make cents?: the effect of promotions on the demand for baseball, *Journal of Sport Management*, 14: 8–27.

10 Sport sponsorship

Overview

This chapter describes the use of sponsorship in sport marketing and explains the major principles and tools of its deployment. Although sponsorship is usually considered a subsection of promotions, it has become so pivotal to sport marketing that it is being treated here as the fifth element of the sport marketing mix. This chapter outlines five essential aspects of sport sponsorship: (1) sponsorship objectives, (2) sponsorship targeting, (3) sponsorship leveraging, (4) sponsorship evaluation, and (5) ambush marketing.

By the end of this chapter, readers should be able to:

- Define the term sport sponsorship.
- Identify potential sponsorship objectives and associated market segments.
- Highlight the key elements of sponsorship targeting.
- Outline the sections of a sponsorship proposal.
- Specify how sponsorship may be augmented through leveraging.
- Highlight the main principles of sponsorship evaluation.
- Explain what is meant by ambush marketing.
- Identify the five main tactics in preventing ambush marketing.

Introduction

Chapter 9 examined promotions as the fourth element of the sport marketing mix. It also introduced the concept of sport sponsorship as a kind of promotional activity. Conventionally in marketing, sponsorship is viewed as a sub-category of personal selling because it involves personal contact between an organisation and a sponsor. Given that sponsorship is not a dominant form of promotions for most non-sport organisations, it is reasonable that in most textbooks it is treated as part of personal selling. However, the prominence of sponsorship in sport marketing demands that it be treated as a variable to be managed in its own right. With this in mind, sport sponsorship is treated here as an equal part of the marketing mix. The chief components of sport sponsorship are highlighted in Figure 10.1, which locates sponsorship within the Sport Marketing Framework.

What is sport sponsorship?

Sport sponsorship has increased dramatically over the past two decades. For many large non-sport corporations like Shell, Coca-Cola, Emirates and Vodafone, sponsoring sport organisations and athletes is an important part of their marketing strategies. Many different kinds of sport organisations and individuals may be sponsored, including individual athletes, clubs and teams, events, leagues, unions, federations, competitions, venues and special causes.

Sport sponsorship occurs when a sporting organisation, club, league, venue, cause or athlete is supported by a separate company (or person). The recipient of the sponsorship is known as the *sponsorship property* or the *sport property*. These legal-sounding terms are indicative of the fact that sponsorship is a business agreement between two parties. A non-legal term for the sponsorship recipient is the 'sponsee'.

> *Chapter Principle 10.1*: The term sport property refers to the recipient of the sponsorship. This could be an athlete, team, event, venue, association, cause or competition.

Sponsorships are supposed to benefit both parties; usually the sport property receives cash, goods, services or expert advice, and the sponsor receives benefits such as promotional rights and the marketing advantages of being associated with a particular sport property. Sponsors hope that by investing in a sport property, they will increase consumers' awareness of their brand, and consequently build their brand equity. It is important to realise, however, that sponsorship can be a high-risk investment. This is mainly because the outcome of the agreement is unpredictable. For example, there is no guarantee that a sponsor will achieve the increased sales, improved brand

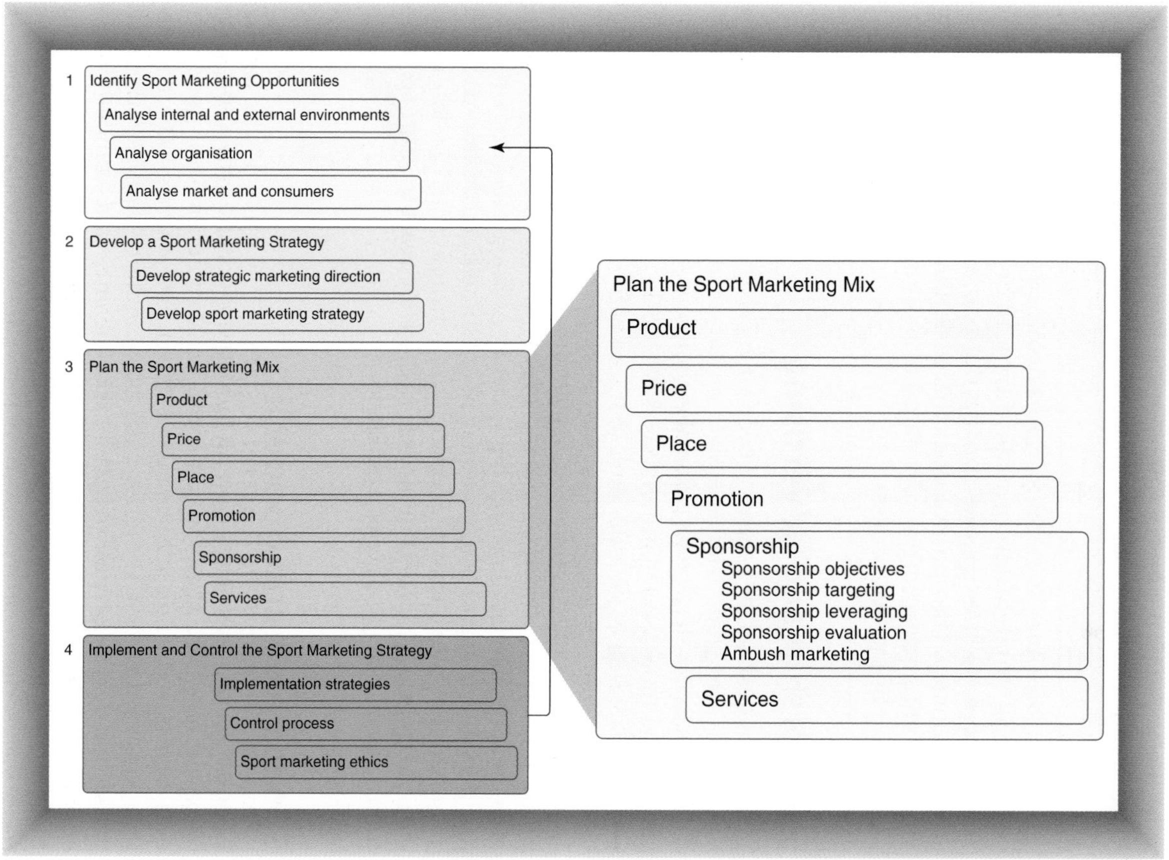

Plan the Sport Marketing Mix

Product

Price

Place

Promotion

Sponsorship
Sponsorship objectives
Sponsorship targeting
Sponsorship leveraging
Sponsorship evaluation
Ambush marketing

Services

1 Identify Sport Marketing Opportunities

Analyse internal and external environments

Analyse organisation

Analyse market and consumers

2 Develop a Sport Marketing Strategy

Develop strategic marketing direction

Develop sport marketing strategy

3 Plan the Sport Marketing Mix

Product

Price

Place

Promotion

Sponsorship

Services

4 Implement and Control the Sport Marketing Strategy

Implementation strategies

Control process

Sport marketing ethics

Figure 10.1 The Sport Marketing Framework.

image or changed consumer perceptions that they are seeking. The risk of sponsorship may be particularly high if individuals are sponsored. Like any investment, risk decreases with diversification. Because any individual athlete can easily fall prey to ill health, injury, poor performance or even personal circumstances that are unfavourably interpreted in the media, it is more likely that a sponsor can lose their investment. On the other hand, the right prominent athlete can be a sponsor's dream.

> *Chapter Principle 10.2*: Sport sponsorship is a business agreement where one organisation provides financial or in-kind assistance to a sport property in exchange for the right to associate itself with the sport property. The sponsor does this to achieve corporate objectives (such as enhancing corporate image) or marketing objectives (such as increasing brand awareness).

Sponsorship and advertising

To really understand the benefits of sponsorship, it is useful to consider the ways in which it is different to advertising. Consumers generally see advertising as a selfish activity; they believe that the company or brand being advertised is out to promote their own interests. Consumers may even suspect that the company is trying to pressure and coerce them into buying the product. This can make consumers sceptical and suspicious about advertisements, and they may deliberately resist by ignoring or wilfully disliking the advertised product. On the other hand, consumers are more likely to think that a sponsorship has some benefits beyond those for the sponsor. Although they may realise that the sponsor is trying to persuade them about something, the approach is more disguised and subtle than advertising, and consumers may be less defensive about responding to it. Consumers may therefore react to sport sponsorship communications with a general goodwill.

Sponsorship and goodwill

Goodwill is an important principle to help understand why sport sponsorships are effective. There are four important dimensions of goodwill that owe their introduction to Meenaghan (2001). First, more goodwill is created for sponsorship of social causes, such as community-based sports organisations than for large profit-seeking sport events and competitions. This opportunity has led some corporations to use sport sponsorship as a form of corporate social responsibility. Second, goodwill is usually greatest when the consumer is personally involved in the sport activity that is being sponsored. In fact, the more that a consumer is personally involved in the sport property, the higher the level of goodwill that is generated. Third, the time at which a sponsor becomes involved with a sport property can influence the level of goodwill associated with it. Sponsors which become involved later might be seen to be 'jumping on the bandwagon' compared with sponsors which are perceived as instrumental to the formation of a strong relationship with a sport property early in its life, or during a downturn. This leads to the fourth observation, which is that there can be some risk of a sponsor losing goodwill when it decides to discontinue the agreement. Consumers might conclude that the sponsor was only involved to exploit the opportunity.

Chapter Principle 10.3: Sport sponsorship generates goodwill among consumers. The amount of goodwill generated can vary depending on the kind of sport property sponsored, the degree of involvement that consumers have with the sport property, the time at which the sponsor becomes involved, and when and how the sponsor ceases the sponsorship.

Fan involvement

One important implication leading from the previous section is that a sponsor is likely to generate more goodwill among consumers who are personally involved with the sport property compared with those who are more casually involved. The idea of fan involvement was introduced in Chapter 3, and is a term that describes the degree to which fans personally identify with a particular sport, competition or athlete, or the level of personal affiliation and engagement they possess in regard to the sport property.

Fan involvement is an important consideration in sponsorship because a sport consumer's response to a sponsorship is driven by his/her level of involvement in the sport property. For example, strongly involved sport consumers show higher levels of sponsorship awareness, a more substantial sense of goodwill towards the sponsor, a greater brand preference for the sponsor and a stronger intention to purchase sponsor's products. Consumers are also more likely to change brands as a result of sponsorship, and because they are knowledgeable about the sport property, they are better able to judge whether there is a logical connection or congruence between the sport property and the sponsor.

Positive responses from highly involved sport consumers are more likely to occur in certain situations. In general, sport consumers tend to be more personally involved in events, teams or individual athletes, and will respond better to the sponsors of these kinds of sport properties, compared with the sponsorship of competitions or a sporting broadcast. In addition, involved fans are more likely to respond positively when there is one clear sponsor of an activity instead of several sponsors competing for attention. All of these points teach us that fan involvement is an important element to consider when looking at sponsorship.

Chapter Principle 10.4: Fan involvement is an important consideration in sponsorship because a consumer's response to a sponsorship is driven by the level of involvement that he/she has with the sport property.

Sponsorship objectives

The sponsors and sport property will have different objectives they want to achieve as a result of a successful sponsorship. The two most common objectives for sponsors are enhancing brand image and increasing brand awareness. For the sport property, the most common objective is to attract financial support, which in turn helps to meet other administrative and developmental goals. While these may be the most common, the objectives of sponsorship can vary greatly, depending on the size of the partners, the nature of the sponsorship relationship, and the type of sport property being supported. For this reason, it is essential that both the owner of the sport property and the sponsor have a clear understanding of the objectives of a sponsorship agreement. By understanding the benefits a sponsor seeks, the sport property is in a better position to 'sell' the idea of the sponsorship, and to ensure that they can provide what the sponsor needs. In the next section, possible sponsorship objectives from the perspective of the sponsor and from the perspective of the sport property are reviewed.

Sponsor objectives

Although there are some non-marketing goals that will be mentioned shortly, for a sponsor, the objectives of a sport sponsorship programme are general marketing goals. This means that most sponsorship objectives can be related to a specific market segment (or segments) that a sponsor aims to reach with the sponsorship programme. Some potential objectives are outlined in Table 10.1 where each has been related to a market segment. The table highlights the fact that sponsorship is a versatile promotional tool because it can reach many different market segments and help to achieve a range of promotional objectives relevant to the sponsor.

At first glance it might appear that the sponsorship objectives highlighted in Table 10.1 are exclusive to the sponsor. After all, one of the main objectives

Table **10.1** Major Sponsorship Objectives for Sponsors

Market Segment	Objective
General public	To promote the public image of the organisation To increase mass media exposure and public relations To increase general public awareness of organisation and/or product To generate goodwill To form a general brand perception To create a favourable community perception through social or cause-related sponsorship

Table 10.1 (Continued)

Market Segment	Objective
Target market	To increase consumer awareness of a product/service/brand To increase sales/market share of a specific product To establish a brand association between the sport property and sponsor To create an 'image transfer', where values are transferred from the sport product or type of sponsorship to the sponsor To develop brand equity (the added value a product has because of the brand name) To develop, manage and/or change brand image (what values and ideas consumers associate with the brand) To promote brand loyalty (e.g. repeat purchasing)
Distribution channel members	To increase sales to channel members (e.g. wholesalers) To promote discounts and deals from channel members (e.g. suppliers) To develop new relationships/new distribution channels (e.g. pouring rights at an event)
Internal stakeholders	To improve staff morale and relations To increase staff satisfaction (e.g. through a sense of pride in the association or through corporate hospitality/entertainment) To promote satisfaction of shareholders (e.g. due to pride in association, improved brand equity/sales/market share) To promote positive communications with the media (e.g. through corporate hospitality, corporate social responsibility)

for the sport property is to attract financial or in-kind support, which the owner organisation might employ in a variety of administrative, promotional or developmental projects. However, the association between the sponsor and the sport property can yield significant branding benefits to both parties. By attracting the 'right' sponsor, the owner of a sport property can influence the way that his/her target market thinks about his/her brand (brand image). A corporate sponsor can add substantial credibility to this image, in turn enhancing the sport property's brand equity, brand loyalty, and even ticket or product sales. Those employed by the sport property might even feel satisfied and proud to know that their organisation has the reputation to attract powerful or important sponsors. In fact, many of the objectives (either directly or indirectly) may be considered relevant to both the sport property owners as well as the sponsor.

> *Chapter Principle 10.5*: The objectives of sponsorship can vary greatly, depending on the size of the partners, the type of sponsorship and the type of sport property being supported. Some common objectives for the sponsor are to enhance sales, to promote the public image of its brand, to increase consumer awareness, to modify its brand image, and to build business relationships.

Sport property objectives

Table 10.2 outlines the major sponsorship objectives of sport organisations as owners of sport properties. Unlike the previous table detailing sponsor objectives, each of the following objectives is not associated with a market segment. This is because a number of the objectives relate to non-marketing areas such as corporate and operational development.

Table 10.2 Major Sponsorship Objectives for Sport Properties

Activity Area	Objective
Corporate objectives	To promote the public image of the sport property through a credible association and brand match up
	To increase mass media exposure and public relations (directly through the use of new funds, or indirectly through PR undertaken by the sponsor)
	To increase general public awareness of the property and/or product (directly and indirectly)
Marketing objectives	To increase consumer awareness of a product/service/brand (directly through the use of sponsor funds/resources, and indirectly through the PR undertaken by the sponsor)
	To increase credibility among consumers (via credibility of sponsor)
	To establish a brand association between the sport organisation and sponsor to create an 'image transfer' from the sport product
	To position or re-position the sport brand in the minds of consumers
	To develop, manage and/or change brand image (what values and ideas consumers associate with the brand)
	To promote discounts and deals from channel members (e.g. from suppliers at an event through offering sponsorship rights)
	To develop new relationships/new distribution channels (e.g. granting exclusive pouring rights at an event)

Table 10.2 (Continued)

Activity Area	Objective
Operational objectives	To obtain funding, resources and/or services to support operation and development
	To increase staff satisfaction (e.g. pride/credibility in the association/free goods and merchandise)
	To promote credibility with stakeholders (e.g. politicians, regulators, shareholders and the media)
	To promote satisfaction of shareholders (e.g. due to pride/credibility in association)

Chapter Principle 10.6: The objectives of sponsorship for the sport property will vary. In addition to attracting financial support, object- ives include increasing credibility, increasing awareness, and man- aging brand image.

Sponsorship targeting

It is more common for the sport property to be the one that introduces the idea of sponsorship to a sponsor rather than the reverse. This is partly because the benefits for the sport property are easier to measure (such as the amount of money received) compared with those for the sponsor. It is diffi- cult, for example, for a sponsor to know how much its sales have increased as a result of the sponsorship compared with how much they have increased because of other promotions and marketing. Therefore, when a sport prop- erty approaches a potential sponsor, it is important that they have a clear idea of what they have to offer or 'sell'. Usually the sport property would approach a sponsor with a written sponsorship proposal designed to high- light the potential benefits of the relationship. There are two central elements to this process: the first is choosing the right potential sponsor, and the sec- ond is writing an appropriate proposal.

Choosing the right sponsor: sponsorship affinity

Attracting the 'right' sponsor for a sport property is not just a matter of locat- ing one that is willing to hand over some cash. Sponsorship relationships are more successful, and more likely to be renewed, when there is the right match between partners. Sponsorship in motor racing provides a good example. Motor racing teams need large sums of money to maintain their competitiveness in an expensive sport; in other words, they need sponsors. The sport consumers who watch motor racing are usually people interested in buying and maintaining their own cars. It stands to reason that companies

199

like BMW and Shell want to reach these consumers in order to influence their buying decisions. Motor racing teams need money from sponsors, and sponsors want to promote their products to the people who watch the motor racing teams.

When companies consider sponsoring a sport property, they focus on two priorities. First, they look for an affinity between the sponsor and the sport property. Second, they look for an affinity between the target markets of the sponsor and those of the sport property. It is important that the brand positioning strategies of both parties match, and that the target market the sport property reaches is the same (or partially the same) as the target market the sponsor is trying to reach. Figure 10.2 shows these two vital components for ensuring a good match between sponsorship partners.

> *Chapter Principle 10.7*: Sponsorship affinity refers to whether there is a good fit or match between the sponsor and the sport property. Two factors are particularly important for ensuring a good match: (1) an overlap of target markets and (2) a match up of brand positioning strategies.

Match up of brand positioning

To recap, brand positioning or market positioning refers to how a sport organisation would like its consumers to think and feel about its brand when compared to competitors. It is the image or perception of the sport brand that consumers carry in their minds. Positioning takes into account the fact that consumers will compare a given sport brand with others in the market. When a company sponsors a sport property, the way that consumers think

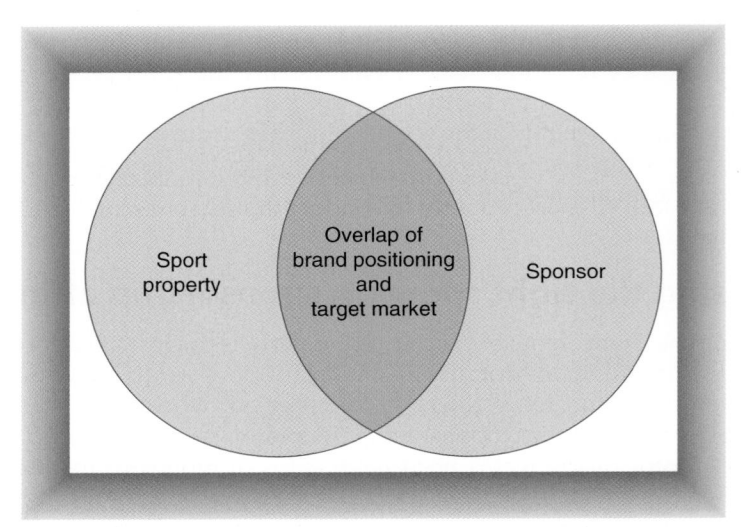

Figure 10.2 Sponsorship Affinity.

and feel about the sponsor and its brand(s) will be influenced by the way they think and feel about the sport property. Equally, the way that consumers think and feel about the sport property will be influenced by the way they think and feel about the sponsor. The key implication is that there must be a match between the brand positioning strategies of both parties. For example, Shell positions many of its motor oil products as being good quality and high performance. This matches the high-performance image of professional motor racing teams and means that there is a strong overlap between Shell and the sponsored teams Ducati and Ferrari.

Interactive case

Log on to the Shell website http://www.shell.com (Shell Directory→Shell Business, Consumer and Corporate Websites→Shell Motorsport→Shell Advance and Ducati) and the Ducati website http://www.ducati.com.
Consider the following questions:

- What kinds of consumers do you believe watch motor cycle racing on TV or at an event? (Think about their age, gender, interests, motivations)
- What kinds of consumers do you think buy Shell motor oil products? (Think about their age, gender, interests, motivations)
- What kind of brand positioning or image do you think that Ducati wants to portray? What about Shell?
- How does the Shell association with Ducati influence what sport consumers might think about their motorcycle oils?
- How might having Shell as a sponsor influence what sport consumers might think about Ducati bikes?
- What kind of brand positioning or image do you think that Shell wants to portray for its motor oil products?

This example should demonstrate that a good match between sponsorship partners involves two elements: (1) a match in the branding image that both partners want to portray and (2) a match in the target audience of the partners. To make sure that there is a good match between the sponsorship partners, it is important for the sport property to conduct thorough research and write a targeted sponsorship proposal.

Sponsorship proposals

The sponsorship proposal should be a specific document that is targeted towards a specific sponsor. Writing a general proposal and sending it to a number of potential sponsors is ineffective because it will be obvious to the sponsors that their brand positioning and target market have not been considered. The proposal should take into account the market position as well as the

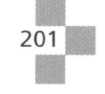

resources of a potential sponsor, and should describe the return a sponsor could reasonably expect from their investment. A sponsorship proposal should generally address a number of key areas including an overview of the sport property, a description of the target audience of the sport property, the goals of the sponsorship programme, the type and period of association, sponsorship benefits and rights, the investment required, the ambush prevention strategy and an evaluation strategy. A detailed outline of the key sections of the sponsorship proposal is provided in Table 10.3.

Table 10.3 Key Sections of Sponsorship Proposal

Covering Letter
  Maximum one page
  Addressed to an appropriate staff member working with the potential
    sponsor. Usually a marketing manager, but could be a sponsorship manager
    in a large company

Cover Page
  Clear, professional and attractive presentation
  Identify the potential sponsor and the sport property

Executive Summary
  An overview/summary of the proposal

Overview of the Sport Property and Its Owner Sport Property
  History, context and social/community significance
  List of current and past sponsors (if applicable)
  References or endorsements from past sponsors (if applicable)
  Media attention (frequency and type, include brief examples)
  Programmes and events organised by the owner sport property (target groups,
    participation numbers, audience demographics, promotional activities)

Target Market
  Identify consumer targets reached by the sport property
  Demonstration of how this consumer audience matches and/or expands the
    target market of the proposed sponsor
  Consider internal and external audiences (e.g. existing consumers, potential
    consumers, local community, general public, suppliers, wholesalers,
    distributors, government, shareholders)

Brand Affinity
  Identify the brand positioning of the sport property
  Demonstrate how this positioning matches or complements the brand
    positioning of proposed sponsor

Goals of the Sponsorship Programme
  What can be realistically achieved for the sponsor (e.g. brand awareness
    among a target group, media exposure, increased sales/market share,
    community involvement/social responsibility, building goodwill, general
    public awareness, staff relations)

Sponsorship Type
  Event, team/individual, competition, venue

Table 10.3 (Continued)

Period of Association
  Duration of agreement

Sponsorship Benefits and Rights
  Detail the rights of the sponsorship agreement
  Note whether these sponsorship rights are exclusive or shared with other
    partners
  Note other benefits for the sponsor (e.g. special seating, client entertainment
    at events, cross-promotional activities, networking opportunities, image
    enhancement)
  Outline different 'packages' available (if applicable)
  Demonstrate how the sponsorship benefits relate to the sponsor's
    mission/vision and business objectives

Investment
  Costs (include varying cost options if appropriate)
  Could include an upfront fee and performance-based incentives
  In-kind investments
  Term/duration of agreement

Ambush Prevention Strategy
  Outline exclusivity of sponsor rights and how their exclusivity will be
    protected

Evaluation Strategy
  Performance measures and targets
  How these measures and targets will be assessed

A number of the key areas described in Table 10.3 have already been discussed in this chapter, such as the goals of sponsorship and the issue of brand/target market affinity. The remaining areas are examined in detail in the forthcoming sections of this chapter, including evaluating sponsorships and ambush prevention strategies.

Chapter Tool 10.1. Sponsorship Proposal: A sponsorship proposal should be researched and written for a specific sponsor (rather than writing a general proposal that is sent out to various potential sponsors). This way the proposal can take into account the market position and resources of the potential sponsor, and it can address issues of sponsorship affinity between the two parties.

A sponsorship proposal should generally address a number of key areas including an overview of the sport property, a description of the target audience of the sport property, the goals of the sponsorship programme, the type and period of association, sponsorship benefits and rights, the investment required/cost, the ambush prevention strategy, and an evaluation strategy.

Sport sponsorship rights

The rights that are given through a sponsorship are sometimes called *entitlements* or *sponsorship assets*. There is a vast array of rights that can be delivered through a sponsorship beyond the obvious ones such as naming rights and signage. Table 10.4 provides a detailed inventory of the kinds of sponsorship rights that a sport property might offer a sponsor during a negotiation.

Table 10.4 Sport Sponsorship Rights

General Sponsorship Rights
 Naming rights to an event, competition or club
 On-site signage rights
 On-site sales rights
 On-site product sampling/trials
 Corporate entertainment and hospitality
 VIP tickets
 Merchandising and promotional give-aways
 Use of venue for sponsor functions
 Athlete/celebrity appearances for sponsor
 Right of first refusal to new sponsorship opportunities
 Use of event volunteers
 Additional advertising opportunities
 Product placement—use of sponsor branded equipment/
  product at event
 Access to mailing lists/databases
 Trademark/logo display on equipment, clothing, media promotions
 Public-speaking opportunities
 Product category exclusivity
 Interactive areas, e.g. message boards, polls, quizzes, game-zones
 Consumer promotion exclusivity
 Non-profit/cause overlay/social responsibility option
 Jumbotron/large-screen signage
 Mobile phone content
 Plasma or LED screens
 Radio (buys or event broadcast)
 Video-on-demand content

Media rights
 Media rights, including photography and footage rights
 Press releases announcements and press kits
 Public service announcements
 Internet content/links
 Newspaper (buys or special event coverage)
 Pre-event and post-event promotional activities
 Print media presence (programmes, guides, etc.)
 Webcast (live stream or on-demand)

Chapter Tool 10.2. Sport Sponsorship Rights: Sport properties can offer a range of sponsorship rights that can be negotiated with potential sponsors into a customised package of benefits. The inventory of sponsorship rights provides the starting point for a suite of rights to be considered.

Interactive case

Log on to the website for one of the following sport organisations, and examine its sponsorship proposals against the proposed version in Table 10.3.

1. Asia Pacific Regatta at http://www.sailmelbourne.com.au (Sponsors→ Information for Potential Sponsors→Download Sponsorship Brochure)
2. Glasgow University Tennis Club at http://www.gutennis.co.uk (click on 'Sponsorship' in left-hand menu)
3. Newfoundland and Labrador Rugby Union at http://www.rockrugby.ca/sponsors/TheRockSponsorshipProposal.pdf
4. South Africa Bungee Extreme Adventure Sports at http://www.sabungee.co.za/sponprp.htm
5. The Maui Jim Hawaii Marlin Tournament Series (big game fishing event) at http://www.konatournaments.com/KTResults/MJ_sponsor2.pdf
6. Capital District Triathlon Club of New York State at http://www.cdtriclub.org/sponsors.html

Sponsorship leveraging

Leveraging sponsorships means getting additional value out of an already existing sponsorship investment. It is concerned with getting the maximum benefit and advantage from the sponsorship through careful integration with other marketing activities. Leveraging also helps to combat ambush marketing, which will be explained shortly. In fact, one of the keys to a successful sponsorship for both parties is leveraging activities. Leveraging helps to build a more positive and long-lasting relationship between the partners because it involves investing time and resources in one another, and seeing the relationship as a strategic alignment.

For a sponsor to make the most of a sponsorship, it needs to invest resources over and above the costs of the sponsorship itself. By paying the sponsorship fee, a sponsor is really only buying the right to associate themselves with the sport property; they must invest more money in order to make the most of this right by communicating the affiliation to their target market. Many sport marketing experts believe that a sponsor will need to invest at least three times more money than the cost of the sponsorship itself in order to leverage successfully. The aim of leveraging is to promote the association between the two brands from every angle possible, and not just leave it up to the sport property.

Sponsorship is only one promotional tool. In order to leverage the value of this tool, it is recommended that sponsors also use the other elements of the promotions mix in order to complement and draw attention to the sponsorship. For example, advertising, public relations and sales promotion activities could all be used in conjunction with the sponsorship to strengthen the effect. Corporate hospitality and an online presence could tie in with sales promotions to maximise the impact of the sponsorship. In fact, all four of the traditional promotions mix elements should be used to properly leverage a sponsorship, that is advertising, public relations, sales promotions and personal selling. Sponsors need to advertise, publicise, promote and personally sell their sponsorship association to consumers in order to create greater impact. Using a suite of promotional elements in addition to the sponsorship can create a kind of synergy, where the whole of the marketing programme is greater than the sum of the individual elements of the promotions mix. This is, of course, the whole point of using a strategic framework as the basis of a sport marketing approach. Thus, it is not enough to just use the other elements of the promotions mix to leverage a sponsorship, but the four elements of the general marketing mix should also form part of an integrated sponsorship leveraging plan. For example, a sponsor may introduce a new product for the duration of the sponsorship, or use special packaging relating to the event. The price of the sponsor's goods or services may be discounted during the event, or a percentage may be donated to a prominent or related cause. Distribution channels (place) may be expanded so that the sponsor's product can be bought exclusively at the event.

It is not only important to consider how to leverage a sponsorship, but also to whom the leveraging efforts should be directed. One good recommendation is that sponsorships should be leveraged towards a choice of three different groups of stakeholders: consumers, employees, and corporate stakeholders including distribution channel members (see Cliffe & Motion, 2005). These three possibilities are outlined in the following sub-sections.

Leveraging sponsorship towards consumers

Many of the promotional activities that were mentioned in relation to leveraging can be aimed directly at a sponsor's target market. Advertising to promote the connection with the sport property, sales promotions that coincide with the event and public relations through high-profile media outlets can all reinforce the sponsorship relationship to consumers. The sponsorship may also give the sponsor access to content about the sport property that its consumers may be interested in. This tactic works particularly well with technology or communications category sponsors who can use their sponsorship of sport properties to provide extra content to their customers.

Leveraging sponsorship towards employees

In the earlier section on sponsorship objectives, it was highlighted that a sponsorship may help to meet internal marketing goals by improving staff morale, increasing staff satisfaction, and creating a sense of staff pride in the organisation. If a sponsor's employees have an emotional connection to the sport property being sponsored, then the sponsorship may help them to develop emotional connections to the workplace. As a result, some leveraging can be usefully directed towards the sponsor's employees, offering them the opportunity to attend games or events and receive corporate hospitality. This can create a positive brand experience and enhance loyalty among employees, which in turn is more likely to lead to quality interactions with customers.

Leveraging sponsorship towards corporate stakeholders

A sponsorship can improve the goodwill and business relationships that a sponsor has with its stakeholders. This might include distribution channel members, shareholders, the media and politicians. For example, corporate hospitality is one concrete way in which sponsors can build positive relationships with their suppliers and other distribution channel members.

Chapter Tool 10.3. Sponsorship Leveraging: Leveraging sponsorships means getting value out of the sponsorship investment. It is concerned with getting the maximum amount of benefit and advantage from the sponsorship through careful integration with other elements of the promotions and marketing mix. For a sponsor to make the most of a sponsorship, it is recommended that it invest resources over and above the costs of the sponsorship itself.

To leverage a sponsorship, a sponsor should use all four elements of the marketing mix, including all of the promotions mix activities.

Leveraging activities should be directed towards three different groups of stakeholders: (1) consumers, (2) employees and (3) corporate stakeholders (including distribution channel members, suppliers, shareholders, the media and politicians).

Corporate social responsibility and cause-related sport marketing

Sometimes corporations or other commercial enterprises seek a beneficial brand association as a result of providing support to a specific charitable or non-profit cause. It is common in these arrangements for sport organisations to partner with corporations in order to provide a high-profile cause. The characteristics of sport tend to make it an attractive partner for social engagement. For example, sport generally enjoys a good media profile, is associated with fun and entertainment, is healthy and encourages social interaction. As a result, sport presents a powerful vehicle for corporations to demonstrate that they are meeting their social and community obligations. Cause-related sport marketing, or its more recent successor sport corporate social responsibility, is effective in heightening the brand awareness of sponsors and tends to connect their brand with a more trusting and caring image. Sport marketers should remain aware of the ways in which sport brands can be employed as platforms for corporate social activity.

Sponsorship evaluation

Some sport marketers believe that the true effects of a sponsorship are impossible to evaluate. For example, sponsorship usually occurs in conjunction with other promotional strategies which makes it difficult to isolate its effects. It is also possible that it is the very interaction of a number of promotional strategies that helps to make a sponsorship work, rather than any one strategy on its own. In other words, different strategies rely on one another to be successful. It is clear that sponsorships are more successful at increasing consumer awareness when they are combined with advertising and other leveraging that reinforces and highlights the sponsorship association. The problem is that this interdependence can make it difficult to evaluate sponsorship on its own.

While it is true that measuring the effect of a sponsorship independent of all other marketing activities is extremely difficult, there are ways in which the success of a sponsorship can be judged. A careful evaluation strategy is important because sponsors expect to receive some objective feedback about the effect of the money they have invested in a sponsorship. Without a clear return on their investment, it is unlikely that a sponsor will continue an association. Even small businesses which sponsor on a more modest level (such as local community clubs) need evidence that the money they commit to a sponsorship will yield benefits. After all, small businesses have far less money to spend and will tend to be discerning about such investments. To be able to demonstrate that sponsorship has a positive outcome for sponsors is the best way to legitimise it as a marketing technique, and to attract and retain sponsors.

> *Chapter Principle 10.8*: To be able to demonstrate that sponsorship has a positive outcome for corporations is the best way to legitimise it as a marketing technique, and to attract and retain sponsors.

The sponsorship evaluation process is a systematic tool for sport marketers to apply to sponsorship evaluation. The sponsorship evaluation sequence is presented in Figure 10.3, followed by guidance about each stage of the evaluation process.

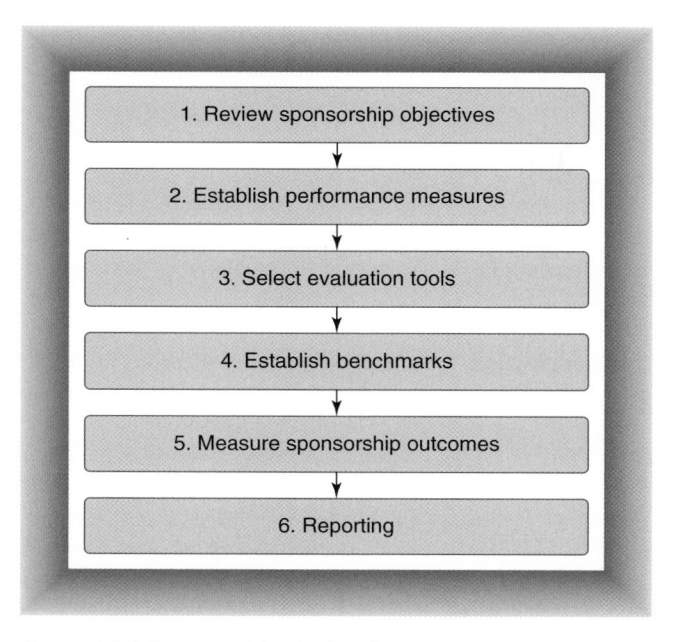

Figure 10.3 Sponsorship Evaluation.

Review sponsorship objectives

To evaluate the success of a sponsorship programme, there must be a clear understanding of what it was aiming to achieve in the first place. Potential objectives of a sponsorship agreement are highlighted at the beginning of this chapter. They are worth revisiting now because they provide the basis for the next step of establishing performance measures.

Establish performance measures

To evaluate whether objectives have been achieved, it is useful to attach a *performance measure* to each objective. A performance measure is a guide for determining whether the sponsorship objective has been achieved. The word *measure* means a way of estimating, calculating or assessing whether a goal has been achieved. It usually involves finding a way to *quantify* or put a number to the objective. Some important basic examples appear in Table 10.5.

Select evaluation tools

Once marketing objectives have been set, and corresponding performance measures allocated, it is possible to choose the evaluation tools that will be used. Each performance measure will be suited to a particular kind of evaluation tool. The key message here is that sponsorship evaluation is best conducted using a range of evaluation tools. Choosing from a 'suite' of evaluation

Table 10.5 Examples of Performance Measures

Sponsorship Objective	Possible Performance Measures
To increase mass media exposure	Number of times the sponsor logo is seen on free-to-air TV during live telecasts per game
To increase the number of people who use the product/service as a result of the sponsorship association	Number of customers who use our service as measured on a post-purchase questionnaire
To increase staff satisfaction levels through corporate hospitality	Satisfaction levels as rated by staff survey, which asks questions about the importance of corporate hospitality
To increase customer awareness of the product	Number of people who have heard of the product in a geographical area as measured by a phone survey
To increase sales	Sales during the sponsored event, compared with sales at the same event last year

tools helps to overcome the limitations of each method on its own; a number or a group of tools are most useful in providing a breadth of information. Table 10.6 outlines the suite of potential evaluation tools.

Table 10.6 has two important lessons. First, the tools selected to evaluate a sponsorship programme should be directly related to its objectives and performance measures. Second, five main kinds of evaluation are used: (1) exposure, (2) consumer awareness, (3) consumer attitudes, (4) sales effects and (5) satisfaction. The most effective and informative sponsorship evaluation programme will use tools from many, if not all, of these five areas. Each is expanded and explained in the following sub-sections.

Exposure

Media exposure monitoring is currently the most widely used form of sponsorship evaluation, mainly because it is one of the easiest methods to use. At its most simple, exposure can be measured by documenting the type, frequency and duration of sponsor name and logo appearances in television, radio, press, print and online sources (such as number of page views or hits). For example, how many times a brand name or logo is observable in print media, or how many seconds it appears on television, may be measured. This can be a simple measure, although it can also become time-consuming if significant volumes of media need to be audited. For larger corporations with sufficient resources, there are software programs that can help with storing and analysing this kind of data. One of the limitations of collecting information about the type, frequency and duration of exposure is that it does not provide any indication of how many people, or what types of consumers

Table 10.6 Evaluation Tools

Objective Area	Type of Evaluation	Aim in Evaluation	Types of Tools
Public image	Consumer attitude	Determine what consumers in the general public think and believe about the brand/product/sport	Surveys and focus groups
Media exposure	Media exposure analysis	Determine the type, frequency and/or duration of exposure Determine readership/viewer statistics and demographics	Exposure audit Numerical estimations of exposure value
Awareness (of general public or a target group)	Consumer awareness	Determine if consumers can recognise and recall the brands involved in the sponsorship (brand awareness), and the association/link between the partners (sponsorship awareness)	Recall and recognition tests through surveys and focus groups
Sales rates or market share	Sales effects	Estimate sales made directly and indirectly as a result of the sponsorship	Tracking of actual sales Consumer self-report survey (claimed sales) Coupons and 'bounce-backs' (sales by proxy) Comparison with competitors' sales to determine market share
Brand association	Consumer attitude Consumer awareness	Determine if there is a link made between the sponsor and the sport property	Surveys and focus groups
Brand equity	Consumer attitude	Determine what consumers think about the brand. What do they associate with it?	Surveys and focus groups
Brand image management	Consumer attitude	Determine the values and ideas consumers associate with the sponsor/sport property Determine how consumers 'position' the brands/products compared to competitors	Surveys and focus groups

(*Continued*)

211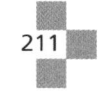

Table 10.6 (Continued)

Objective Area	Type of Evaluation	Aim in Evaluation	Types of Tools
Brand loyalty	Consumer attitude Sales effects	Establish whether the sponsorship affects long-term associations with a brand	Tracking of purchases Loyalty programmes Focus groups and consumer surveys
Satisfaction (consumer, channel member, staff, stakeholder) and positive relationships	Satisfaction	Determine the levels of satisfaction that are generated through the sponsorship agreement	Surveys and focus groups

were exposed. It is therefore useful to also gather information about the readership of the particular publication, the viewer statistics, and the demographic profile of viewers/readers.

Most sport marketers agree that this information is still insufficient on its own, and that it is necessary to put a monetary value on the media exposure that has been obtained. For example, some sponsors may calculate how much it would cost them to pay for advertising of the same frequency and duration as the sponsorship exposure. This usually involves a mathematical calculation which considers the duration and time of exposure, estimated audience levels, television ratings, the size/location of the exposure as well as the standard cost for advertising at that time. Other methods apply different kinds of advertising rates together with weighting systems that try to put a value on the different kinds of exposure, and even the 'favourability' of the exposure. There are also statistical models that try to estimate the proportion of the target population that was exposed to the media coverage in question.

There are two main problems with these methods of 'valuing' exposure. The first is that they equate sponsorship exposure with advertising, while the second is that they are based on estimations that may not be valid. The assumption that sponsorship exposure and advertising have the same impact on consumers is unproven and questionable. When compared to sponsorship exposure, an advertisement is a targeted communication that is designed to convey a specific message to the consumer. The message that is conveyed to a consumer through a sponsorship alliance is more subtle and complex, requiring an understanding of the consumers' attitudes and beliefs about the two brands both separately and together. Furthermore, it is also unreasonable to assume that all consumers pay complete or even partial attention to a sponsor's logo

212

Table 10.7 Measuring Media Exposure

Measuring Media Exposure

At its most simple, media exposure can be measured by documenting the type, frequency and duration of media exposure, as well as readership/viewer statistics, and their demographic profile. There are many methods which try to put a monetary value on media exposure; these provide a 'best guess' based on assumptions and estimations, and their validity is therefore questionable (although it may still be persuasive)

Media exposure can be one important element of sponsorship evaluation, particularly if it is combined with other methods

---

while exciting sporting action is occurring. This does not mean that the sponsorship alliance is worthless, but it does imply that sponsorship exposure is not the same as advertising. The value of sponsorship is ultimately not found in the value of air time, but in the way that a match up of brand images can influence consumer attitudes and purchase behaviour.

To make the approach even more dubious, mathematical methods for putting a 'value' on exposure may be invalid. They may not accurately measure what they say they are measuring. What these formulas try to deliver is a 'best guess' based on assumptions and estimations. There is significant variability in the methods, rates and weighting systems that different approaches use, so it is impossible to compare the results of one with another. There is also the tendency towards inflating the advertising rates against which sponsorship exposure is compared, making sponsorship appear better value than it really is. However, to make a business case for the commencement or maintenance of a sponsorship agreement, these kinds of calculations may be persuasive and have a role to play in evaluation. They are most useful if used on a continuing basis where results can be directly compared from one year to the next. Using the same method consistently can help establish whether there has been a change in exposure. There are specialised sponsorship evaluation consultancies that conduct media exposure measurement for a fee.

In concluding this discussion about measuring media exposure, it is important to remember that media exposure does not in itself reveal anything about consumer intentions. If a logo was seen on television for a total of 45 seconds, there is no information about the impact it had on the people watching it. For example, did it change or strengthen their awareness or attitudes towards the sponsor's brand? While it might be important that consumers are exposed to a sponsor's product or brand, this in itself may not be sufficient to change their attitudes or buying habits. However, if these limitations are taken into account, measuring media exposure can still be one important element of sponsorship evaluation, particularly if it is combined with other forms of evaluation. It can also be an important tool for small sporting organisations which may not have sufficient money to spend on more complex evaluations. The key points to remember about measuring media exposure are summarised in Table 10.7.

Consumer awareness

One of the common objectives of a sponsorship agreement is to increase the awareness consumers possess about a sponsor's product or brand. The most common methods used to test consumers' awareness of a brand or product are based on the ideas of recognition and recall. Testing recognition usually involves showing consumers a list of sponsor's names or logos, and asking which ones they recognise. Sometimes false companies may be added to the list (i.e. companies that are not sponsors) to test the degree to which consumers mistakenly associate brands with a sponsorship just because they are on a list. Testing recall is different because it involves asking consumers to recall sponsor brands spontaneously, without any cues. For example, a consumer may be asked to list the companies or sponsorships that he/she associates with a sport event, without receiving any prompting. Recalling a brand name without any prompting is obviously more difficult, so this is considered a better test of awareness than recognising a brand on a list once prompted.

When using recognition and recall tests, it is possible to test consumers' awareness of two different aspects of the sponsorship: (1) the individual brands (or products) of the sponsor and the sport property and (2) the link or association between the sponsor and sport property. In other words, it is possible to look at evaluating brand awareness as well as sponsorship awareness. Surveys which look at the link between the sponsor and sport property are called association measures.

There are a number of factors which may affect whether a consumer recalls a brand's sponsorship association. These include how long consumers have been exposed to the sponsorship, how strongly they associated previous sponsors with the sport property, how the sponsorship message is delivered, how interested and involved the consumers are with the sport property, the role of other promotional strategies used (such as advertising) to reinforce the sponsorship, and the size of the sponsor. It is also important to realise that recall of a sponsorship can change over time. For example, it may increase just before and during a big sport event, but may die away a few weeks after it has finished.

The ability of consumers to recognise and recall sponsorship partners is typically tested during phone surveys and face-to-face surveys, although it is also possible to incorporate them into a focus group analysis. One of the important things to consider when designing a survey or focus group is how consumers will be selected to take part. This will be influenced by the objectives set for the sponsorship agreement. For example, if the aim is to increase awareness in the general public, then this would be best tested with a large, random sample, which of course can be an expensive and difficult undertaking. However, if the aim is to increase awareness within a more specific target group, then an alternative method for selecting participants such as purposeful sampling (e.g. approaching people at an event, or from a membership list) would be appropriate. Measuring consumer awareness is summarised in Table 10.8.

Table 10.8 Measuring Consumer Awareness

Measuring Consumer Awareness

Consumer awareness is most commonly measured by testing recognition and recall of a brand, product or sponsorship alliance

Recognition is when a consumer is able to identify the brand/product/alliance from a list. This means that he/she has been prompted to remember it

Recall is when a consumer remembers the brand/product/alliance without prompting or recognising from a list

Recognition and recall tests can measure brand awareness (of the individual partners in the sponsorship) as well as sponsorship awareness (the alliance between the partners)

Table 10.9 Measuring Consumer Attitudes

Measuring Consumer Attitudes

Consumer attitudes are the beliefs that a consumer has about a product or brand. There are a number of different types of consumer attitudes that are commonly evaluated including: (1) perceptions about positioning, (2) the fit between the sponsor and sport property, (3) the perceived sincerity of the sponsor, (4) purchase intentions and (5) affinity measures

Consumer attitudes are often measured on surveys with Likert scales using 'agree' and 'disagree' items, and short-answer questionnaires

Consumer attitudes/image affects

While media exposure and consumer awareness evaluations are popular ways to assess the success of a sponsorship, they do not uncover anything about the impact of sponsorship on consumer attitudes. Finding out what consumers really think about a product, brand or sponsorship is not an easy task. It is easier to find out if consumers can recognise and recall a brand, compared with finding out what beliefs they have about the brand, and what values they associate it with. However, discovering what consumers think can be extremely valuable. For example, consumers' attitudes are more likely to give an indication of their likely buying behaviour than awareness measures alone, although the link between attitudes and behaviour is not direct or causal.

Consumer attitudes are often measured through surveys with Likert scales ('agree' and 'disagree' items), and with short-answer questions that ask consumers to give an unprompted response. There are a number of different aspects of consumer attitudes that can be evaluated including (1) perceptions about positioning, (2) the fit between the sponsor and sport property, (3) the perceived sincerity of the sponsor, (4) purchase intentions and (5) affinity measures. Each is discussed in the following sub-sections and summarised in Table 10.9.

215

Positioning perceptions

One important kind of consumer attitude evaluation involves trying to understand how consumers conceptualise a sponsor's brand compared to others. In order to uncover such complex issues, surveys and short answer questionnaires ask consumers to indicate what they associate with the brand, such as values, features or symbols. For example, do they associate the brand with prestige, reliability or family values? A questionnaire may also ask how consumers compare the sponsor's brand to others. For example, do they see it as better value or more dependable than other brands? Obviously, before it is possible to design and implement a consumer attitude survey which evaluates consumer beliefs about positioning, it is vital that there is clear information about how a sponsor sought to position their brand in the first place. The key questions are: What values, features and images do consumers associate with a sponsor's brand?; and, How do consumers compare a sponsor's brand to others?

Sponsor and sport property fit/sponsorship congruence

A sponsorship will be more effective if there is a strong fit or match up between the sponsor's brand and the sport property. The level of fit, or congruence, that consumers perceive relates to the degree to which they think that there is a logical connection between the two. For example, there is an obvious congruence between a sport event like a tennis grand slam and a sponsor which manufactures tennis products. To explore whether consumers perceive a good fit between the sponsor and sport property, survey questions may be posed to determine the characteristics they associate with each, or what consumers think each symbolises or stands for. The researchers can then assess the similarity.

Sincerity of the sponsor

Consumers are more likely to think favourably about a sponsor if they believe that the sponsor is motivated by a sense of community and philanthropy rather than just financial gain.

Purchase intentions

It is often difficult to accurately measure sales that have resulted directly from a sponsorship. One of the ways around this problem is to find out if consumers intend or plan to purchase the sponsor's product. Purchase intentions are therefore a proxy for actual sales, in that they represent a substitute, or a stand-in measure. Purchase intentions can also be considered a proxy for actual behaviour, that is for actually buying and consuming a product. It is obvious, however, that planned behaviour and actual behaviour can be quite different.

Affinity measures

216

The word 'affinity' in the context of sponsorship evaluation, refers to whether or not consumers feel an attraction to a sponsor's product or brand. More specifically, it refers to the degree to which consumers feel that a sponsor's product or brand is 'their kind of brand'. For example, does it give the consumer the sense of identity that they are seeking? Or, do consumers think that it suits other people that they would like to be similar to? Questions of this kind have a relationship to product and brand positioning because they are designed to find out whether the way that consumers think about a sponsor's product/ brand reinforces the way that they would like to think about themselves.

Sales effects

Linking any promotional activity, including sponsorship, to an increase in sales is problematic. One of the main reasons is that a sponsor will usually implement a whole range of different promotional strategies, making it difficult to separate out which strategies have led to which sales. However, in some instances, it can actually be easier to track sales effects that have been stimulated by sponsorship, compared with other promotions. For example, food or beverage rights at a sport event give the sponsor exclusive or preferential sales rights to consumers at the event. It is a simple task to calculate the sales that have been made at the sponsored event.

It is more difficult, however, to determine if there is an indirect increase in sales as a result of the event. For example, did more consumers choose to use a sponsored product after the event as a result of its affiliation with the sponsored property? These kinds of sales are sometimes called claimed sales because consumers may 'claim' that they bought a product as a result of being exposed to it in a certain way. Claimed sales can be measured through surveys which ask consumers to indicate their awareness of the sponsorship, their exposure to the sponsor and their reasoning for purchase. Sometimes brief surveys may even be done at the point of sale to find out what has led the consumer to their decision.

It is also possible to estimate sales by proxy. This means trying to estimate sales by using a 'stand-in', like a coupon or token that is redeemed at the point of sale. For example, if the coupon has been distributed at a sport event and the consumer uses it at the point of sale, then the sale can be associated with the sponsorship. One of the complicating factors of this method is that coupons and tokens often include an incentive for people to redeem them, like offering a discount. This makes it difficult to determine if the sale was made as a result of the sponsorship or the discount promotion. However, while this may make it difficult to accurately estimate sales by proxy, it can be an effective way of leveraging a sponsorship programme. Table 10.10 summarises the important issues associated with measuring sales effects.

To review, three different types of *sales measures* are used in sponsorship evaluation. They are (1) actual sales, (2) claimed sales and (3) sales by proxy. Sales effects measures can make a contribution to a sponsorship evaluation, but they do have two major limitations. First, they do not accurately reflect the effect on sales flowing from a sponsorship. Second, the major benefit of sponsorship may actually be less related to sales and more relevant to the positive effects on consumer attitudes and therefore brand equity.

Table 10.10 Measuring Sales Effects

Measuring Sales Effects

It can be difficult to directly attribute sales to the impact of a sponsorship agreement. Sometimes it may be possible to calculate actual sales, such as when a food or beverage company sponsors an event and makes sales at that event

If it is not possible to measure actual sales, it may be feasible to estimate claimed sales, by surveying consumers about why they purchased a product

Finally, sales can be measured by proxy, which involves estimating sales by using a 'stand-in' like a coupon or token that is redeemed at the point of sale

---

Satisfaction

The final area for evaluating sponsorships is related to satisfaction. A sponsor may aim to increase customer, staff or even shareholder satisfaction through the sponsorship. For example, the sponsor may offer staff corporate hospitality at a sporting event with the aim of improving staff morale and loyalty. It logically follows that if this is an objective, then measures using a satisfaction rating of some kind are required.

Establish benchmarks

Once a suite of evaluation tools has been selected to evaluate the sponsorship, it is important to establish a benchmark. Benchmarks are used to determine the 'status quo' before the sponsorship promotions commence. This is essential to find out whether an objective has been achieved over and above the original levels prior to the commencement of the sponsorship relationship. For example, if the objective is to increase brand awareness among a specific target market, then there must be evidence of what the awareness levels were before the sponsorship agreement began. A benchmark therefore works as a point of reference in the evaluation strategy.

Measure sponsorship outcomes and report

The final two stages of the evaluation process are to measure the outcomes of the sponsorship programme and then report these formally to the sponsor. Measuring the outcomes of a sponsorship means using the suite of evaluation tools again after a set duration during which the sponsorship has been in place. These results should be considered against the benchmarks obtained from the previous step to assess whether the desired goals have been realised. The results of the evaluation should be formally reported to the sponsor, along with any recommendations about improvements that can be made or ways in which the sponsorship can be leveraged for even better results in the future.

> *Chapter Tool 10.4. Sport Sponsorship Evaluation*: A step-by-step process of sponsorship evaluation should include: (1) review sponsorship objectives, (2) establish performance measures, (3) select evaluation tools, (4) establish benchmarks, (5) measure sponsorship outcomes and (6) reporting.
>
> The tools that are chosen to evaluate the sponsorship programme should be directly related to the sponsorship objectives and performance measures originally set.
>
> There are five main kinds of sponsorship evaluation to select from: (1) exposure, (2) consumer awareness, (3) consumer attitudes, (4) sales effects and (5) satisfaction. The most effective and informative sponsorship evaluation programme will use tools from many, if not all, of these five areas.

Ambush marketing

The word 'ambush' refers to a trap or a surprise attack on a competitor. In the sponsorship world, *ambush marketing* is a term used when a company creates the impression that it is associated with a sport property, whereas in reality they have no affiliation at all. Ambush marketing is planned to establish an artificial association with an event in order to obtain some of the benefits and recognition of an official sponsorship, without having to invest any money. Typically, ambush marketing involves an intrusion on the physical space of a sport property or sport event, making use of a particular diversion or grab for attention in order to wrestle the association away from the actual sponsor.

Ambush marketing occurs most often with large sporting events, where the ambushing company deflects attention away from the official sponsors and onto themselves, without having made the appropriate investment into the sport property. Ambush marketing is sometimes called 'parasitic' marketing because a company is 'free-loading', like a parasite, on the back of the official sponsor. In these situations, consumers can become confused and even believe that the ambushing company is an actual sponsor. Before more stringent legislation was introduced, the earliest attempts at ambush marketing were quite clumsy. For example, the ambush company would park a hot-air balloon with their logo on it above a competing brand's sponsored event, or would hand out free memorabilia at the event. Ambush marketing was popularised by the bitter rivalries of companies fighting for the same market, like Coke and Pepsi, and Nike and adidas.

Ambush marketing attempts to undermine the brand equity of official sponsors at the same time as it aims to increase the brand equity of the ambusher. Ambush strategies can be effective. In terms of the recall and recognition of consumers, non-sponsors can often be perceived as genuine and official sponsors, and they may even become more memorable than the official sponsors because they have employed particularly unusual devices and tactics for stealing the attention of consumers.

> *Chapter Principle 10.9*: Ambush marketing refers to a strategy where a company (other than an official sponsor, and often a competitor to the official sponsor) creates the impression that it is associated with the sport property. This is achieved by attracting attention and by giving the false impression of a relationship with the sport property.

There are many ways in which ambush marketing can be undertaken. The most obvious is by the illegal use of official logos or merchandise, or by making false claims about being an official sponsor. Because there are clear laws in most countries that prohibit this kind of behaviour, legal action can be undertaken in response to it. However, some aggressive companies continue to mount ambushing campaigns in ways that may not cause a clear-cut breech in law, and even in ways that may be completely legal. Meenaghan (1996) has shown that there are five main ambush marketing strategies that companies may legally use, often with several approaches used at the same time. The five include the ambushing of advertising, broadcast, sub-categories, athletes or promotions. Each is described in detail in the following sub-sections.

Advertising ambush: buying advertising time around an event

An advertising ambush can occur when a non-official sponsor implements an advertising campaign that coincides with the sport event. This could simply involve buying normal advertising time and space, and the ambusher may argue that it is well within its rights to promote its brand by purchasing legitimate airtime during sporting events. However, the official sponsor is more likely to believe that it has been ambushed. More aggressive advertising ambushes can even imply that there is a link between the ambusher and the event.

An advertising ambush can use any of forms of advertising that have been detailed in Chapter 9. For example, television commercials, magazine and newspaper advertisements, radio spots, posters, billboards, Internet pop-ups, and advertisements on buses and bus stops. Virtual billboards at sporting events offer another avenue through which companies can attempt to ambush. In the 1996 Atlanta Olympics, Nike 'ambushed' Reebok's official sponsorship of the event by covering many of the city's billboards with the 'Swoosh' symbol. This was a way of linking Nike brand awareness with the Olympic event at a low cost, especially when compared with the cost of sponsorship. In another example, Nike bought a large amount of television advertising time during the 1998 Soccer World Cup, which was officially sponsored by adidas. It used the advertisements to promote its sponsorship of the Brazilian team, and reportedly achieved awareness ratings rivalling adidas.

220

Broadcast ambush: sponsoring the broadcast of an event

By sponsoring the broadcast of a sport event, a company can create the impression that it is associated with the sport property. It has, in fact, paid for the right to be associated with the broadcast itself, but the awareness that this generates can spill over onto the sport event as well. Interestingly, a broadcast sponsor has the opportunity to associate itself with the sport to a much larger television audience than the event sponsor, who may only be reaching those people in attendance.

The practice of ambush marketing actually became prominent through a campaign by Kodak, which used a broadcasting ambush strategy as well as a sub-category ambush (discussed in the next sub-section). This occurred during the 1984 Los Angeles Olympic Games, which were officially sponsored by Fujifilm. Kodak became the sponsor of the Olympic broadcast as well as the 'official film' of the US track-and-field team. This created confusion in the minds of many consumers, who believed that Kodak was the official sponsor of the whole event.

Sub-category ambush: sponsoring a sub-category of a sport event

It is common for sport events to offer different categories of sponsorship. In addition to an overall sponsorship of the event, they may also offer sponsorships of smaller categories in the event. An ambusher can invest less money by sponsoring a small element of the event, and then aggressively promote its association. This can even convince the public that the sub-category sponsor is actually a major event sponsor. As noted earlier, the key to success in this form of ambushing is effective sponsorship leveraging. With this tactic, the best approach is to invest only small amounts in the sponsorship itself, and support it with substantial investments in leveraging, giving the impression of a major event sponsorship. When this approach works, it is far less expensive than paying for a major sponsorship.

Athlete ambush: sponsoring an athlete or team

Sponsors may also support an individual athlete or a team who is usually allowed to seek own endorsements. For example, at the 1996 Atlanta Olympics, Nike gained major visibility by sponsoring Michael Johnson, who wore distinctive Nike gold shoes as he won the 200- and 400-metre races (footage that was replayed over and over again), even though Reebok was the major sponsor of the Games.

Promotions ambush: using non-sponsorship promotion

An ambushing company can also use non-sponsorship promotional strategies that coincide with a sport event to create an association. For example, at the

221

2003 Rugby World Cup in Australia, Vodafone as the sponsor of one of the competing teams handed out branded hooters and flags during games, and placed large blow-up Vodafone dolls outside the stadium. Other strategies can include giving away branded T-shirts or temporary tattoos for spectators to wear, which will be seen on the television broadcast. There are limitless examples of promotional ambush strategies, so the list could go on: conducting competitions, giving away official merchandise as prizes without permission, unauthorised websites, live screenings, mobile phone content, unofficial corporate hospitality, unofficial merchandise, unauthorised publications, virtual advertising, advertisements that wish athletes good fortune or congratulate them and promotions that show famous sporting landmarks in the background.

Chapter Tool 10.5. Ambush Marketing Methods:

1. Buy advertising time during the event (advertising ambush)
2. Sponsor the broadcast of an event, not the event itself (broadcast ambush)
3. Sponsor sub-categories of the event (sub-category ambush)
4. Sponsor a team or athlete (athlete ambush)
5. Use imaginative, non-sponsorship promotions during the event (promotions ambush)

Interactive case

Consider the case of ambush marketing at the Olympic Games. Download and read the article 'Ambush marketing: an Olympic event' by Tripodi and Sutherland (2000).
http://www.premiership.com.au/pdf/Ambush%20Marketing.pdf

Ambush prevention

The idea of ambush marketing probably appears unfair to most people. Whether or not it is illegal, however, often depends on the particular details of the ambushing campaign. Even if an ambushing campaign is clearly illegal, the time and costs of settling a dispute through the courts may be considered excessive, unreasonable and counter-productive. Some commentators have claimed that even when it is not illegal, ambush marketing is an immoral practice, although this is a controversial position. Putting aside the legal and ethical issues of this practice, the fact remains that ambush marketing is a problem for both the official sponsors and the sport property, and it is vitally important to consider what strategies can be implemented to avoid the problem occurring in the first place. Thus, the professional sport marketer must know how to use ambush marketing at some times, and defend against it at others.

It is obvious that ambush marketing has a detrimental impact on official sponsors. It can limit their ability to recoup their investment because it reduces positive impact on consumer awareness and attitudes. Ambush marketing can also negatively affect the sport property itself. This is because it can damage the relationship with the official sponsor, and make it more difficult to secure future sponsorships. It is therefore important to understand when ambush marketing is most likely to occur, and what strategies can be implemented to prevent it. It is generally considered to be more effective to block out ambushers than to instigate legal action because of the significant cost and difficulty in establishing that something illegal has occurred.

There are five major elements of an ambush prevention strategy. The first three of these elements have been outlined by Townley et al. (1998, p. 341), who describe them as the 'holy trinity of commercial rights protection'. In addition to protecting commercial rights, an ambush prevention programme should consider how the design of the sponsorship programme may itself create opportunities for ambushing that could be minimised, and how the official sponsorships can be leveraged to minimise ambushing. The five elements of ambush prevention are: (1) control of intellectual property, (2) control of the event environment and locality, (3) control of the event partners, (4) design of the sponsorship programme and (5) leverage official sponsorships. Each is described next.

Control of intellectual property

The intellectual property relating to a sport event can include names, logos, mascots and merchandise. Controlling the use of these properties is really only possible through legal avenues, such as contracts, copyright law, trademark registration and other specialised legislation. Logos and emblems are usually protected by copyright legislation as an original work of art. It is important with these works to negotiate with the designer to have the copyright transferred to the sport property. Names and logos can be protected legally in a given country if they are registered as a trademark. Different legislation and registration systems operate in different locations, so it can be difficult to track and protect these rights. In the case of large sport properties, such as the Olympics or the World Cup, governments in the hosting country may enact specific legislation to protect logos, names and slogans that are related to the event.

For the sport property, controlling intellectual property means ensuring that trademarks are registered in the relevant region and copyright ownership is clarified in contracts. Usually the sport property will also implement a policy of indicating that a trademark or copyright exists, such as through the use of the letters ™ or © wherever the word or logo appears. It is wise to realise, however, that while copyright, trademark and other legislation may deter ambushers from using a logo or other forms of intellectual property, it does not guarantee that they will not. It may be effective in some cases to use legal teams to put further pressure on ambushers to stop their use of a proprietary logo or name. Although it can be costly and difficult, the sport property may choose to settle the matter in court.

Control of the event environment and locality

To prevent an ambush at a sport event, the organisers need to plan for what is called a 'clean' venue. This means that there is no signage, promotions or advertising appearing within the grounds that promote competitors of the official sponsors. This includes the stadium itself, bars and eating areas, toilets, buildings that are visible to the spectators or television cameras, or even the airspace above the stadium. In practice, this means that there must be teams of workers monitoring the event and removing any ambushing material. The terms and conditions of admission can reserve the right for event organisers to refuse entry or eject patrons if they are seen to be participating in an ambush strategy.

The environment surrounding the event may also be controlled, although the extent to which this can be achieved may depend on the available budget and cooperation of local authorities and media. For example, it may be feasible to prohibit promotions by competitors occurring at the event entry, or in nearby streets. Sport events that make use of a wide geographical area, such as marathons and other long-distance events, can pose significant problems. In an extreme example, the organising committee of the 2004 Athens Olympic Games implemented a clean venue policy where 10 000 billboards were cleared from buildings and rooftops in Athens, while all the remaining billboards were reserved for the strict use of the Games' official sponsors.

Control of the event partners

In addition to the obvious partners of a sport event (athletes, teams, sponsors, suppliers and merchandisers), other partners can include licensed broadcasters, media and local authorities. Some of these partners will have a contract with the sport event (athletes, sponsors, broadcasters, suppliers and merchandisers), which should bind them to comply with anti-ambush strategies. The other parties such as local councils, police, and local media are not necessarily obliged to support the anti-ambush strategies, but efforts should be made to inform and negotiate with them to play a role.

Controlling broadcasters

When a sport event organiser negotiates a contract with an event broadcaster, it is essential for it to consider the protection of its sponsors. For example, broadcasters can be contractually bound to give the event sponsors the first opportunity to purchase broadcasting rights as well as advertising time in and around the event. Broadcasters can also be contractually obligated to give the official event sponsors the right to veto their competitors from becoming broadcast sponsors, programme sponsors and/or buying advertising time during the event. It is common for event organisers to reduce the cost of a broadcast sponsorship in exchange for more control over who the broadcasters subsequently sell advertising time to.

Controlling sponsors, suppliers and merchandisers

Sponsors, suppliers and merchandisers for a sport property or event could deliberately or inadvertently help an ambush to occur. For example, official merchandise could be provided to an ambusher who plans to use the goods as prize give-aways without permission. Similarly, official sponsors could facilitate an ambush by participating in joint promotions with non-sponsors. The contracts that are signed with these parties should therefore prohibit behaviour that may lead to ambushing. For example, sponsors can be prohibited from undertaking joint promotions related to the event, unless the organisation they intend to partner with is also an official sponsor. Sponsors can also be prohibited from sharing their sponsorship rights or from sub-licensing them to another, non-official sponsor. All promotional materials can be subject to prior approval by the event organisers.

The contracts that are signed between the sponsors and sport organisers can give the sponsors certain rights to protect their interests. For example, it can give them the right to approve the promotional material of other licensees and sponsors before it is distributed. Sometimes it can ensure them the first opportunity to advertise in official publications. These rights are often called 'rights of first refusal' because they give the sponsor the first opportunity to be involved, or to refuse if they so wish.

Controlling athletes, teams and sport associations

Ambushing can occur through the sponsorship of a team or athlete. On the one hand this is a legitimate agreement, and the athletes/clubs have the right to seek support and endorsement. However, problems can arise if this sponsorship clashes with the overall sponsorship of an event or property. The ability to control this problem will vary from event to event depending on variables such as the relative bargaining power of the event compared with the athletes/clubs, and the regulations of the event itself. However, there are restrictions that may be considered as part of the contractual agreement. For example, athletes may be restricted from wearing branded clothing or footwear; all promotions related to the event may be subject to the event organiser's approval; participants may be required to use specific products or services (those of a sponsor) at the event; and there may be restrictions on participants filming or documenting events.

Design of the sponsorship programme

The way that a sponsorship programme is designed may have an impact on whether ambush marketing campaigns will occur. This is because ambush marketing is most likely to happen under certain circumstances, as highlighted by Lagae (2005). These situations can include when there is a wide variety of sponsorship categories and many sponsors per category, a high cost of official sponsorship, a strictly limited number of sponsors allowed into the event, or side events that are happening outside the main event. For example, if there is a broad variety of sponsorship categories, and/or there are many sponsors per category, it is harder for consumers to keep track of who the official sponsors are. This 'clutter' can lead to confusion about who is and who is not involved. It becomes easier for ambushers to take advantage of this confusion, and lead sport consumers to believe that they are officially involved in the event. However, it is also possible that the sponsorship agreement has strict exclusivity rules that limit the opportunity for companies to become legitimately involved, potentially leading them to unofficially try to grab some attention.

Leverage official sponsorships

Leveraging official sponsorships means getting the maximum amount of benefit and advantage from the agreement through planning additional and integrated marketing activities. If the official sponsors themselves are not promoting their involvement well enough, this may provide the opportunity for an unofficial sponsor to step in and fill the gap. Sponsors who make the most of their agreement can also minimise the impact of an ambush if it does occur. As outlined in the earlier section on leveraging sponsorships, sponsors and sport properties may use other elements of the promotions mix to complement and boost the sponsorship, as well as use the other elements of the marketing mix.

> *Chapter Tool 10.6. Sport Sponsorship Evaluation*: There are five major elements of an ambush prevention strategy: (1) control of intellectual property, (2) control of the event environment and locality, (3) control of the event partners, (4) design of the sponsorship programme and (5) leverage official sponsorships.

Interactive case

Log on to the Beijing Olympics website and read the 'Beijing 2008 Olympic Marketing Plan Overview'.
http://en.beijing2008.cn/bocog/sponsors/n214077622.shtml

Case Study—Sponsorship and the *Tour de France*

By Sharyn McDonald

The *Tour de France* was first raced in 1903. Prior to television's inception, the *Tour de France* provided a commercial marriage between bicycle manufacturers sponsoring the cyclists and print journalists covering the event. The Tour first appeared on television in 1948, and by 1960

footage taken from motorcycles and helicopters was being broadcast. There were 50 million television viewers in 1973, and by 2006 the *Tour de France* had become one of the world's most publicised sporting events with 150 million television viewers in 170 countries.

Sponsorship of the Tour began to change after 1929 because corporate supporters began to finance teams and provide prize money. International sponsors responded to the growth of media coverage and the Tour became an attractive and lucrative opportunity for promoting brand awareness and recognition. In 1995, Tour sponsors, Coca-Cola and Nike, were ranked first and fifth in a consumer poll that recognised French sport sponsorship. This level of exposure has attracted some of the world's leading companies to invest in teams. Today, there are between 20–22 teams bearing their primary sponsor as a team name, with approximately nine riders per team.

Former world number one cyclist Lance Armstrong helped increase the popularity of the *Tour de France* in the United States. Riding for the Discovery Channel Pro Cycling Team, Armstrong won the Tour an unprecedented seven times. However, his retirement has had a negative impact on viewing figures in the United States. Nevertheless, several US based sponsors remain reliant on the Tour's international exposure.

The danger of such a well-publicised event is the potential for unfavourable brand associations from scandals. Sponsors of the *Tour de France* have been faced with alleged doping incidents leading to doubts over future sponsorships. Dutch financial company, Rabobank, Swiss bike manufacturer, BMC, and German truck company, MAN, made news headlines when they publicly considered dropping out as team sponsors in the wake of the doping scandals revealed in the 2007 Tour. German broadcasters, ARD and ZDF, responded to the drug scandal by ceasing coverage part way through the Tour.

The *Tour de France* has overcome difficulties in the past. During the 1940s and 1950s, the race experienced financial problems, which prompted organisers to seek new sponsors. The first drug speculation was reported as early as 1924, and the popularity of the event has continually increased despite alleged cover-ups. Scandals, declining attendance and the possible withdrawal of financial support threaten the future of the *Tour de France*. The competitive nature of sport sponsorship suggests that corporations may invest elsewhere if the negative publicity does not subside.

For more information see:

(2003). Chronology of the Tour 1902–2003, *International Journal of the History of Sport,* 20(2): 267–273.

Mignon, P. (2003). The Tour de France and the doping issue, *International Journal of the History of Sport,* 20(2): 227–245.

Reed, E. (2003). The economics of the tour, 1930–2003, *International Journal of the History of Sport,* 20(2): 103–127.

Skidmore, S. (2007). U.S. Sponsors of Tour de France Hang On. *Associated Press.*

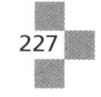

SportBusiness.com (2007). *Another Sponsor Considers Tour Future*. Available at:
http://www.sportbusiness.com/news

SportBusiness.com (2007). *German Commercial Channel Swoops for Tour de France Rights*. Available at:
http://www.sportbusiness.com/news

Steephill.tv. (2007). *Tour de France 2007 Live Dashboard*. Available at:
http://www.steephill.tv/2007/tour-de-france/

Principles summary

- Chapter Principle 10.1: The term sport property refers to the recipient of the sponsorship. This could be an athlete, team, event, venue, association, cause or competition.
- Chapter Principle 10.2: Sport sponsorship is a business agreement where one organisation provides financial or in-kind assistance to a sport property in exchange for the right to associate itself with the sport property. The sponsor does this in order to achieve corporate objectives (such as enhancing corporate image) or marketing objectives (such as increasing brand awareness).
- Chapter Principle 10.3: Sport sponsorship generates goodwill among consumers. The amount of goodwill generated can vary depending on the kind of sport property being sponsored, the degree of involvement that consumers have with the sport property, the time at which the sponsor becomes involved, and when and how the sponsor ceases the sponsorship.
- Chapter Principle 10.4: Fan involvement is an important consideration in sponsorship because a consumer's response to a sponsorship is driven by the level of involvement that he/she has with the sport property.
- Chapter Principle 10.5: The objectives of sponsorship can vary greatly, depending on the size of the partners, the type of sponsorship and the type of sport property being supported. Some common objectives for the sponsor are to enhance sales, to promote the public image of its brand, to increase consumer awareness, to modify its brand image and to build business relationships.
- Chapter Principle 10.6: The objectives of sponsorship for the sport property will vary. In addition to attracting financial support, objectives include increasing credibility, increasing awareness, and managing brand image.
- Chapter Principle 10.7: Sponsorship affinity refers to whether there is a good fit or match between the sponsor and the sport property. Two factors are particularly important for ensuring a good match: (1) an overlap of target markets and (2) a match up of brand positioning strategies.
- Chapter Principle 10.8: To be able to demonstrate that sponsorship has a positive outcome for corporations is the best way to legitimise it as a marketing technique, and to attract and retain sponsors.

- Chapter Principle 10.9: Ambush marketing refers to a strategy where a company (other than an official sponsor, and often a competitor to the official sponsor) creates the impression that it is associated with the sport property. This is achieved by attracting attention and by giving the false impression of a relationship with the sport property.

Tools summary

Chapter Tool 10.1. Sponsorship Proposal
Chapter Tool 10.2. Sport Sponsorship Rights
Chapter Tool 10.3. Sponsorship Leveraging
Chapter Tool 10.4. Sport Sponsorship Evaluation
Chapter Tool 10.5. Ambush Marketing Methods
Chapter Tool 10.6. Sport Sponsorship Evaluation

Review questions

1. Identify all kinds of sport properties that can be sponsored.
2. What are the major reasons sport properties and sponsors decide to enter sponsorship agreements?
3. What are the variables that affect consumer goodwill about a sponsorship?
4. Provide a good example of a sponsor and sport property relationship that enjoys a high level of affinity.
5. Describe the process of sponsorship evaluation.
6. Explain why sponsorship leveraging is so pivotal to successful associations.
7. Outline the legal approaches to employing ambush marketing in sponsorship.

Relevant websites

http://www.shell.com	(Shell)
http://www.ducati.com	(Ducati)
http://www.premiership.com.au	[Premiership International Services (consultants)]
http://en.beijing2008.cn	(2008 Beijing Olympic Committee)
http://www.sailmelbourne.com.au	(Asia Pacific Regatta)
http://www.gutennis.co.uk	(Glasgow University Tennis Club)

229

http://www.rockrugby.ca	(Newfoundland and Labrador Rugby Union)
http://www.sabungee.co.za	(South Africa Bungee Extreme Adventure Sports)
http://www.konatournaments.com	(The Maui Jim Hawaii Marlin Tournament Series)
http://www.cdtriclub.org	(Capital District Triathlon Club of New York State)

Further reading

Amis, J. & Cornwell, T.B. (2005). *Global Sport Sponsorship*, Berg, Oxford.

Crompton, J.L. (2004). Sponsorship ambushing in sport, *Managing Leisure*, 9: 1–12.

Payne, M. (1998). Ambush marketing: the undeserved advantage, *Psychology and Marketing*, 15(4): 323–331.

Ségiun, B., Teed, K. & O'Reilly, N.J. (2005). National sports organisation and sponsorship: an identification of best practices, *International Journal of Sport Management and Marketing*, 1(1/2): 69–91.

Speed, R. & Thompson, P. (2000). Determinants of sports sponsorship response, *Journal of the Academy of Marketing Science*, 28(2): 226–238.

References

Cliffe, S.J. & Motion, J. (2005). Building contemporary brands: a sponsorship-based strategy, *Journal of Business Research*, 58: 1068–1077.

Lagae, W. (2005). *Sport Sponsorship and Marketing Communications: A European Perspective*, Prentice Hall, Essex.

Meenaghan, T. (1996). Ambush marketing: a threat to corporate sponsorship, *Sloan Management Review*, 38(1): 103–113.

Meenaghan, T. (2001). Understanding sponsorship effects, *Psychology and Marketing*, 18(2): 95–122.

Townley, S., Harrington, D. & Couchman, N. (1998). The legal and practical prevention of ambush marketing in sports, *Psychology and Marketing*, 15(4): 333–348.

Tripodi, J.A. & Sutherland, M. (2000). Ambush marketing: an Olympic event, *Journal of Brand Management*, 7(6): 412–422.

11   Sport services

Overview

This chapter introduces sport services marketing. It highlights the principles and tools instrumental in delivering quality service and in establishing customer satisfaction. The chapter also explains the importance of developing strong relationships with sport fans and customers. In addition, the services marketing mix is outlined, which emphasises the significance of participants, physical evidence and processes.

By the end of this chapter, readers should be able to:

- Define the term services marketing.
- Outline the differences between sport goods and services.
- Identify the three elements of the services marketing mix.
- Discuss the key variables of quality service.
- Explain the difference between outcome and process quality.
- Discuss approaches for measuring service quality.
- Define the term customer satisfaction.
- Explain the concept of delighting the customer and the situations in which it is a useful sport marketing strategy.
- Outline the six-step process of customer relationship marketing.

Sport services

This text has introduced the four traditional elements of the sport marketing mix: product, price, place and promotion as well as sponsorship as an extension of promotion. To these, services is now added as an extension to the product. The chapter begins with a review of the characteristics of sport services before starting to explain the sport services mix, services quality, customer satisfaction and relationship marketing. Figure 11.1 shows the elements of sport services within the Sport Marketing Framework.

Defining a sport service

Although sport is regularly packaged into tangible goods such as merchandise or sport equipment, most sport is actually experienced as a service. It may be useful at this point to review the differences between sport goods and services. Chapter 6 presented four ways in which sport goods and services can be differentiated: tangibility, consistency, perishability and separability. Each is explained in more detail next.

Tangibility

When a sport product is tangible, it is a physical thing that can be touched, seen, felt and sometimes even smelt. Sport goods are tangible because they are physical, and are often objects that can be taken away like a DVD or a scarf. Sport services are intangible because they cannot be seen or touched. They do not exist beyond the memory of their experience. Sport services are like a performance, where a sport organisation or athlete does something (performs) to give a consumer an experience. Sport consumers do not actually own the service, and cannot take it home to keep; they just experience it for a certain amount of time.

In fact, most sport goods and services are a mixture of tangible and intangible elements. This is because many physical sport products have a service or an idea element. The most obvious example is that a sport good is bought by a consumer because of the benefits they will receive from it, and benefits are, of course, intangible in nature. In addition, many sport services are sold together with something tangible. For example, a membership to a football club may come with a package including club stickers, badges and regular newsletters. In many instances, sport consumers purchase a mixture of goods, services, benefits and ideas.

Consistency

232

Consistency is a second way in which sport goods and services can be separated. Consistency refers to the uniformity of quality from one time that a

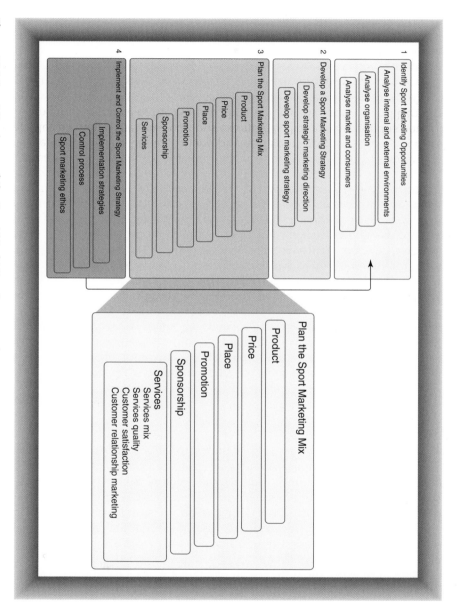

Figure 11.1 Sport Services and the Sport Marketing Framework.

sport product or service is delivered to the next. Sporting goods usually have a high degree of consistency. For example, there is not much change in the quality of one sporting shoe compared with another of the same brand and style from one purchase to the next. And, there is no difference at all between two DVDs with the same sport content. On the other hand, sport services usually have far more variable quality. The quality of a sport experience may change depending on a range of factors including who is providing the service as well as the special conditions of its offering (e.g. weather), and the variable performance of athletes and teams. Many sport services come in the form of a sporting competition or infrastructure in which individuals participate. For sport participants, the organisational service they experience could be inconsistent from week to week. For example, the quality of refereeing, pitch or court, changing rooms, weather and innumerable other variables will affect their experience of sport service consistency, including the personal athletic performance of participants.

Perishability

Perishability refers to whether a sport product or service can be stored and used at another time. Sporting goods (like clothing and equipment) tend not to be perishable, although there are exceptions like nutritional supplements that have a specific life span. Basketballs, cricket bats and bicycles can be stored if they are not bought by a consumer without any fear that it will damage the product. Sport services cannot be stored. For example, there is no way to store any unsold tickets to a sport match in order to sell them at another time. Once the game has been played, any seats that were not filled are lost forever. Similarly, if only five customers have arrived for an aerobics class in a leisure facility at a given time, the vacant positions represent unsold potential that can never be reclaimed. Of course, as observed in Chapter 6, many sport services are combined with sport products to make up for the perishability of sport services. An example is a DVD recording of a game.

Separability

Separability is a term that is used to describe whether a sport product or service is manufactured or produced at the same time as it is consumed. Sporting goods are manufactured well before they are used. For example, a hockey stick is made, delivered to a wholesaler and/or retailer, placed on the shelf and bought by a consumer at some point typically months or years after the initial production. Another way of looking at this is that the quality of the good (the hockey stick) is separated from the quality of service at the sport store where it is bought. It is possible to separate the item from the person selling it, although sometimes one can affect the other. Sport services are made and consumed at the same time. At a live sport event, the competition is created at the same time as it is consumed by fans.

Chapter Principle 11.1: There are four characteristics which illustrate the difference between sport goods and services: tangibility, consistency, perishability and separability. Sport services are intangible because they exist only as an experience. Sport services tend to be inconsistent because they are affected by variables that are difficult to control. Sport services are perishable because they can only be offered and experienced once at any point in time. Sport services are inseparable because they are consumed at the same time as they are produced.

Services mix

The special nature of sport services (when compared with sport goods) means that the marketing of services can be quite different to the marketing of goods. This has led some commentators to argue that there is a need to augment the conventional sport marketing mix, which was originally devised with goods in mind. Although many supplementary ideas have been suggested to help marketers work directly with services, one approach introduced by Booms & Bitner (1981) has become popular, which involves the use of three additional 'Ps': participants (staff and customers), physical evidence (tangible elements of the service) and processes (the system of service delivery). These additional 'Ps' are not just the concern of sport marketers, but are also under the influence of administration and human resources staff, therefore demanding an integrated approach from everyone in a sport organisation. In this respect, the three service mix 'Ps' should not be seen as equivalent to the four conventional marketing 'Ps' that are described in Chapters 6–9. Nevertheless, they do provide some useful clues to the marketing of sport services. The three Ps of the sport services mix are described next.

Participants

Because a sport service is consumed at the same time as it is produced, both staff and other consumers can influence perceptions of service quality. This is particularly true for 'high contact' services like fitness centres and sporting competitions. In fact, the 'staff' in these examples is actually part of the service. For example, a sport masseur is part of the massage service, just as athletes are part of a sporting match. The quality and management of employees (and athletes) is therefore an important part of sport services marketing. Furthermore, in sport events other consumers are especially important elements to the service as they have a powerful impact on atmosphere. This means that for sport organisations, the ways in which they allow consumers to interact with one another is a fundamental consideration of the service structure.

Physical evidence

The physical evidence of a sport service includes the environment in which it is delivered, and any other visual or tangible elements. For example, the physical environment of a tennis competition includes the stadium, the food and beverage facilities, the seating and the scoreboard. Other tangible elements could include the design of tickets, programmes and merchandise. Not only are these characteristics important components of the service, they are significant because consumers use physical evidence as clues to the service quality. In fact, the more intangible a service, the more important it is to include physical elements to reinforce service quality.

Processes

Processes in sport services marketing refer to the steps that a consumer progresses through to receive a service, as well as those in which a service provider has to perform to deliver the sport service. For example, to attend a rugby match, a sport fan may have to queue for a ticket, travel on public transport, wait again in queues to enter the ground, submit to a security screening, find the right seat, locate some food and beverages and eventually exit. It is therefore important that consumers are educated to understand and anticipate what processes they have to experience to receive a service. It is also important for these processes to be conducted in an appropriate way so that they do not take away from customers' perceptions of the quality of the service.

> *Chapter Principle 11.2*: The sport services mix is made up of participants, physical evidence and processes. Participants are those people involved in delivering and receiving a sport service. Physical evidence is the tangible or visual elements of a service such as a sport stadium. Processes represent the steps involved in delivering a sport service.

An approach to sport services marketing

Although the three services mix elements were originally developed for services marketing, they are relevant to the marketing of sport services as well. Chapter 6 showed that most sport products contain intangible elements, and that most sport services include tangible elements. This means that almost all sport marketing involves making decisions about both product and service elements. For example, although sport equipment, memorabilia and merchandise are tangible products, they are sold to consumers through service outlets which can have an influence over consumer perceptions of the product. This fact can be troublesome for manufacturers who do not have control over the sales-related service of their goods.

In addition, it is obvious that the three elements of the services mix interact in ways that make their independent management difficult. For example, those who deliver a sport service are constrained by the physical environment (evidence) that houses their services and by the processes they employ. As a result, it is difficult to develop tactics for the services mix (participants, physical evidence and processes) in a sport marketing plan in the same way as it is done for product, price, place and promotions (and sponsorship as a major part of promotions). In fact, sport services are really just a prominent part of a sport product strategy, and should therefore remain consistent with overarching product strategy. The challenge for sport marketers is to determine where to invest their limited resources to create the best service outcomes for consumers.

One way to approach this challenge is for sport marketers to decide *what* is to be done across the services mix that will lead to a better *quality* of service, stronger *relationships* with consumers and higher levels of their *satisfaction*. The remainder of this chapter explains how service quality, customer relationship building and customer satisfaction are the critical success areas behind the successful marketing of sport services.

> *Chapter Principle 11.3*: There are three key principles behind the successful marketing of sport services: service quality, customer relationship building and customer satisfaction.

Service quality

Chapter 6 indicated that product quality is one of the central factors influencing the development of brand equity (brand equity is the added value that a product has because of its brand name). This is also true for service quality. Consumers are more likely to be loyal to a service (leading to greater brand equity) if they perceive that it is of high quality.

> *Chapter Principle 11.4*: Sport consumers are more likely to be loyal to a service if they perceive it to be of high quality.

Because of the relative characteristics of sport goods and services, there are different aspects to their quality management. Chapter 6 introduced the elements of product quality, noting that they can be measured relatively easily in terms of whether the product conforms to specifications, how long it lasts and how quickly it is fixed when there are problems. Service quality, on the other hand, is more complex to define because it involves the assessment of an individual consumer's experience.

Service quality can be seen as a consumer's general judgement about the value, superiority or excellence of a service. However, it is difficult to measure this judgement because each consumer will have a unique idea about what a value, excellent or superior service involves. For example, one consumer might believe that the key quality feature of a service is staff courtesy, whereas another might think it more important that the service is delivered on time. To get around this problem, a useful way to understand service quality is to consider it the degree to which a service meets the needs and expectations of consumers. When a consumer's expectations are not met, they are likely to perceive that the service quality is low. When a consumer's expectations are met or exceeded, they are likely to perceive that the service quality is high. There are some obvious connections between service quality and customer satisfaction which are explored later in this chapter.

> *Chapter Principle 11.5*: Service quality can be seen as the degree to which a service meets the needs and expectations of consumers.

The important next question is what kinds of expectations consumers might demand from a service. There are five quality elements that are commonly used to describe expectations of service quality. These five areas were originally developed by Parasuraman et al. (1988). They are reliability, assurance, empathy, responsiveness and tangibles. Each is briefly described in Table 11.1.

> *Chapter Principle 11.6*: There are five areas that are commonly used to describe expectations of service quality. These five areas are reliability, assurance, empathy, responsiveness and tangibles.

Outcome and process quality

When service quality is defined in terms of customer expectations it means that quality is determined by customers, not sport organisations. It is whether the service conforms to customers' specifications rather than those of the sport organisation, which will determine if service quality exists. Customers will make a judgement about whether a service is meeting their expectations at two points in time: first, they will evaluate what the service delivered after it has been consumed (outcome quality); and, second, they will evaluate how the service is delivered during consumption (process quality). A customer's judgement about service quality does not therefore rely just on the outcome of a service, but also on judgements about how a service is delivered. In some instances it may be difficult for customers to judge the outcome quality of a service. For example, assessing the immediate results of a fitness or health consultation with a personal trainer or a sports medicine practitioner would be impossible without specific knowledge. As a result, when customers have difficulties interpreting outcome quality, they tend to rely on how the service was delivered (process quality) to make their judgements.

> *Chapter Principle 11.7*: Customers will make a judgement about whether a service is meeting their expectations at two points in time: first, they will evaluate what the service delivered after it has been consumed (outcome quality); and, second, they will evaluate how the service is delivered during consumption (process quality).

Table 11.1 Five Elements of Sport Service Quality

Quality element	Explanation	Examples
Reliability	The ability to provide a service in a consistent and dependable way. Whether customer expectations of the service will be met every time	Is the service performed right the first time? If a service is promised within a certain time, is it delivered? Is the service the same quality regardless of the time of day or staff member who delivers it? Are reports or statements free of errors?
Responsiveness	The willingness to help customers, and to provide them with the service on time	Does the sport organisation respond to problems quickly? Are employees willing to answer customer questions? Are times for delivery/completion of service given to the customer?
Assurance	The level of confidence and trust that a customer holds in the service	Do employees appear to know what they are doing? Are employees able to use equipment and technology skilfully and quickly? Are the materials provided up-to-date?
Empathy	The ability to get to know customers and their needs, and to deliver a personalised service	Do employees try to get to know the needs of the customer? Is the organisation flexible enough to accommodate the customer's schedule? Do employees recognise regular clients and address them by name?
Tangibles	Physical features of the service (e.g. information booklets, equipment, appearance of staff, facilities, sport venue)	Are the facilities attractive? Does the equipment look modern? Are employees dressed appropriately? Are written documents attractive and easy to understand?

Having introduced the five elements of service quality, as well as the ideas of outcome and process quality, it is now relevant to explore the relationships between them. Process quality (how a service is delivered) is strongly connected to the service quality elements of 'empathy', 'assurance' and 'responsiveness', as they describe how the service is delivered to the customer. For example, whether employees are willing to answer questions (responsiveness), whether they recognise customers (empathy) and whether they appear to use equipment quickly and skilfully (assurance) are features of how the service is being delivered to the customer.

The service quality elements of 'tangibles' and 'reliability' are more strongly related to outcome quality. The physical quality of facilities, equipment,

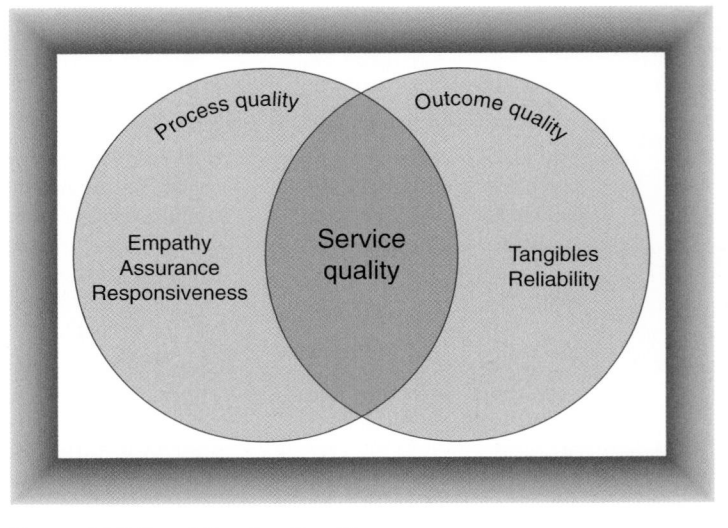

Figure 11.2 Sport Service Quality.

documents and staff appearance (tangibles) is not primarily associated with how a service is delivered, but is part of what is delivered. Furthermore, customers will usually make judgements about how reliable a service is (reliability) after it has been delivered (such as whether a service is performed right the first time, on time, regardless of who is delivering it). This relationship between the five elements of service quality, process quality and outcome quality is shown in Figure 11.2.

> *Chapter Principle 11.8*: The service quality elements of empathy, assurance and responsiveness are particularly important to customers' evaluations of process quality. Tangibles and reliability are particularly important to customers' evaluations of outcome quality.

Measuring service quality

While it is clearly important to understand how customers think about service quality, it is even more useful to be able to measure customers' perceptions of service quality. There are numerous survey instruments which have been developed for organisations to use to measure how their customers respond to the elements of service quality. One of the most well-known is called SERVQUAL, which was developed by Parasuraman et al. (1988, 1991). This survey instrument is designed to determine if there is a difference (or a gap) between what customers expect of a service and what they believe they actually receive. The survey collects data which can provide a measurement of the gap between expectations and perceptions. Naturally, such a measure is advantageous because it can be calculated again at a later date to see if any improvements have been made. There is also an adaptation of SERVQUAL (called TEAMQUAL) that was developed for use in professional team sport settings by McDonald et al. (1995).

Interactive case

Log on to the following site where some sample questions from SERVQUAL are listed.
http://www.businessadvantage.ndirect.co.uk/SERVQUAL.htm
A full list of SERQUAL questions can be found in the original article by the survey authors Parasuraman et al. (1988).

After reading the SERVQUAL questions it should be obvious that the survey covers a wide range of service quality areas. These may be considered the *core* areas of service quality for any industry or organisation. Customers, however, may also have specific expectations about certain industries or organisations. For example, clients at a boxing gym may not be interested in 'modern' looking equipment, but desire and expect 'back-to-basics' facilities that come with the stench of sweat. For this reason it is important to also understand the unique expectations that customers have through careful market research.

Identifying gaps in service quality

As noted earlier, the SERVQUAL survey instrument helps to identify if there is a gap (a difference) between what customers expect from a service, and what they report they receive. Research has identified that there are four kinds of common gaps which affect customers' perceptions of quality (Parasuraman et al., 1985). Collectively, these 'gaps' represent a powerful tool for sport marketers to employ when considering service quality. Gaps do not necessarily need to be assessed through quantitative surveys. Sport marketers can gain insight into the aspects of their services that need to be considered simply by understanding that there are four kinds of gaps between expectations and service delivery.

The idea of 'gaps' shows sport marketers that there are some practical things that can be done to improve service quality. First, they can try to find out what their customers actually expect from the service, rather than rely on what they assume customers want (this addresses gap 1). Second, they can make sure that what the customers expect is provided for in the service 'specifications', such as the features of the service and the way it is delivered (addressing gap 2). Third, sport marketers can monitor whether these service specifications are followed through in the actual delivery of the service by staff (addressing gap 3). Finally, sport marketers can make sure that the

241

service delivery claims are accurate when they are promoting them (addressing gap 4).

Chapter Tool 11.1. Service Quality Gaps:

Gap 1   When there is a difference between what a customer expects, and what the service provider thinks that the customer expects.

Gap 2   When there is a difference between what the service provider thinks that the customer expects and the actual service specifications.

Gap 3   When there is a difference between the specifications of the service, and the actual service that is delivered.

Gap 4   When there is a difference between what the service provider says they are going to deliver, and what is actually delivered.

Building relationships with sport consumers

The idea of relationship marketing was first discussed in the 1980s and 1990s. Definitions of relationship marketing typically include statements about attracting, maintaining and improving customer relationships. The word relationship is used because of the fact that two parties are involved (most obviously a supplier and a customer) who interact with one another. Relationship marketing recognises the importance of keeping current customers, as well as attracting new ones, and emphasises that the relationship with customers needs to be managed well to encourage loyalty. It also recognises that organisations rely on networks, and interaction between many different people, not just consumers, to deliver a service and/or product. For example, relationships between suppliers and market intermediaries are also important.

A useful definition of relationship marketing was provided by Harker (1999). He suggested that relationship marketing occurs when an organisation engages in proactively creating, developing and maintaining committed, interactive and profitable exchanges with selected customers (partners) over time. This definition indicates that relationship marketing is concerned with seven components: (1) the creation of a relationship, or the initial attraction; (2) the development or enhancement of that relationship; (3) the maintenance or preservation of that relationship; (4) the interaction between two parties who cooperate and exchange things; (5) the potential for lasting, long-term relationships; (6) the emotional elements of these relationships, such as commitment and trust; and (7) the potential for these relationships to be profitable and rewarding for both parties.

> *Chapter Principle 11.9*: Relationship marketing involves creating, developing and maintaining a connection between sport organisations and sport consumers that leads to interactive, rewarding and long-term exchanges. Relationship marketing recognises the importance of keeping current customers, as well as attracting new ones, and highlights that the relationship with customers needs to be managed well to encourage loyalty.

Relationship marketing focuses on the one-to-one relationships between parties, often the buyer and seller, or sport fan and sport organisation. It is also concerned with the quality and long-term potential of this connection, and the fact that both parties can derive a benefit from it. The idea of relationship marketing has more recently been instrumental in the development of customer relationship management (CRM).

Customer relationship management

Relationship marketing has made way for the concept of CRM. CRM involves using information technology to better manage customer relationships. More specifically, it involves using information technology to collect information about sport consumers to keep track of their consumption activities, and to create long-term relationships with them.

> *Chapter Principle 11.10*: CRM involves the use of information technology to create and maintain ongoing, long-term relationships with sport consumers, leading to high levels of loyalty, and improved sales.

Like relationship marketing, the aim of CRM is to create stronger connections between sport consumers and sport organisations. It involves acquiring relevant information about current and potential sport customers, such as their buying patterns, preferences, consumption habits, motivations and purchasing triggers. Much of this information can be collected at the point of sale and is later used to stimulate communication with customers.

Shopping on Amazon provides a simple example. If a consumer were to search for this text, the Amazon CRM software will subsequently suggest that other consumers who bought this book also purchased others, which are listed, and will likely be associated with sport or marketing in some way. This example shows that CRM involves communicating with consumers on a one-to-one basis, in a way that is quite different to mass marketing. It helps an organisation to anticipate the behaviour of their consumers to improve sales and customer loyalty. In a sport context, most professional clubs and teams

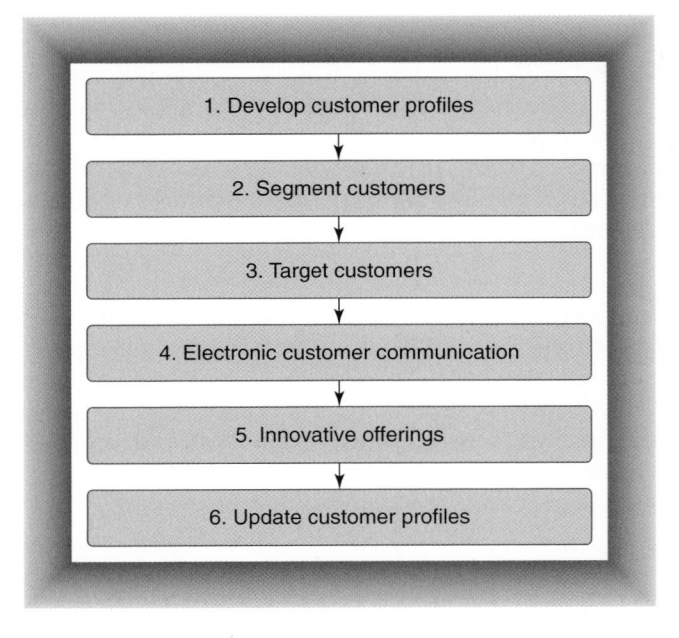

Figure 11.3 Six-Step Process of CRM.

use CRM systems to enhance their contact with customers. A standard CRM system can be used to collect data relevant to creating new opportunities for contact with consumers. For example, the software can generate an automatic e-mail message to the parents of a junior member of a club a few weeks before their birthday. The message might offer to sell the latest club merchandise at a 'birthday' discount. In general, the software is capable of analysing thousands of sales, looking for patterns that might help sport marketers to anticipate the needs of their customers. Among the most helpful information, the software can provide guidance on customer preferences, which customers purchase the most, patterns in demand at different times of the year and which products are the most successful.

Agrawal (2003) suggests that CRM involves a six-step process that has been adapted to form the steps identified in Figure 11.3. It should be observed that the process has similarities to the overall sport marketing framework that guides this text because it involves the basic processes of collecting information, segmenting consumers, and developing and implementing a strategy.

Develop customer profiles

Sport organisations gather a wide range of data for CRM including the buying patterns, preferences, shopping habits, motivations and purchasing triggers for both current and potential customers. Typically, such information is collected at the point of sale and is added to a consumer history 'file', which gives a picture of needs, values and behavioural patterns over time. It is also important to collect sales revenue information so that it can be linked with customer histories. This way it is possible to link specific customer profiles to specific consumption behaviour. It is also possible to keep track of what follow-up and support is requested by a customer after their purchase, as this can help sport marketers to more accurately calculate what it has cost to make the sale to that customer.

Segment customers

CRM software provides additional information that can be used in segmentation. This information can lead to sophisticated patterns of consumption that can provide the basis for specific segmentation categories. For example, consumers can be segmented according to their attendances, merchandise purchases, social club activities or even their online presence. Sport marketers can employ CRM data to help them make decisions about the most appropriate deployment of their marketing resources.

Target customers

Targeting customers involves choosing which sport consumers are going to be the focus of marketing efforts. With CRM, this process includes making a number of estimations about the sport organisation's relationship with the customer such as (1) the likely costs of delivering the sport product or service to that customer, (2) the likely revenue that will be generated through their purchases and (3) the likely value of that customer to the sport organisation over the lifetime of the relationship (this is called customer lifetime value, CLV).

Electronic customer communication

The basic vehicle of CRM is information technology, which of course develops with technological progress. Currently, CRM mainly makes use of database software, websites, mobile or cellular phones and call centres to get messages to consumers. For example, sport consumers may receive messages on their mobile (cellular) phones offering them live sport, scores, replays, tickets or discounted merchandise. However, the technology being employed by sport marketers to communicate with consumers is changing all the time. So important is the application of 'new' media that Chapter 12 is dedicated to it.

Innovative offerings

The key to this step is that sport consumers should be offered opportunities based on their demonstrated needs and buying habits. If the information collected in step one about customer preferences and habits is accurate, it should provide a guide as to what to offer customers next.

Update customer profile

Throughout the process of offering sport customers new products and services, it is important to continue to keep track of how they respond. Over time sport marketers can learn more about consumer habits and preferences, and any changes that occur can lead to an appropriate response.

Chapter Tool 11.2. Customer Relationship Marketing Process:
The six-step process of CRM is briefly as follows:

1. *Develop Customer Profiles*: Information could include buying patterns, preferences, shopping habits, motivations for both current and potential customers, and revenue information. This gives a picture of customer needs, values and behavioural patterns over time.
2. *Segment Customers*: Segmentation is usually based on buying habits, shopping patterns, preferences etc.
3. *Target Customers*: Choose which customers are going to be the focus of marketing efforts. This usually involves estimating (1) the likely costs of delivering the sport product or service to those customers, (2) the likely revenue that will be generated through customer purchases and (3) the likely value of those customers to the sport organisation over the lifetime of the relationship.
4. *Electronic Customer Communication*: CRM uses information technology such as database software, websites, mobile and cellular phones, and call centres to get messages to customers.
5. *Innovative Offerings*: Sport customers should be offered opportunities based on their demonstrated needs and buying habits.
6. *Update Customer Profiles*: Keep track of customer responses, and learn more about their habits and preferences over time.

Customer satisfaction

There are a wide range of emotional and psychological experiences associated with a sport service that are relevant to satisfaction. In fact, it is reasonable to identify at least five different states of satisfaction: satisfaction as contentment, pleasure, relief, novelty and surprise (Oliver, 1989). These states are described in Table 11.2.

Whether a customer experiences one of the states of satisfaction recorded in the table depends on what they are expecting out of the service in the first place. A customer will evaluate how a service has performed after they have used it, and compare it with the expectations they had prior to consumption. If the customer judges that there is a difference or discrepancy between what they expected and what they received, they will experience a strong reaction to the service. The reaction may be positive or negative, depending on whether the service fell short or exceeded expectations. In other words, there are degrees of satisfaction and dissatisfaction.

Table 11.2 Five States of Satisfaction

Satisfaction as ...	Characterised by...	Example
Contentment	Habit/continual consumption, low arousal	A leisure facility continues to offer a clean pool as part of their services
Pleasure or relief	Increased pleasure or decreased unpleasant emotions/perceptions (relief)	A sport physiotherapist may help to decrease pain and distress (relief) A close match where a consumer's team wins may stimulate positive emotions (pleasure)
Novelty	New performance/ experience	A consumer's local fitness centre installs state-of-the-art equipment
Surprise	When the unexpected happens, or the expected does not	Spectators witness an unexpected, record-breaking performance When returning a pair of used, faulty running shoes a consumer expects the staff to decline to assist, but they are helpful instead

Chapter Principle 11.11: Customer satisfaction is a judgement that customers make after they have experienced a sport service where they compare what they expected from it with what they believe they actually received. When expectations are met or exceeded, customers are satisfied, and when expectations are not met, customers are dissatisfied.

Satisfaction and quality

Satisfaction and service quality are strongly linked as they represent different sides of the same coin. Both ideas are concerned with what a customer expects from a service. It is important to realise, however, that although these concepts are connected, they are not the same thing. One of the main ways in which they are different is that satisfaction relates to a specific experience (or series of experiences) of consuming a product or service, whereas a customer's perceptions about the quality of a service are not linked to one specific experience. Furthermore, it is also possible for a customer to believe that a service is high quality, even if they have never consumed it. For example, many sport fans would believe that the Wimbledon tennis event offers a high-quality service, although most would never have attended. It is also possible to feel satisfied by a service while still feeling that it is not a high

247

quality. A good example of this may be a customer who is satisfied by a service because it was inexpensive, even if it was of low quality, like cheap tickets to a sport event that are a long way from the action. Customers can be satisfied by a service that is low in quality if it meets their needs.

Service quality is also different from satisfaction in that customers usually judge quality based on service attributes, and their ideas of what an excellent service should entail. On the other hand, customer satisfaction is affected by many things (other than the service attributes), which are out of the control of the service producer, such as the weather, and parking availability. From this perspective it is likely that customer satisfaction, rather than customer perceptions of service quality, gives a better indication of the sport organisations that perform better in the marketplace.

If a customer experiences satisfaction repeatedly from a sport service, this can lead to a belief that the service is of a high quality. In addition, as service quality increases, satisfaction also tends to increase. In fact, satisfaction can be affected by a customer's perceptions of service quality. Even though satisfaction and quality are two different ideas, they influence each other.

Customer satisfaction and sport marketing

Customer satisfaction is an important concept for sport marketers to understand for two reasons. First, it encourages sport marketing efforts to remain focused on the needs of customers, making these needs and associated perceptions of sport products a priority. As Chapter 1 stressed, the most basic idea in sport marketing is that of meeting the needs of consumers. Second, customer satisfaction can influence not only a customer's intention to purchase, but also their repeat purchasing over time. Simply put, a satisfied customer is more likely to be loyal than an unsatisfied one.

> *Chapter Principle 11.12*: Focusing on customer satisfaction ensures that sport marketers make the needs and perceptions of their customers a priority, which in turn leads to stronger loyalty to the sport organisation and its products.

Delighting the customer

An idea related to customer satisfaction is that of delighting the customer. It occurs when a customer's expectations are exceeded to a surprising degree, resulting in an extremely positive emotional state. In these circumstances, the customer is more than just satisfied. They may feel excited, exhilarated or other positive emotions that have a strong physiological element.

The importance of the concept of delight is best understood in the context of satisfaction. As the previous section established, customers compare what they expect from a service with how it actually performs. If the service performs worse than they expected they are likely to feel dissatisfied, but if it meets or exceeds their expectations they are likely to feel satisfied. It is the degree to which the service exceeds expectations that determines whether a customer experiences satisfaction or delight. If the service exceeds expectations within a normal range, customer may simply feel satisfied. For example, if a parent receives a free coffee when waiting to pick up their child from a karate class at a leisure centre, then they might experience satisfaction slightly above the normal expectations. However, if a service performs to a surprisingly positive degree, then a customer might experience delight. The key here is that delight comes about when the service has performed to a level that the customer could not have reasonably expected. For example, if a sport fan's seat was upgraded at a sport event as the result of a loyalty programme, then they might experience delight. The difficulty for sport marketers is that eliciting delight can only occur if the service performs to a surprisingly high level, and this means that the sport organisation must put in substantial extra effort and resources. There are three types of delight that are useful for sport marketers to manipulate.

> *Chapter Principle 11.13*: Customer delight occurs when a customer's expectations are exceeded to a surprising degree, resulting in an extremely positive emotional state. Delight transpires when the customer is more than just satisfied. This can happen when a service exceeds a customers' expectations of what they think is normal or reasonable from that particular sport service.

Assimilated, re-enacted and transitory delight

A general principle is that when customers are delighted they are more likely to be loyal to a sport service than if they were merely satisfied. However, it is also true that delight can increase customer expectations, which will make customer satisfaction much more difficult in the future. How then can a sport organisation know whether it is beneficial to try to delight their customers? Rust and Oliver (2000) offer some guidance on this matter. They show that there are three different types of delight—assimilated, re-enacted and transitory—which each have a different effect on customer experiences and expectations.

Assimilated delight

Feelings of delight do not stay permanently with a customer; they will not continue to feel the physical intensity of delight (such as excitement or exhilaration) indefinitely, although they are likely to remember the experience. If a customer remembers being delighted the last time they used a service, their expectations may be raised well above normal. This may be termed assimilated delight, because the customer has incorporated the things that delighted them into their expectations of what is normal. The customer may

249

even tell others about the features of the service, and as a result others may also come to expect a high level of performance as normal. Worse, competing organisations may hear about what is being offered and duplicate it themselves, which of course will mean that there is nothing unique about the original service. As a result, sport organisations have to carefully consider whether the cost of providing a delighting feature is worth it.

Re-enacted delight

Re-enacted delight occurs when a customer savours the memory of being delighted. A good example is a fan who experienced delight at attending an exhilarating sport match, and then enjoys remembering and re-living the experience over and over again. They may watch replays, chat about it on the Internet or attend other matches at the same venue or between the same teams to recreate the original feelings. It is as if they can re-experience the original delight in different situations.

Re-enacted delight can happen when customers realise that the delighting experience is unique and cannot be easily recreated. They realise that they cannot reasonably expect it to happen on a regular basis. This is often true of experiences of sport participation and spectating. A sport organisation may therefore be able to encourage re-enacted delight by creating one-off or once-per-season special events that customers will remember fondly in the future. The organisation can also help customers and participants to develop strong memories through recreations, ceremonies and memorabilia related to the delightful event, as well as DVD recordings.

Transitory delight

The final type of delight, transitory delight, transpires when customers forget that they had once been delighted. This means that they will not expect the delighting features to be present when they use the service again in the future; they may be delighted all over again as if it is the first time! For example, if a customer attributes the delightful experience to pure chance or fate, they may decide that it is unlikely to happen again. They may also attribute good service to one particular staff member, not the organisation, and therefore not expect the same service again in the future. It is possible, in these scenarios, that a customer's reaction to the experience is fleeting, and they forget about what delighted them after some time has passed.

Should delight of sport customers be a goal?

From the previous section is should now be clear that delighting the customer will sometimes pay off, but other times it may not. For example, with assimilated delight it is possible that customer expectations will be raised and this will make it more difficult to satisfy customers in the future. Furthermore, although delighting the customer may help profitability in some situations, it is probable that customers dissatisfaction hurts a sport

250

organisation more than delight helps it. This means that it is generally more effective to focus on reducing dissatisfaction and complaints (therefore increasing overall satisfaction), rather than focusing on trying to achieve the next level of 'delight'. The most important point to take away from these comments is that sport marketers must be aware of the situations in which delighting the customer can be profitable, and the times when it may be a counterproductive investment.

It is important to know whether customer satisfaction/delight has a strong influence on customer behaviour. For example, will delight result in loyalty, word of mouth promotion, or will it be overlooked as irrelevant? One way to find out this kind of information is through market research and pilot programmes. In addition, the role of competitors is important. For example, competitors with substantial resources will find it easier to imitate novel services. In this instance there may be limited advantage in raising expectations.

Chapter Principle 11.14: Providing customer delight in a sport service can lead to higher levels of loyalty, word of mouth promotion and an advantage over competitors. However, it is essential to know how customer satisfaction/delight influences customer behaviour. It is also important to consider how capable competitors are of copying any innovative service features. It is usually better to invest resources in decreasing customer dissatisfaction than in increasing customer delight.

Case Study—'Sport Rage' and Participant Satisfaction

By Sharyn McDonald

There has been a dramatic increase in the number of media reports describing the antics of disruptive parents at children's sporting events. Sometimes parents are forced to remove their children from team sports due to the overly competitive and aggressive atmosphere generated by other parents and coaches. This phenomenon, known as 'sport rage', occurs as a result of pushy parents and win-at-all cost coaches who place enormous performance pressure on children.

Those clubs which fail to control parents and coaches who behave inappropriately face not only player recruitment pressures but also the potential loss of officials and sponsors. In some instances, behavioural problems have caused sporting clubs to defend themselves in court. In addition, clubs which continue to condone or ignore abusive behaviour face the possibility of a future generation of rule-intolerant, abusive players who are inclined to emulate the behavioural outbursts they witnessed in their youth. Surveys targeting youth sports have revealed that 84 per cent of officials and youths have witnessed parents acting violently, 45 per cent of children had been verbally abused and a further 17 per cent have been physically assaulted during a game.

251

In Australia, the New South Wales state government has implemented programmes to target anti-social behaviour during youth sport. They have created a series of fact sheets that target both parents and clubs, outlining the consequences of bad behaviour and how clubs should respond. In the absence of a policy to deal with disruptive parents, many clubs provide electronic links to these fact sheets via their websites. Another initiative developed by the New South Wales government targeted 10- to 13-year olds offering education through role play. Piloted in four schools within the same municipal region, students had the opportunity to experience a variety of roles including scoring, coaching, refereeing and playing as well as assuming the role of a parent. This provided the students with alternate perspectives on participation in sport, where they were encouraged to make a pledge to be fair while watching and participating in sport.

Educational programmes to reinforce the importance of fair play have also been used to improve the behaviour of parents. The non-profit organisation, the National Alliance for Youth Sports, offers parents in the United States an innovative programme called the Parents Association for Youth Sports (PAYS). The programme began in 1999 and 100 000 families have since undertaken the training. Parents can either attend a presentation or enrol online. At a cost of $6, parents watch a 20-minute interactive video training session and receive a handbook, *SportingKid* magazine, and a membership card. Upon completion of the training, parents are encouraged to follow a 'Parents' Code of Ethics' which promotes positive experiences in youth sports and holds parents accountable for their actions.

The behaviour associated with sport rage can cost clubs their reputation and reduce the enjoyment of sport for both spectators and players. When parents or their children feel unsafe or threatened in sporting environments, sport rage becomes a major obstacle in the delivery of a high-quality and satisfying sport service.

For more information see:

National Alliance for Youth Sports (2003). *Parents Association for Youth Sports*. Available at:
http://www.nays.org/IntMain.cfm?Page=13&Cat=2

New South Wales Government (2007). *Sport Rage*. Available at:
http://www.dsr.nsw.gov.au/sportrage/

Wren, D. (2007). *Violent Parents—The New Contact Sport*. Available at:
http://www.magic-city-news.com/Doug_Wrenn_44/Violent_Parents_-_The_New_Contact_Sport7433.shtml

Principles summary

- Chapter Principle 11.1: There are four characteristics which illustrate the difference between sport goods and services: tangibility, consistency, perishability and separability. Sport services are intangible because they exist only as an experience. Sport services tend to be inconsistent because they are affected by variables that are difficult to control. Sport services are perishable because they can only be offered and experienced once at any point in time. Sport services are inseparable because they are consumed at the same time as they are produced.

- Chapter Principle 11.2: The sport services mix is made up of participants, physical evidence and processes. Participants are those people involved in delivering and receiving a sport service. Physical evidence is the tangible or visual elements of a service such as a sport stadium. Processes represent the steps involved in delivering a sport service.
- Chapter Principle 11.3: There are three key principles behind the successful marketing of sport services: service quality, customer relationship building and customer satisfaction.
- Chapter Principle 11.4: Sport consumers are more likely to be loyal to a service if they perceive it to be of high quality.
- Chapter Principle 11.5: Service quality can be seen as the degree to which a service meets the needs and expectations of consumers.
- Chapter Principle 11.6: There are five areas that are commonly used to describe expectations of service quality. These five areas are reliability, assurance, empathy, responsiveness and tangibles.
- Chapter Principle 11.7: Customers will make a judgement about whether a service is meeting their expectations at two points in time: first, they will evaluate what the service delivered after it has been consumed (outcome quality); and, second, they will evaluate how the service is delivered during consumption (process quality).
- Chapter Principle 11.8: The service quality elements of empathy, assurance and responsiveness are particularly important to customers' evaluations of process quality. Tangibles and reliability are particularly important to customers' evaluations of outcome quality.
- Chapter Principle 11.9: Relationship marketing involves creating, developing and maintaining a connection between sport organisations and sport consumers that leads to interactive, rewarding and long-term exchanges. Relationship marketing recognises the importance of keeping current customers, as well as attracting new ones, and highlights that the relationship with customers needs to be managed well to encourage loyalty.
- Chapter Principle 11.10: CRM involves the use of information technology to create and maintain ongoing, long-term relationships with sport consumers, leading to high levels of loyalty, and improved sales.
- Chapter Principle 11.11: Customer satisfaction is a judgement which customers make after they have experienced a sport service where they compare what they expected from it with what they believe they actually received. When expectations are met or exceeded, customers are satisfied, and when expectations are not met, customers are dissatisfied.
- Chapter Principle 11.12: Focusing on customer satisfaction ensures that sport marketers make the needs and perceptions of their customers a priority, which in turn leads to stronger loyalty to the sport organisation and its products.

- Chapter Principle 11.13: Customer delight occurs when a customer's expectations are exceeded to a surprising degree, resulting in an extremely positive emotional state. Delight transpires when the customer is more than just satisfied. This can happen when a service exceeds a customer's expectations of what they think is normal or reasonable from that particular sport service.
- Chapter Principle 11.14: Providing customer delight in a sport service can lead to higher levels of loyalty, word of mouth promotion and an advantage over competitors. However, it is essential to know how customer satisfaction/delight influences customer behaviour. It is also important to consider how capable competitors are of copying any innovative service features. It is usually better to invest resources in decreasing customer dissatisfaction than in increasing customer delight.

Tools summary

Chapter Tool 11.1. Service Quality Gaps
Chapter Tool 11.2. Customer Relationship Marketing Process

Review questions

1. Identify the elements of the sport services mix. Provide an example of how each is relevant to the marketing of sport services.
2. Explain what sport service quality is and compare it with sport goods quality.
3. Provide an example of each of the five areas of service quality.
4. Explain how customer satisfaction and dissatisfaction come about.
5. What is the relationship between service quality and customer satisfaction?
6. How does CRM lead to opportunities for customer loyalty?
7. Under what circumstances is customer delight worth pursuing?

Relevant website

http://www.businessadvantage.ndirect.co.uk/SERVQUAL.htm (Service Quality Survey)

Further reading

Chelladurai, P. & Chang, K. (2000). Targets and standards of quality in sport services, *Sport Management Review*, 3(1): 1–22.

Constantinides, E. (2006). The marketing mix revisited: towards the 21st century marketing, *Journal of Marketing Management*, 22: 407–438.

Greenwell, T., Fink, J.S. & Pastore, D.L. (2002). Assessing the influence of the physical sports facility on customer satisfaction within the context of the service experience, *Sport Management Review*, 5: 129–148.

Payne, A. & Forw, P. (2005). A strategic framework for customer relationship management, *Journal of Marketing*, 69(4): 167–176.

References

Agrawal, M.L. (2003). Customer relationship management (CRM) and corporate renaissance, *Journal of Services Research*, 3(2): 149–171.

Booms, B.H. & Bitner, M.J. (1981). Marketing strategies and organization structures for service firms. In J.H. Donnelly & W.R. George, *Marketing of Services*, American Marketing Association, Chicago, pp. 47–51.

Harker, M.J. (1999). Relationship marketing defined? An examination of current relationship marketing definitions, *Marketing Intelligence & Planning*, 17(1): 13–20.

McDonald, M.A., Sutton, W.A. & Milne, R. (1995). TEAMQUAL: Measuring service quality in professional team sports, *Sport Marketing Quarterly*, 4(2): 9–15.

Oliver, R.L. (1989). Processing of the satisfaction response in consumption: A suggested framework and research propositions, *Journal of Consumer Satisfaction, Dissatisfaction and Complaining Behaviour*, 2: 1–16.

Parasuraman, A., Berry, L. & Zeithaml, V. (1991). Refinement and reassessment of the SERVQUAL scale, *Journal of Retailing*, 67(4): 420–450.

Parasuraman, A., Zeithamal, V. & Berry, L. (1985). A conceptual model of service quality and its implications for future research, *Journal of Marketing*, 49: 41–50.

Parasuraman, A., Zeithamal, V. & Berry, L. (1988). SERVQUAL: A multiple-item scale for measuring consumer perceptions of quality, *Journal of Retailing*, 64(1): 12–40.

Rust, R.T. & Oliver R.L. (2000). Should we delight the customer? *Journal of the Academy of Marketing Science*, 28(1): 86–94.

12 Sport marketing and the new media

Overview

The purpose of this chapter is to examine the application of 'new media' to sport marketing. It explores the kinds of technologies and tools that are available to sport marketers using new media and considers the influence that new media has on the sport marketing philosophy. The chapter contains more 'Interactive Activities' than others because the new media tools described are best experienced to be fully appreciated.

By the end of this chapter, readers should be able to:

- Define the terms new media and new media marketing.
- Define the advantages and disadvantages of new media marketing.
- Describe how new media marketing relates to the Sport Marketing Framework.
- Identify the six key principles of new media marketing.
- Describe the six-step process of engaging consumers with new media marketing.
- Outline the five broad categories of new media technologies.
- Study new media options by logging into cutting-edge existing sites.

Introducing the new media

The term 'new media', like the term 'marketing', can mean different things depending on the context. An instructive starting point is to define what is meant by the term media. Generally, the term refers to communication with the general public by organisations such as broadcasters, print newspapers, magazines, radio stations and any other group interested in disseminating information. These organisations are, in fact, designed specifically for the purpose of communicating with the general public. This chapter takes a broader view and refers to media as any instrument or means of communicating information. It is important to take a broad view like this because technology has provided the sport marketer with so many innovative ways of communicating with the general public that they no longer have to rely only on traditional 'media' organisations.

New media is often described as electronic or digital media and is usually associated with the Internet, computers, and forms of mobile communications. To phrase this more generally, new media refers to communications that are generated by electronic means or through recent technological platforms. New media refers to technologically sophisticated platforms or vehicles for transmitting and communicating information. It is important to note from this definition that not all forms of new technology are new media. Put simply, only those technologies which are capable of transmitting information to the general public (or a targeted consumer segment) are considered new media.

> *Chapter Principle 12.1*: New media refers to communications that are generated by electronic means, or through recent technological platforms. It refers to technologically sophisticated platforms or vehicles for transmitting and communicating information.

Manovich (2002) has attempted to identify more specific criteria which can help determine whether a technology qualifies as new media. His five standards are listed in Table 12.1.

Manovich's standards highlight the fact that new media technologies are capable of sending and receiving digital content or information, which is not limited to using a computer. Digital content is delivered through many other devices such as mobile or cellular phones, PDAs and MP3 music players.

Table 12.1 Manovich's Five Standards of New Media

1. New media is represented numerically, with ones and zeros
2. New media is modular, that is, it has individual elements that maintain their independence even when they are combined into larger objects
3. The processes involved in creating, manipulating, and accessing the media are able to be automated
4. New media is variable, or able to exist in nearly infinite versions
5. New media is increasingly able to translate into differing file formats

The information can even be transferred seamlessly from one digital technology to another and from one digital format to another (for example from a mobile phone to a computer). Another feature of new media is that data, or information, is accessible in real time. Because of these and other features of new media technologies, they have exerted a major influence on society and the way we communicate with one another, just as the printing press did when it was first introduced in the 15th century. New media is especially important in sport marketing because it permeates all aspects of consumers' lives in Western society.

> *Chapter Principle 12.2*: New media is represented numerically, and it is modular, automated, variable and transferable to differing file formats and able to be customised.

To some extent new media can be seen as the latest technological trend, but it also has serious implications for sport marketing. New media is more than technology; it has come to refer to a different style of marketing where sport marketers can communicate in novel ways with sport consumers. New media is also important because it creates additional opportunities in sport, such as new assets (like website and mobile digital rights), and new possibilities in licensing and merchandising (such as computer games). Although the types of technologies that are available continue to change and develop, the principle remains the same: sport marketers can use advanced technology to communicate with their customers and sell them extra products and services that are associated with sport.

The popularity and prevalence of new media technology means that it provides sport marketers with innovative ways of communicating with consumers. Many of these new media communication approaches are far more rapid, responsive and interactive than other marketing strategies. For example, compare the one-way content of television with the opportunity to customise a replay directly to a consumer's mobile phone. Not only are new media platforms fast and direct, they are also inexpensive compared with traditional techniques of sport marketing. Even more importantly, new media enables sport organisations to develop messages that are personalised to key target audiences.

> *Chapter Principle 12.3*: New media technologies provide sport marketers with new ways of communicating with consumers and novel approaches to their marketing activities. Many of these approaches are far more rapid, responsive, interactive and inexpensive when compared with other marketing strategies; they are also more able to be customised to key target audiences.

Interactive case

Log on to the NFL team, Dallas Cowboys website: http://www.dallascowboys.com.

Navigate through the various toolbars on the site to learn about the new media tools the team uses to communicate with fans and consumers. Click on 'Fans' in the top toolbar and then select 'RSS'. Read about what RSS (Really Simple Syndication) means.

The Dallas Cowboys website shows an extensive range of ideas that sport marketers can use to communicate with fans using new media technology. The site gives fans the opportunity to access video and audio information as well as the standard text. Importantly, it also allows fans to connect and talk with one another. The site is set up so that fans can easily read and create blogs, chat on the fan forum, access RSS feeds, receive instant e-mail alerts, watch live broadcasts, download audio podcasts (of games highlights, interviews and press conferences) and even watch video of game highlights and repays. Another benefit of RSS technology for the Dallas Cowboys is that it enables the organisation to monitor the kind of information that is being published and posted about it. In a marketing context where it is increasingly difficult for sport organisations to control what is being said about them, RSS may provide one tool to help watch out for and respond to both positive and negative press.

The Dallas Cowboys example demonstrates the impact that new media is having on the way products are being delivered in the sport market. Consumers can even watch sport in completely new ways thanks to advances in digital television, which allows a choice of camera angles, the personalisation of menus and settings and to rewind live television. Not only is new media revolutionising the delivery of sport, the reverse is also true; sport represents essential content for new media technologies. For example, organisations such as phone companies are eager to use sport content (such as games results) for mobile phone services. Other new media providers are keen to use sport in other ways such as creating editorials and articles, generating opportunities for customer participation, setting up discussion forums, as well as betting and purchasing opportunities. These examples highlight the fact that sport and the media enjoy a symbiotic relationship, meaning that although sport and media organisations are very different, they have come to be dependent on one another. Sport provides the content and new media provides the distribution. New media technology is a central part of this relationship.

New media sport marketing: adapting the sport marketing philosophy

At its most simple, new media sport marketing refers to the use of new media technologies in marketing programmes. However, new media marketing means more than just using up-to-date technology within a traditional marketing programme. It also refers to a novel marketing approach that recognises the complex social and technological world that sport consumers occupy. To be effective, new media marketing must do more than just use new technology. It also has to respond to the changing lifestyles and expectations of sport consumers.

Sport consumers are inundated with marketing messages. Despite the technological options, sport marketers must compete with a vast range of entertainment and communication technologies. There is an enormous amount of 'clutter' in the marketing environment, and sport marketers must find ways to cut through it. In this new environment, conventional marketing strategies are becoming less effective. As a result, sport marketers must be aware of the ways in which sport consumers' lives have changed, and the corresponding new expectations they have of sport products and marketing programmes. For example, sport consumers have limited discretionary leisure time, consume more media from a greater variety of media outlets, belong to numerous virtual networks and tend to be fragmented as an audience (leading to the erosion of mass media effectiveness). Sport consumers also possess new expectations including personalised experiences, interactivity, choice and control, the opportunity to multi-task (Generation M) and access to user-generated content.

New media sport marketing recognises that consumers are exposed to an immense amount of marketing and have a wide range of sport product choices at their fingertips. As a consequence, sport consumers are less likely to be convinced by mass media sales pitches. In fact, consumers can be resistant to traditional marketing strategies such as advertising campaigns. It is important to note that the new media marketing approach does not render the standard principles of marketing obsolete, but it does give the sport marketer new principles to wield that are relevant to the current environment. The presence of new technological tools should therefore sharpen sport marketers' thinking about the pace of marketing and the nature of interaction and communication with consumers.

Chapter Principle 12.4: New media sport marketing is customised communication with targeted sport consumers that is generated by electronic means or through technologically sophisticated platforms that facilitate the transmission of information.

There are six key elements of new media sport marketing that can be employed by sport marketers to engage better with consumers. These are customisation, modularity, sticky branding, networked communication, inclusivity and permission. The principles are illustrated in Figure 12.1 and are described next.

Chapter Principle 12.5: New media marketing is targeted and personalised interaction which is based on the principles of customisation, modularity, sticky branding, networked communication and permission.

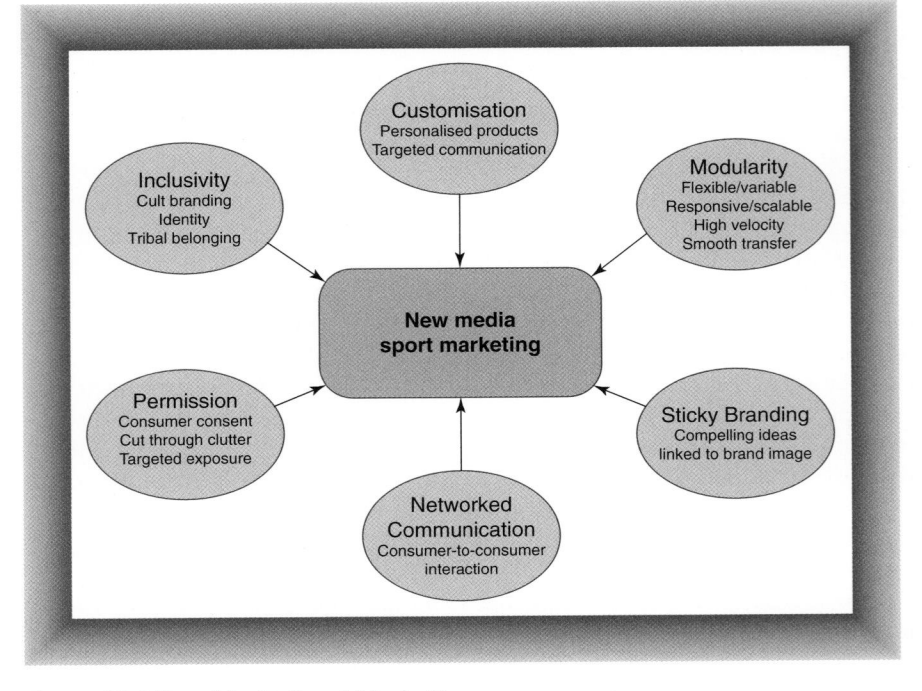

Figure 12.1 New Media Sport Marketing.

Customisation

As opposed to a mass marketing approach, new media sport marketing is targeted and customised. New media technology gives marketers specific information about the behaviours and preferences of their consumers. As a result, marketing can become more specialised and nuanced, directed precisely towards the personal needs and choices of customers. New media options are instrumental in converting scattered mass marketing into surgical direct marketing.

The concept of behavioural targeting through digital television is one example of potential customisation. Although not in use at present, digital television technology is capable of tracking a consumer's viewing habits and passing this information on to advertisers, who can subsequently provide targeted offerings. Google currently tracks user behaviour in a similar way, learning about each consumer's search interests and the kinds of advertisements they may each respond to. Another example of customisation was presented in the previous chapter on sport services marketing, which explained the importance of developing customer relationships. It described how computer software can collect relevant information at the point of sale about current and potential consumers, such as their buying patterns, preferences, shopping habits, motivations and triggers. This information is helpful for sport marketers to anticipate what other products the consumer may be interested in, and to make offers and suggestions based on consumer profiles.

New technology is also changing the way in which sport products are designed and personalised. Nike, for example, allows customers to design their own customised footwear. In the 1990s, the technological sophistication required to offer reasonably priced, customised footwear to the general public was not available. Now, however, Nike is able to capitalise on technology, and is able to cater to consumers' demands for individualised products that give them a sense of personal identity and control.

> *Chapter Principle 12.6*: New media sport marketing messages should be customised or targeted and adapted to specific consumers and their needs.

Interactive case

Log on to the Nike ID website and follow the steps required to design a customised pair of Nike ID shoes: http://www.nikeid.com

Modularity

A modular object is composed of elements or units that conform to a regular standard and can stand alone in functionality or combine with other modules to provide new functionality. This allows flexibility and variety in the way the elements are used. For example, Lego blocks can be joined and arranged in an incredible variety of constructions. New media marketing technology is often structured in a modular fashion, such as sports betting websites, which provide a set format (or 'unit') for setting up a betting account and standardised systems for using its interactive services. Another simple example is e-mail. It can stand alone as an independent form of communication, or it can be linked into other forms such as mobile devices, Facebook, electronic newsletters and automated databases.

From a new media marketing perspective, modularity means that communication with consumers can be fast, responsive, simple and flexible. It is important that the marketing message is fast because the more quickly an idea passes from one consumer to another, the larger the number of consumers who will come into contact with it before it dies out. Velocity is also important in dealing with customer enquiries, orders and demands. Sport consumers expect services to operate responsively and products to be delivered almost instantaneously.

New media sport marketing can provide fast and responsive solutions to consumers, and allows an unprecedented level of responsiveness to changing demand levels. A modular system can be scaled up and down easily, meaning that it can easily adjust to servicing small or large numbers of people as demand changes. A club's Internet message board, for instance, may need to be able to receive and organise increased traffic after a significant event such as a season final win or a player scandal.

New media modularity should also enable smoothness of information transfer between consumers. In his book *Unleashing the Ideavirus*, Godin (2000) uses the term smoothness to refer to the ease with which consumers can spread a particular marketing idea to other consumers. Sport marketers need to consider how smooth or easy it is to access the new media product or service. Being able to access and spread ideas through the click of one button is an ideal example—that is how Hotmail spread. The ideal scenario is to have an idea or product that is so smooth that once someone is exposed to it, they are instantly hooked. Examples of functions that make ideas effortless to transfer are 'Tell-a-friend' tools on websites; 'save to my web' and 'e-mail this page' icons; 'furl this site' links; and 'forward to a friend' functions.

> *Chapter Principle 12.7*: A modular new media marketing programme (including product design) is the one structured in a standardised and automated way which incorporates flexibility, responsiveness to changes in demand and ease of transfer.

Interactive case

Log on to some of the websites listed below to see the ways in which sport betting agencies are using new media technologies to provide services to consumers and to encourage them to interact with other consumers.

http://www.tab.com.au: On this site, you will see a live odds service, news, results and information, as well as live audio and video.

http://www.bookmaker.com: Consumers can access live lines which refresh every 10 minutes, betting rewards/loyalty programmes and office pools.

http://www.vip.com: Users of this site can participate in free contests against other users, interact via links to a message board (via the 'random thoughts' link) and download the service to their mobile phones and PDAs.

http://www.2betdsi.com: On this site, virtual horse racing software runs simulated horse racing every 10 minutes 24/7. Mobile phone betting, office pools and contests against other betting enthusiasts are also available.

The sport betting industry is increasingly using sophisticated software to enable online betting as well as consumer-to-consumer interaction. Not only do these sites provide news, results and information, they also offer live audio and video, live odds service, reward programmes, free contests against other consumers, mobile betting, office pools and even message boards.

Sticky branding

An idea or product has to stand out from the crowd to last or even to be noticed at all. People will respond to an idea if it is compelling or gripping in some way. In the case of sports, what the sport marketer ultimately wants is for an idea to stick that says something about the sport brand. An all-male professional sport league, for example, may wish to attach ideas of masculinity, drama, and physical power to their brand to attract male viewers. This could be achieved by posting game highlights and physical clashes on YouTube or through posting imagery on their website of heavily muscled players captured in dramatic poses.

The key point here is that the sport brand must be linked with ideas that are 'sticky'—or that take hold in consumers' minds—and that are consistent with the positioning strategy for the brand image. As consumers may respond to many different kinds of ideas, the key is to identify those that are consistent with the marketing strategy. Some of the more effective 'sticky' ideas are funny, sexualised, thought-provoking, offering financial profit, horrible, shocking, beautiful, hyper-real, attention-grabbing, involving sensory bombardment, unconventional and unpredictable. A sticky idea may also be one that meets a niche need or fills a market gap.

Chapter Principle 12.8: Sticky branding occurs when new media sport marketing ideas take hold in consumers' minds in ways that are consistent with the positioning strategy for the brand.

Interactive case

Seth Godin wrote a book called *Unleashing the Ideavirus* in 2000, which has now become the most downloaded electronic book ever. Godin suggests that marketers should get consumers to pass on information to one another by taking advantage of new media technologies and viral marketing techniques. This means that consumers should talk and market to each other. In Godin's (2000, p. 6) own words, marketers should 'ignite consumer networks and then get out of the way and let them talk'.

Download and read Seth Godin's book *Unleashing the Ideavirus*. It can be downloaded on http://www.ideavirus.com for free and is a case study on viral marketing in itself. Godin identifies eight components of viral marketing, described in Table 12.2.

Viral marketing is a powerful tool when the trend for using e-mail to communicate is taken into account. A study by the marketing firm Sharpe Partners (2006) suggested that 90 per cent of Internet users share content with other people via e-mail, with 63 per cent of them sharing content at least once per week with up to six recipients. This gives an indication of the power of 'word of mouse'. However, it is important to note what kind of content is most commonly sent. The study indicated that in descending order people were most likely to send (1) humorous material such as jokes or cartoons, (2) news, (3) religious and spiritual information, (4) games, (5) business and personal information and (6) sport- or hobby-related information. This gives some further indication of what ideas might be 'sticky' for use in viral marketing. In particular, sport information can be combined with humour or news.

Viral marketing is not the only example of the principle of networked communication in sport marketing, although it is a powerful one. There are many

Table 12.2 Components of Viral Marketing

Sneezers

Sneezers are those people who are more likely to tell their friends about a new idea or product. They spread ideas around through word of mouth or mouse. Sneezers are important to viral marketing, and sport marketers need to identify who they are and give them encouragement and incentives to spread the word around.

According to Godin, there are two kinds of sneezers: promiscuous sneezers and powerful sneezers. Promiscuous sneezers will pass on their favourite ideas or products to almost anyone, anytime. They are not usually influential opinion leaders, but by sheer volume of how often and how many people they tell, they can be effective spreaders of an idea. They can be motivated by money or other incentives. A powerful sneezer is an opinion leader, someone of influence who is respected and admired by a group of people. For example, a powerful sneezer could be a celebrity, a star player, a local hero or an industry expert. The trick with powerful sneezers is recognising that their influence cannot be bought. If David Beckham publicly endorses lots of different products, fans will become increasingly suspicious that he does not actually use all of them.

Hive

A hive is a group of people who have something in common. For example, they may share ways of communicating, they may have a collective history or they may all follow certain rules or 'typical' ways of behaving. Sport fans who follow a certain club are an excellent example of a hive.

Velocity

Velocity is a measure of how quickly an idea spreads from one person to another person. The faster an idea spreads, the greater the number of people who will get 'infected' by the idea before it dies out.

Vector

A vector is the path that a virus takes as it moves through a group of people. It may move through an audience with a certain demographic (such as men aged 18–35 or college/university students), or it may start up in a sub-group (such as fans of one particular sport team) and then break out into the bigger population.

Medium

The medium is the vehicle or the means by which an idea is transmitted. An idea has to have a way of moving and being transmitted from one person to another. It is a medium which gives an idea its ability to move. A medium could be an image, a movie, a slogan or phrase, a logo, a video clip or even a celebrity.

Smoothness

Smoothness refers to how easy it is for a person to spread a particular ideavirus. Being able to spread the idea through the click of one button is an ideal example. Very smooth viruses, like Hotmail, spread themselves with virtually no effort at all. Just the act of using the product spreads the virus. The ideal scenario is to have an idea or product that is so smooth to pick up that once someone is exposed to it, they are instantly hooked.

Persistence

Persistence refers to whether an idea or product is used for a long time by each person. Some ideas fade out, but ideas that stick around will get passed on to new people for months and even years. Persistence basically refers to how long a sneezer will sneeze.

Table 12.2 (Continued)

An idea is likely to be more persistent if it takes advantage of people's daily-routines (such as using the Internet, carrying a mobile phone, etc.). In addition, the more the people within a hive use a product or idea, the more often others in that hive will be reminded of it.

Amplifier
An amplifier is something which increases the strength of an idea or product as it gets passed along. It is something which gets the message across to a larger audience, such as television advertising, a magazine article or Internet chat rooms and fora.

other effective tools that can be used, such as social networking sites, Web pages and social bookmarking/photo-sharing services. Following are a number of activities that offer the opportunity to explore and reflect on the marketing potential of these networking hubs. First, consider the increasingly influential phenomenon of social networking sites, such as Facebook and MySpace. These sites allow consumers to read blogs, participate in fora and communicate interactively with sport organisations, players and other fans.

Networked communication

The fourth principle of new media marketing is networked communication, which refers to the use of new media to facilitate communication between consumers. It allows a network of communication to develop, rather than just a one-way projection of information to the customer. Put very simply, it means getting consumers to talk to each other. The idea of networked communication is based on the idea that instead of telling consumers about certain products, it is more productive to get consumers to talk to each other about the products. This is easier than ever before because new media platforms allow an interactive approach where marketers can organise consumers to communicate with one another. For this reason, new media sport marketing tends to be focused on marketing activities that bring consumers together, such as online communities, blogs, podcasts and message boards. New media is not just a set of tools for communication but is also a hub of consumer interaction and commercial activity.

Networked communication provides consumers with a personalised experience, and because of this it is sometimes called engagement marketing. It stresses the importance of fostering the interaction between consumers in way that encourages word of mouth (word of mouse) communication to facilitate their interest in the sport product. This is based on the premise that consumer-to-consumer (C2C) marketing is more powerful than business-to-consumer (B2C) marketing as occurs with traditional advertising.

Viral marketing is a prominent example of networked communication using new media technologies. A virus is an infectious agent that replicates itself and spreads from one living thing to another. Although it may start out in small numbers, in the right environment a virus will grow exponentially.

Viral marketing is a term that describes any marketing message that is designed to be passed on from one consumer to another. Like a virus, the aim of viral marketing is to encourage rapid communication from one person to another, until thousands, or even millions of people have been 'infected'. Viral marketing is therefore a systematic approach that aims to encourage people to share a marketing message with their personal contact network.

> *Chapter Principle 12.9*: Networked communication is based on the idea that instead of telling consumers about products, it is more productive to get consumers to talk to each other about them.

Interactive case

Log on to a couple of the MySpace pages listed below to see the way in which networking software is enabling sport properties to embed their brand into social networks.

Roger Federer
http://profile.myspace.com/index.cfm?fuseaction=user.viewprofile&friendid=40967163

Dallas Cowboys Cheerleaders
http://www.myspace.com/dallascowboyscheerleaders

Manchester United
http://www.myspace.com/manutd

The Tibetan Olympic Team: Team Tibet 2008
http://profile.myspace.com/index.cfm?fuseaction=user.viewprofile&friendID=190132567

In addition to well-known services such as MySpace and FaceBook, there are other innovative sites that give sport consumers a chance to interact and network with other fans who share their interests. The two websites Furl (from File Uniform Resource Locators) and Flickr are the excellent examples. Furl (http://www.furl.net) offers people a way to organise and share a personal file of websites and content they have enjoyed. A similar site (http://del.icio.us) also offers social bookmarking so that participants can see what other people have bookmarked. Flickr (http://www.flickr.com) provides a visual networking forum, where people can post and share photographs of subjects that interest them.

Inclusivity

The principle of inclusivity in new media marketing is closely related to the idea of networked marketing. Because new media can provide consumers with a platform for communication and interaction, it lends itself to offering them something to belong to. Sport consumers are motivated by a psychological need to feel as if they 'belong' to a group. New media sport marketing can be conducted in such a way that sport consumers feel 'included' in virtual groups.

Virtual worlds such as Second Life are powerful examples of how new media is being used by consumers to develop identities and cultivate belonging within a social world. In September 2007, the provider of host broadcast services for the FIFA World Cup (Infront Sports and Media, 2007) launched a virtual world called Empire of Sports. The site offers multi-sports gaming, which are integrated within the idea of a sporting lifestyle and industry. Players compete through sporting 'avatars' to win multi-player competitions in sports such as football, basketball, tennis, skiing, bobsleigh, athletics and gym games. Players start as novices and must train, eat nutritious food, purchase equipment and practise to improve their skill and performance. The platform offers virtual clubs, leagues, fan clubs, and competitions ranging from 'grassroots' to professional. Those who are more interested in the management of sport can sign up to become chairmen or managers of sporting clubs and shape the virtual world from behind a virtual desk. There are also options for promoting media rights and content. Infront has even made licensing agreements with 'real world' sporting brands to tap into the existing passions of sport consumers. This is clearly an opportunity for sporting clubs and leagues to not only secure licensing income but to offer their fans a new platform for consumer-to-consumer interaction.

> *Chapter Principle 12.10*: Inclusivity refers to the use of new media marketing to fulfil the need to 'belong', which in turn fosters the development of identity. New media marketing can be conducted in such a way that sport consumers feel 'included' in virtual groups.

Interactive case

Log on to the Empire of Sports website (http://www.empireofsports.com). Read about the features of this virtual world, access some news releases of interest and view the screenshots, photographs and videos to better understand the product on offer.

A virtual world such as Empire of Sport offers consumers a unique way to connect with a 'tribe' of like-minded fans. It is also a tool for fans to explore new and different identities. After all, someone with little athletic ability could rise to the top of one of the virtual leagues and develop their 'true potential as an athlete', in the words of the site. For sporting organisations in the 'real world', sites such as this represent a distinctive opportunity for exposure to a niche market and even for spin-off sales such as merchandise and licensing. However, it is worth noting that there are risks involved for the sport property, as they are unable to control the content on the site. For example, consider a scenario where a professional sporting club licenses their brand to be associated with a virtual club, and that virtual club consistently loses or has a reputation for cheating and rough play. Does this virtual behaviour reflect badly on the real brand?

Permission

The sixth principle of new media marketing is permission. Some of the traditional approaches to marketing are based on the idea of 'interruption', or marketing at consumers. For example, an advertisement on television can be seen to 'interrupt' a viewer with an unanticipated message as they watch a programme. Marketers hope that even though the viewer was not expecting to see their advertisement, it will nevertheless influence their brand perceptions and purchase intentions. Another simple example of interruption marketing is Internet banner advertising, where a banner unexpectedly appears on a computer screen in an attempt to entice the operator to click through to a website. In both of these examples, the communication of information is one way: from the marketer to the consumer. Many consumers are resistant to these kinds of advertising campaigns. In addition, such advertising strategies are largely ineffective because the market is flooded with them and consumers have learnt to tune out to their invasive messages.

In contrast to 'interruption' marketing, new media sport marketing is based on the idea of 'permission'. This is often referred to as permission marketing and refers to the use of new media to communicate with consumers who have given their permission to receive customised messages, usually via e-mail, mobile or cellular phones and PDA devices. Not only does this help to overcome the problem of consumers' inboxes overflowing with spam, it also helps marketers to segment and target consumers more accurately and therefore cut through the advertising clutter. Usually consumers will sign up to receive messages on the organisations' websites.

Of course it is true that cutting-edge technology can be used to market to consumers without their permission. However, this approach has a number of problems and may backfire on sport marketers. One example is the trend known as 'Bluejacking', which has developed thanks to the popularity of Bluetooth capabilities in mobile phones, PDAs and laptops. Bluejacking involves sending instant, unsolicited messages over Bluetooth to reach mobile and cellular phones, PDAs and laptops within range. For example, it is possible to set up a broadcast system so that when a person walks past a sporting goods store, or a sporting billboard, an instant message can be sent to their phones.

While Bluejacking may seem like an effective way to reach potential customers, there is a danger in exploiting the ability to contact consumers directly. As technologies such as Bluetooth become more common, consumers may become inundated with messages and content, even if they have not asked for it and do not want it. This could lead to consumers developing negative associations with the organisations that send such unsolicited material. Another problem with Bluejacking is that it only offers a mass-market approach; it does not help sport organisations to send specific messages to key target markets. This means that when using new media technology to market directly to consumers there is a trade-off between reaching consumers and respecting consumer control and privacy.

Subscription-based short message service (SMS) instant messaging may be a viable alternative to Bluejacking that takes advantage of mobile phone technology while seeking consumer permission. For example, a sport stadium could message members to inform them about parking, short queues, half-time food and beverage specials, merchandise deals, games results on other courts/arenas and perhaps in the future instant video replays. Requiring fans to complete a simple registration to receive this content means that relevant messages are sent to interested recipients.

Chapter Principle 12.11: Permission in new media sport marketing refers to the effectiveness of communicating with consumers who have consented to receive customised messages, rather than to send random, untargeted and uninvited marketing communications.

Compared with traditional marketing, new media sport marketing can help sport organisations to spread messages quickly to a large but targeted audience at a relatively low cost. However, there are disadvantages as well. First, it is not possible to control the content which is generated through networked communication and interaction. This exposes sport properties to the risk of negative opinions and public perceptions. Second, it is often difficult to control the timing of some aspects of the marketing campaign. Technological innovation creates both opportunities and challenges for sport organisations. It is also important to note that new media sport marketing should not replace traditional marketing principles. In fact, new media marketing should be considered a (potentially powerful) marketing strategy that can be used within the Sport Marketing Framework. A summary of the new media sport marketing principles appears in Table 12.3.

The new media sport marketing process

To review, the six elements of new media sport marketing are *customisation, modularity, sticky branding, networked communication, inclusivity* and *permission*. When these ideas are understood as a package, they suggest that there is a process involved in engaging consumers with new media marketing. First, sport organisations must make *contact* with consumers using compelling ideas to capture their attention and the features of modularity to ensure the contact is fast, flexible and smooth. Once contacted, consumers may respond to the customised offerings and engage in *conversation* via the networked and interactive capabilities of the platform. Conversation leads consumers to make social *connections* with other users, with whom they can share *content*. Over time this interaction leads to the development of a deeper sense of *community* and belonging to the other users, the platform, and the sport property.

271

Table 12.3 Summary of New Media Sport Marketing Principles

Principle	Description
Customisation	The marketing message, as well as the products themselves, should be targeted and customised to specific consumers and their needs
Modularity	The marketing programme (including product design) should be structured in a standardised and automated way which allows it to be flexible, responsive to changes in demand, and quick and easy to pass from one person to another
Sticky branding	The brand must be linked with ideas that are 'sticky'—or that take hold in people's minds—and that are consistent with the marketing plan for the brand image
Networked communication	New media allows a network of communication to develop between consumers, as well as between consumers and the organisation. Networked communication is based on the idea that instead of telling consumers about your products, it is more productive to get consumers to talk to each other about your products
Inclusivity	Through networked communities and user interaction, new media technologies can fulfil the need to 'belong', which in turn fosters the development of identity. New media marketing can be conducted in such a way that people feel 'included' in virtual groups
Permission	This refers to the fact that it is often more effective to communicate with customers who have given their permission to receive customised messages, rather than to send random, untargeted and uninvited information

A sport consumer may then become a *convert*: someone convinced of certain beliefs and ideas that are shared through the platform, which, in the best-case scenario, include the sticky ideas that have been attached to the brand image. This process is represented in the diagram in Figure 12.2.

Even though sport consumers may not be receptive to some traditional marketing strategies, they still want to participate in sport-related consumption in both traditional and novel ways. This means that sport marketers must engage the sport consumer and find ways for them to identify and belong to the sport product and organisation. Sport marketers must utilise personalised strategies in their marketing programmes. Fortunately, new technology allows sport marketers to develop an unprecedented combination of consumer interaction and marketing customisation. The tools of new media sport marketing are available to almost all sport organisations and therefore represent an unprecedented level of access to consumers that has conventionally been the purview of only the most well-resourced sport organisations.

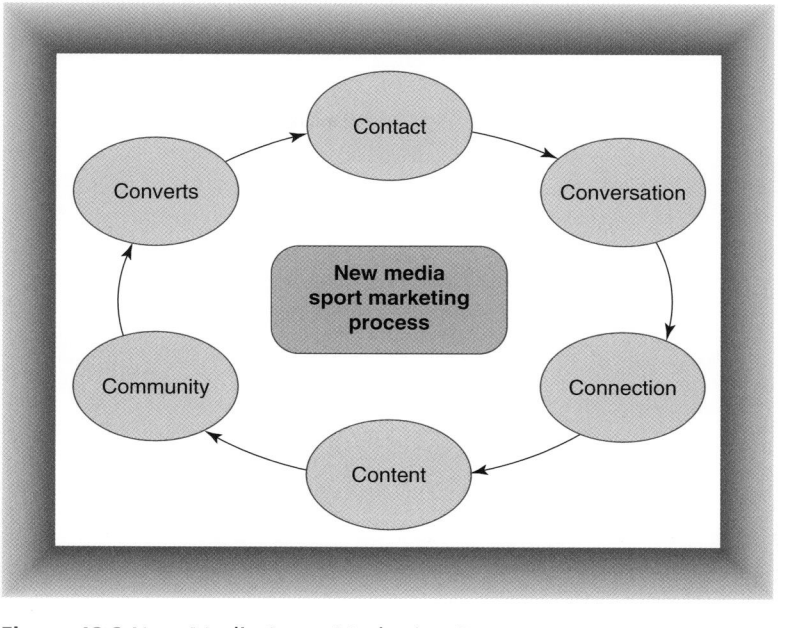

Figure 12.2 New Media Sport Marketing Process.

New media sport marketing tools

The new media sport marketing principles outlined in the previous section can be used to help achieve the positioning strategy specified as an outcome of following the Sport Marketing Framework. In this section, some tools for implementing new media sport marketing principles are outlined.

The introduction of new media into the sport marketing realm means that the context of marketing is changing and that there are more tools for communicating with sport consumers than there has ever been before. In general, the most popular tools of marketing, such as advertising, are only available to those organisations with plenty of resources. However, with the use of new media tools, any sport organisation can be seen and heard. Sport organisations may also be able to collect market research data more easily than ever before and therefore understand their customers better. There is software, for example, that sport marketers can use to monitor blogs written about their brand that will report on certain keyword or phrases. This potentially enables sport marketers to monitor positive, negative and incorrect information that is being published about them, and also to learn about the attitudes and needs of their consumers. Similar software such as RSS enables the search and retrieval of news headlines or stories. These examples exemplify how important it is for sport marketers to understand the different types of new media tools that are at their disposal, and to continue to keep up-to-date with

273

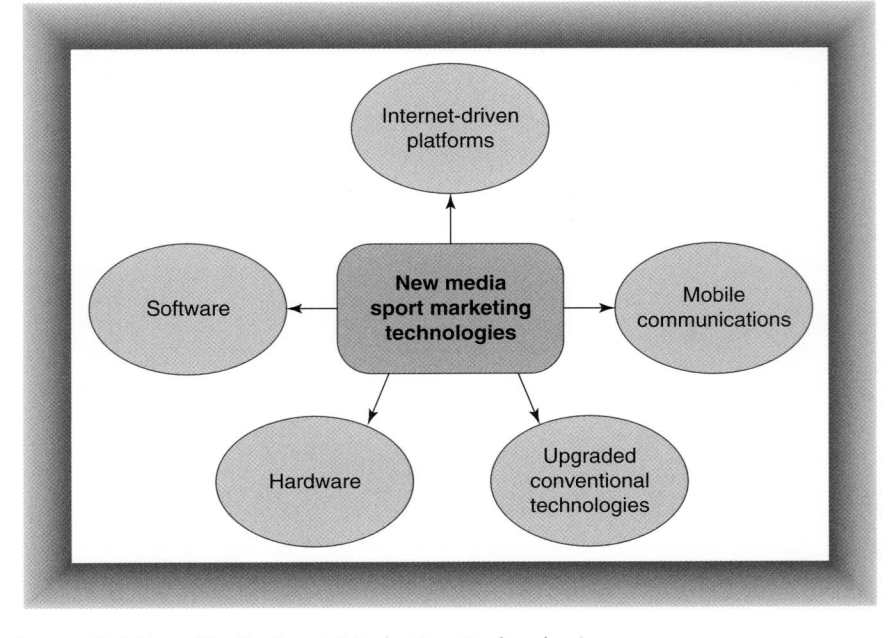

Figure 12.3 New Media Sport Marketing Technologies.

developments in new media technologies. In this section, the dominant new media tools that were available at the time of writing are outlined.

New media technologies can be classified into five tools, although some overlap between categories is inevitable. They are (1) Internet-driven platforms, (2) mobile communications, (3) upgraded conventional technologies, (4) hardware and (5) software. These categories are illustrated in Figure 12.3.

Following are some further examples of each new media technology tool. These lists are not exhaustive and, given the pace of new media development, new devices and software will continually be added. Despite the likelihood that these examples will become dated soon after the printing of this text, they will continue to provide a useful starting point for thinking about each category.

Internet-driven platforms

Internet-driven platforms include the increasingly sophisticated methods of communicating that the World Wide Web supports, such as blogs and social networking sites, e-mail, web video, podcasts, vodcasts, websites, pop-ups, spam, virtual worlds, wikis, electronic commerce (such online and mobile payments), Myspace and Facebook. The use of YouTube and other similar user-generated video sites is another popular example of Internet-driven technology being used in sport marketing. The National Hockey League (NHL) was the first major sport league to provide content for the YouTube community. Commencing in late 2006, the NHL began providing daily video highlights of regular season games, which are available within 24 hours of the original broadcast, in addition to other off-ice footage. Since then many other leagues have followed suit, including the NBA, and in November 2007, the International Fight League (IFL). By broadcasting snippets of compelling content to an audience eager for thrills and entertainment, these leagues are hoping to expose their athletes, coaches and events to a much larger audience than they have ever been able to access before. Both the NHL and the IFL have also negotiated revenue-sharing partnerships with YouTube, which allows them to show advertisements in conjunction with the video content.

> *Chapter Tool 12.1. Internet-Driven Platforms*: They include methods of communicating that the World Wide Web supports, such as blogs and social networking sites, e-mail, web video, podcasts, vodcasts, websites, pop-ups, spam, virtual worlds, wikis, electronic commerce (such as online and mobile payments), Myspace, Facebook and YouTube.

Interactive case

Log on to YouTube on the Internet and NHL video page. This can be accessed by typing 'NHL' into the search box or by accessing the following page: http://www.youtube.com/NHLVideo

Take note of the functions that have been set up which enable viewers to interact with the NHL and with other fans.

Mobile communications

Mobile communications include the communication tools that are associated with mobile or cellular phones and any wireless communication system. Examples include Bluetooth, mobile phones, PDAs, wireless, SMS, multimedia messaging service (MMS), 3G mobile/cellular phones and PS2, which are free from the restrictions of traditional land-based connections. Mobile communications such as these can be used to distribute information using either a push or pull strategy. A push strategy involves sending unsolicited communications to consumers, such as through a SMS. A pull strategy involves providing free information, such as weather reports, game updates and news headlines that the consumer has given permission to receive.

The use of SMS technology provides an example of how mobile communications can be used to market goods and services. An SMS message can do much more than simply convey information. An emerging trend is the use of mobile phone coupons (much harder to lose than paper coupons) where a barcode can be sent to a consumer and scanned at the point of sale. Using this technology, sport leagues, events, and retailers can offer exclusive promotions to consumers who have given permission to receive regular deals.

Competitions can also been designed to make use of mobile phone technology, such as competitions for game tickets. There are, of course, important issues to consider when using SMS technology. Scharl et al. (2005) suggest that there are a number of key success factors to consider when designing an SMS marketing programme, including four success factors of the message itself and four factors relating to the device.

SMS message success factors

1. *Content* should ideally be short, funny or informative and eye catching. It should include information regarding how to stop messages and use appropriate abbreviations (especially with younger users).
2. *Timing of transmission* should minimise the risk of annoying consumers and is best sent during business hours or after midday in the case of students.
3. *Customisation* is paramount. The more targeted the content of the mobile content, the more likely it is to be successful, although this also raises issues of privacy and consumer control.
4. *Consumer control and privacy* requires permission to be sought to send mobile content that the recipient will be interested in. This also minimises the spam problem for consumers who can easily become overwhelmed by advertising clutter.

Device success factors

1. *Graphics and capacity.* The limitation of character numbers is an issue at present which restricts the possible applications of this medium. MMS applications are, however, helping to create programs which are eye-catching and attention grabbing.
2. *Transmission process.* Problems with unsent and delayed messages can reduce the impact of SMS marketing campaigns, especially in the case of time-limited promotions such as last-minute tickets. Future technology may, of course, address this issue.
3. *Product fit.* The needs and habits of mobile communications users suggests that this technology fits best with promotions for products that are frequently purchased, low priced, technical and targeted towards a younger demographic.
4. *Viral impact.* The potential for recipients to forward messages on to their friends has the potential to increase the impact of a campaign at no additional cost to the promoter.

In addition to the potential for messaging information to consumers, mobile communications are increasingly capable of delivering personalised content and even streaming broadcasts. Mobile communications can be used to access information, replays, live footage and statistics about prominent sport events and games from anywhere in the world, including from the game venue itself. Some venues rent out PDAs for this purpose at games, but it is more likely that consumers will use their own PDA on a fee for service or subscription basis. Of course, the same system can be used to send person-alised marketing communications to consumers. Consumers can even decide whether they want to purchase something on offer on the spot via their PDA or phone. BBC Sport now provide their website content via Palmtops, computers or mobile/cellular phones free of charge, allowing consumers to access the news stories about their favourite sports any time and anywhere (http://news.bbc.co.uk/sport2/hi/2823593.stm).

The wireless feature of mobile communications allows roaming connectivity between different portable and permanent technologies such as phones, laptops, handheld computers and diaries, and the Internet. This integration will make portable real time and recorded sport viewing from virtually any location in the world a possibility in the short term and an inexpensive one in the medium term. Handheld, wireless computers are already available and will shortly be pervasive enough for displaying sporting events, replays and highlights. It is also likely that they will be employed during events for similar functions.

> *Chapter Tool 12.2. Mobile communications*: These include the communication tools that are associated with mobile or cellular phones and any wireless communication system. Examples include Bluetooth, mobile phones, PDAs, wireless, SMS, MMS, 3G mobile/cellular phones and PS2, which are free from the restrictions of traditional land-based connections.

Interactive case

Log on to the website for the NFL Europe and Canada (http://www.nfl.com and http://www.nflcanada.com) and explore the ways in which they encourage fans to interact and network.

Team and league websites can also be constructed to allow fans and consumers to network and communicate interactively. Official NFL websites are a good example of this functionality. These sites offer numerous opportunities for fans to interact with one another and even to have an impact on the league itself. In addition to sophisticated services such as the NFL shop, video highlights and news, the sites offer 'fan challenge' competitions, the ability to vote for players and coaches of the week, fan balloting for players who will be included in the Pro Bowl and general blogs.

Upgraded conventional technologies

Upgraded conventional technologies refer to the technological advances that have been made with devices such as televisions, radios and video recorders. Examples include digital television broadcasts, interactive television, digital video recorders, TiVo (the TiVo device stores television programmes onto non-removable hard disk storage much like all digital video recorder devices), graphical user interfaces, satellite radio and electronic kiosks.

One of the innovations seen in many upgraded technologies is the introduction of increased interactivity and customisation. The BBC used an upgraded TV platform to provide interactive Olympic coverage during the Athens 2004 Olympic Games. More than six million digital TV viewers in the United Kingdom tuned into the BBC by using the 'red button' on their remote control which allowed them to access an interactive portal. This provided over 2000 hours of extra and exclusive television footage, as well as a medals table, winners section and news stories.

In addition to the benefits of interactivity, there are several ways in which digital data can be used to enhance the sport watching experience. First, it can be viewed like ordinary video or television transmissions and also offers increased flexibility so that events may be watched over the Internet. As wireless connectivity to the Internet improves in quality, cost and convenience, the option of watching a sporting event on the run through a personal computer, phone, diary or pad will become more prevalent. Second, digital can be used to cover specific players or aspects of the sporting event. The viewer can be the director if they choose, selecting camera angles, players, activities or replays at their discretion. Third, digital can be employed to create new statistics associated with the event. The technology provides more options for measuring and monitoring. These statistics can also be stored for each player or team and revisited later for analysis or even for use in game play. Fourth, digital technologies enable real time interaction such as gaming. As viewers watch the big game, they can link in to play in direct competition through their home gaming console or computer interface. As data are stored historically, game players will be able to create their own teams based on real game performances.

Chapter Tool 12.3. Upgraded Conventional Technologies: These refer to the technological advances that have been made with devices such as televisions, radios and video recorders. Examples include digital television broadcasts, interactive television, digital video recorders, TiVo (the TiVo device stores television programmes onto non-removable hard disk storage much like all digital video recorder devices), graphical user interfaces, satellite radio and electronic kiosks.

Interactive case

Log on to Flickr (http://www.flickr.com) and perform a search for 'Yankee Stadium'. Consider who is posting these images and what positioning information it conveys about the facility.

Sites such as Flickr offer sport organisations a unique avenue for promotion and for reaching fans and potential consumers. The most obvious application involves sport teams, clubs and stadiums posting their own, attention-grabbing photographs, and links to sites such as these so that fans can post their own. Other less obvious opportunities are also available, such as promoting sponsors through the images that are posted and setting up competitions for the best images posted during a given time frame.

Hardware

Hardware refers to the physical objects and equipment that make up new media technology, such as computer systems, games devices, portable equipment, game consoles and multimedia (CD, DVD). New technology has already produced prototype pocket PCs with sufficient processing power to access and replay almost every sporting moment ever broadcast.

Another trend in information technology hardware is the increasing ability for devices to perform multiple tasks and to interact seamlessly with other equipment. A partnership between Apple iPod and Nike, for example, has seen the development of technology which enables 'communication' between an iPod Nano and Nike running shoes. The Nike+ shoes are designed with a pocket under the insole which can house a sensor. A receiver is then inserted into the dock connector of an iPod Nano which collects information wirelessly from the sensor during activity. The software then provides a 'Nike + iPod' menu option on the Nano. The feature is able to provide workout-based voice feedback which provides progress reports on time, distance and pace, and even congratulates the participant on reaching a personal best. The package also provides Nike sport music content, the ability to choose workout options (such as time, distance or calorie goals) and the ability to store and display the results of up to 1000 individual workouts.

> *Chapter Tool 12.4. Hardware*: It refers to the physical objects and equipment that make up new media technology, such as computer systems, games devices, portable equipment, game consoles and multimedia (CD, DVD).

Interactive case

Log on to the Apple website (http://www.apple.com/ipod/nike/) to view the marketing associated with the Nike + iPod system. Consider the needs of people who would use this product (runners), including both practical and psychological needs. Reflect on how the physical devices themselves have been designed and constructed in order to meet these needs.

Software

Where hardware refers to the physical equipment involved in new media technology, software enables that equipment to operate. Software includes both the systems software which enables the technology to function (such as the operating system and the utilities), as well as the applications software which run the users' programs. Software is therefore the interface which ultimately makes all new media technologies function.

Virtual reality software is an example which promises to dramatically change the way spectators view sport in the future. The virtual nature of spectatorship will offer spectacular opportunities for sport enterprises to improve their revenues, particularly if they are a genuinely international property. For example, virtual reality will allow remote users to 'sit' anywhere in the stadium. Like pay-per-view television, the number of virtual reality participants will determine profitability, except virtual reality provides more opportunities for discriminatory pricing.

Software development has also been pivotal to the success of the Nike + iPod sport kit introduced in the previous activity. Not only does software provide the 'Nike + iPod' menu on the iPod Nano, there is a Nike Plus website which includes software functionality for synchronisation and networked communication with other runners worldwide. Once connected to a computer system, the iPod Nano 'synchs' workout data not only to iTunes but also to the website Nikeplus.com, where the user can view their data, set and track goals and even challenge other runners to compete in virtual races. The Nike + iPod system therefore shows how innovative hardware and software can work together to provide new experiences for sport participants.

Chapter Tool 12.5. Software: It includes both the systems software, which enables the technology to function (such as the operating system and the utilities), and the applications software, which run the users' programs.

Interactive case

Log on to the Nike Plus website (http://www.nikeplus.com) to view the software functionality associated with the Nike + iPod system. Consider which software functions enable users to communicate with others and to develop a sense of belonging. Compare the Nike approach to marketing the Nike Plus system to the Apple approach.

Future possibilities and dangers

There are a range of imminent and promising technologies that are almost certainly going to have an impact on sport marketing in the future. Many of them will diminish the gap between the most powerful and well-resourced sport organisations and those which have traditionally struggled for exposure. Smaller sports will find that web broadcasting and all its digital opportunities are their best bet for finding a stable niche. Other exciting developments are being seen in the development of state-of-the-art cameras that can be embedded in eyeglasses and even contact lens style cameras that fit over the retina. With athletes wearing such devices, the data could be transmitted directly to viewers who could choose an athlete to follow as well as a choice of angles and replays.

While new media technologies can offer significant advantages for sport marketers, there are also dangers associated with new media marketing. Sport organisations must have the tools to ensure that the relationships they cultivate with fans bridge the gap between commerce and community. In turn this necessitates the careful management of customer input into products and services. Sport enterprises will have to work hard to ensure that experiences are created for sport consumers that are superior to those they might receive through other discretionary leisure pursuits. Technology has the sometimes unwelcome potential of converting services or customer experiences into commodities. To fortify the sporting experience, sport organisations must continue to focus on understanding the feelings of belonging in sport supporters.

Case Study—New Media in Traditional Baseball

by Sharyn McDonald

As a sport steeped in tradition, baseball has been slow to adopt new technology. Although large-screen replays are commonplace in football games, baseball organisers have been concerned that they might lead to unnecessary pressure on the umpires. However, other forms of technology have found their way into baseball as a result of being responsive to the entertainment needs of fans.

Fans and spectators of baseball tend to be particularly interested in statistics, which have become readily available via the Internet and mobile (cellular) phones. Baseball fans can subscribe to receive player alerts for up to 25 players, customised statistics, team scores and news via text messaging. The Major League Baseball website, mlb.com, offers fans the chance to view footage using MLB.com 'Gameday' technology. Fans can view live datacasts of every game with cameras covering the strikezone, base runners and team line-ups, using their mobile (cellular) phones. MLB.TV subscribers have the opportunity to watch six games live, player-tracking alerts, clickable line scores and extended highlights.

However, it is not only baseball fans who have been utilising the features of this new technology. Players are utilising video uploads to assess their performance and to study the opposition. Instead of having to remain in one location to evaluate their game, players have the portability of video footage, which can be uploaded onto iPods. The players are able to study video footage of opponents and watch it at their convenience. Current players can also use their own historic footage to improve their skills. When their performance is lagging or in need of refinement, they can view footage of themselves in their prime to replicate their best technique.

For those players yet to reach the major league and who are still trying to be discovered, this technology is an important marketing tool. They have the opportunity to be video-captured by one of the numerous scouts who collect and package data on prospective and current players. Teams such as the Colorado Rockies and the San Francisco Giants issue laptops and iPods to coaches and scouts for the purpose of recruitment. With video imagery, scouts can compare players they have seen from anywhere in the world. This exchange of information is two-way. College team coaches are sending clips of their teams to attract prospective high school students, and high school students are sending files of their game highlights to college recruiters. This provides an opportunity for talented players from remote areas or distant countries to promote their skills to recruiters. Baseball is played in over 100 countries around the world, but many aspire to play in Major League Baseball in the United States. It may only be a matter of time before talented players can be discovered through self-promotion over the Internet.

For more information see:

Associated Press (2006). *Rockies Using Video iPods to Study Swings, Hitters*. Available at: http://sports.espn.go.com/mlb/news/story?id=2486924 (accessed 16 June 2006).

Krazit, T. (2007). *Tech Scores with Pro Teams*. Available at: http://www.cnet.com/ 4520-13388_1-6765903-1.html (accessed 1 September 2007).

Koprowski, G.J. (2006). *Athletes, Sports Fans Cultivate Creative Uses of iPods*. Available at: http://www.macnewsworld.com/story/51381.html (accessed 28 June 2006).

Principles summary

- Chapter Principle 12.1: New media refers to communications that are generated by electronic means or through recent technological platforms. It refers to technologically sophisticated platforms or vehicles for transmitting and communicating information.
- Chapter Principle 12.2: New media is represented numerically, and it is modular, automated, variable and transferable to differing file formats and able to be customised.
- Chapter Principle 12.3: New media technologies provide sport marketers with new ways of communicating with consumers and novel approaches to their marketing activities. Many of these approaches are far more rapid, responsive, interactive and inexpensive when compared with other marketing strategies; they are also more able to be customised to key target audiences.

- Chapter Principle 12.4: New media sport marketing is customised communication with targeted sport consumers that is generated by electronic means or through technologically sophisticated platforms that facilitate the transmission of information.
- Chapter Principle 12.5: New media marketing is targeted and personalised interaction which is based on the principles of customisation, modularity, sticky branding, networked communication and permission.
- Chapter Principle 12.6: New media sport marketing messages should be customised or targeted and adapted to specific consumers and their needs.
- Chapter Principle 12.7: A modular new media marketing programme (including product design) is the one structured in a standardised and automated way which incorporates flexibility, responsiveness to changes in demand and ease of transfer.
- Chapter Principle 12.8: Sticky branding occurs when new media sport marketing ideas take hold in consumers' minds in ways that are consistent with the positioning strategy for the brand.
- Chapter Principle 12.9: Networked communication is based on the idea that instead of telling consumers about products, it is more productive to get consumers to talk to each other about them.
- Chapter Principle 12.10: Inclusivity refers to the use of new media marketing to fulfil the need to 'belong', which in turn fosters the development of identity. New media marketing can be conducted in such a way that sport consumers feel 'included' in virtual groups.
- Chapter Principle 12.11: Permission in new media sport marketing refers to the effectiveness of communicating with consumers who have consented to receive customised messages, rather than to send random, untargeted and uninvited marketing communications.

Tools summary

Chapter Tool 12.1. Internet-Driven Platforms
Chapter Tool 12.2. Mobile Communications
Chapter Tool 12.3. Upgraded Conventional Technologies
Chapter Tool 12.4. Hardware
Chapter Tool 12.5. Software

Review questions

1. In what ways is new media different from traditional media?
2. Describe the key characteristics of new media approaches in sport marketing.
3. Provide an example of each of the following principles: customisation, modularity, sticky branding, networked communication, inclusivity and permission.

4. What implications do new media sport marketing principles have for conventional sport marketing techniques?
5. Provide some examples of how mobile communications might be pivotal to the future of marketing communications within venues.
6. Speculate on the future of sport marketing related software. Provide an example that you think might be developed in the future.

Relevant websites

http://www.dallascowboys.com	(Dallas Cowboys NFL team)
http://www.nikeid.com	(Nike ID)
http://www.tele-efficiency.com	(Web marketing and telecommunications company)
http://www.ideavirus.com	(E-book written by Seth Godin on viral marketing)
http://www.myspace.com	(Pages for Roger Federer, the Dallas Cowboys Cheerleaders, Manchester United, The 2008 Tibetan Olympic Team)
http://www.flickr.com	(Photo-sharing website)
http://www.nfl.com	(NFL Europe)
http://www.nflcanada.com	(NFL Canada)
http://www.tab.com.au	(Tabcorp Holdings Australia)
http://www.bookmaker.com	(Bookmaker.com Costa Rica)
http://www.vip.com	(VIP.com Netherlands Antilles)
http://www.2betdsi.com	(Diamond sportsbook Costa Rica)
http://www.empireofports.com	(Online, multi-sport gaming platform)
http://www.zdnet.co.uk	(Business Website United Kingdom)
http://www.youtube.com	(YouTube video-sharing)
http://www.apple.com/ipod/nike/	(Apple)
http://www.nikeplus.com	(Nike Plus)
http://www.sharpe-partners.com/	(Sharpe Partners)

Further reading

McIntyre, P. (2007). Watch out! Your TV will soon be watching you, *The Age*, Melbourne, Australia. Available at: http://www.theage.com.au/news/security/watch-out-your-tv-will-soon-be-watching-you/2007/07/04/1183351332572.html (accessed 5 July 2007).

Wilson, R.F. (2000). The six simple principles of viral marketing. *Web Marketing Today*, Issue 70, February 1. Available at: http://www.tele-efficiency.com/Documentation/Principles_viral_marketing.PDF.

Pikas, C.K. (2005). BLOG searching for competitive intelligence, brand image, and reputation management, *Online*, 29(4): 16–21.

Scharl, A., Dickinger, A. & Murphy, J. (2005). Diffusion and success factors of mobile marketing, *Electronic Commerce Research and Applications*, 4(2): 159–173.

References

Godin, S. (2000). *Unleashing the Ideavirus*. Do You Zoom, Inc. Available at: http://www.ideavirus.com

Manovich, L. (2002). *The Language of New Media,* MIT Press, Boston.

Infront Sports and Media. (2007). Infront Sports & Media takes sports marketing into the virtual world (Press Release 4 June 2007). Available at: http://www.empireofsports.com/press/20070604_InfrontTakesSportsMarketingIntoTheVirtualWorld.pdf

13

Sport marketing implementation and control

Overview

This chapter presents the final stage of the Sport Marketing Framework, the process of implementing and controlling the sport marketing strategy. It introduces the strategies available for enhancing the success of the implementation process. The chapter explains how to develop a control process for implementation, and shows how its use can help evaluate and improve a sport marketing strategy. The final section of the chapter provides a summary of the philosophy, process, principles and tools of sport marketing highlighted in the text.

By the end of this chapter, readers should be able to:

- Describe the importance of implementation and control strategies in a sport marketing strategy.
- Explain how implementation differs from planning sport marketing strategies.
- Identify the key concepts behind successfully transforming a sport marketing strategy into action.
- Outline the steps of a control process.
- Understand how to link the control process to improved strategic decisions.
- Debate the ethical and social responsibilities of sport marketers.

Introduction

The first three stages of the Sport Marketing Framework—(1) Identify Sport Marketing Opportunities, (2) Develop Sport Marketing Strategy and (3) Plan the Sport Marketing Mix—have been explained. It is now time to outline the final stage of the Framework, which is to *implement and control* the sport marketing strategy. The implementation and control process is shown in Figure 13.1, within the Sport Marketing Framework.

Implementing a sport marketing strategy means putting the plans that were devised into action. Controlling a sport marketing strategy means keeping the implementation of marketing activities consistent with the plan and the measures that were put in place to indicate success. In practice, control is all about ensuring that a plan's objectives are going to be achieved, and taking action to correct any problems if it looks as though things are not going as they should. As a result, a central function of control is to evaluate implemented marketing activities to see if they have achieved what they were supposed to. To evaluate a sport marketing plan means to assess it, or to weigh up its positive and negative outcomes to reach a view on its performance. In the end, it is essential to determine how successful a sport marketing strategy has been, or else there is no way of knowing what worked and what did not, and no way of improving in the future. This chapter provides the principles and tools underpinning the successful development of an implementation and control process.

> *Chapter Principle 13.1*: Implementing a sport marketing strategy means putting the plans into action.

Implementation strategies

When it comes to executing a sport marketing plan, it might seem simple enough to follow the plan, but many sport organisations find that it is much harder than it sounds. A marketing plan may be innovative, but if it is not implemented properly it will fail. While it is common for sport marketers to discover that executing a strategy is more difficult than they anticipate, there are five sport marketing implementation tools that greatly increase the probability of success, as illustrated in Figure 13.2.

> *Chapter Principle 13.2*: The implementation success of a sport marketing plan is enhanced through the use of five implementation tools: (1) Leadership and commitment, (2) Communication and delegation, (3) Teamwork and projects, (4) Rewards and reinforcement and (5) Control and feedback.

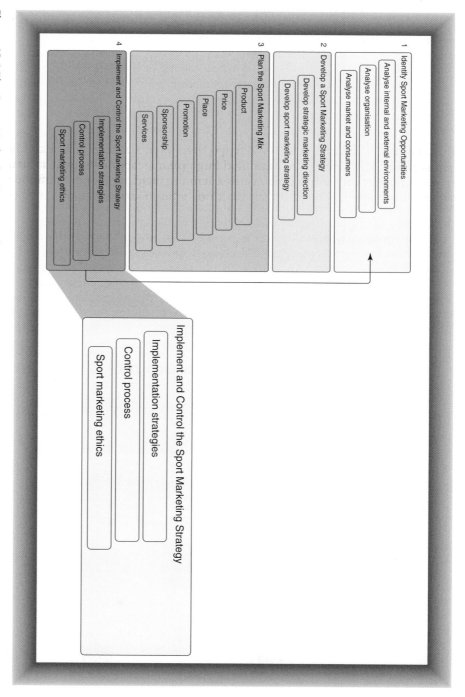

Figure 13.1 The Sport Marketing Framework.

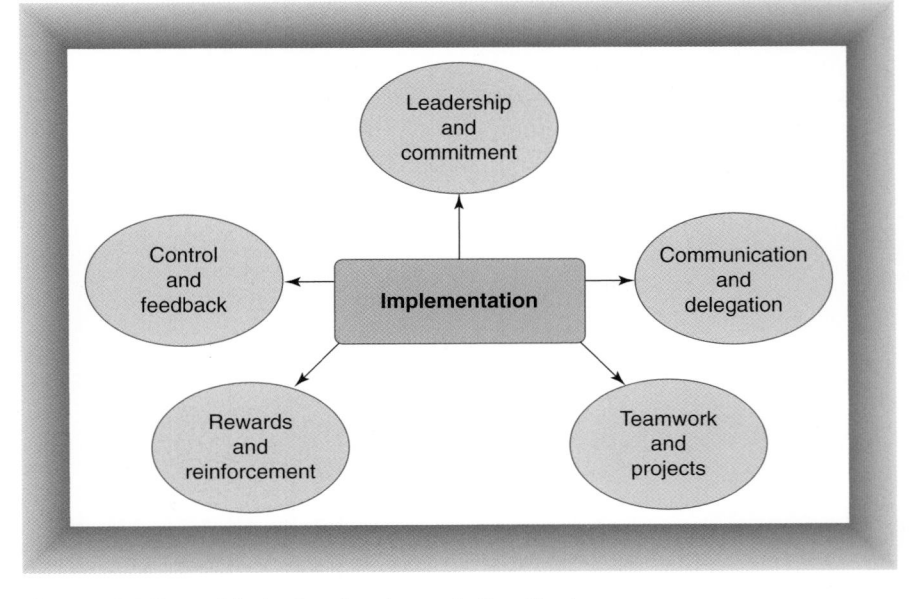

Figure 13.2 Sport Marketing Implementation Tools.

Leadership and commitment

A sport marketing plan is more likely to be successful if there is a clear leader or group of leaders who take responsibility for its implementation. In practice this ensures that the sport organisation is committed to the plan it has devised. The role of the leader is to co-ordinate and organise marketing activities, as well as to manage the control process.

There are a number of levels at which leadership or initiative is required in the implementation of a sport marketing plan. Implementation begins with senior management leaders who have to develop and oversee the timeline associated with the marketing plan and every activity within it, along with the allocation of whatever resources are needed to take action. Any marketing plan will need resources to make it a reality. Every activity in a sport marketing plan will have a corresponding cost for implementation such as staff time and training, the research and development of products and promotions, and even the need to pay for specialist consultants or external contractors if the right expertise is not available internally. It is important not to underestimate the investment in staff time that will be needed. Developing and implementing a marketing plan will not only need the time of marketing staff, but also administration staff and management.

> *Chapter Tool 13.1. Leadership and Commitment*: A sport marketing plan is more likely to be successful if there is a clear leader or group of leaders who take responsibility for its implementation. Leadership and commitment involves the designation of a timeline and the allocation of resources.

Communication and delegation

It is important that all members of the sport marketing team have a good understanding of the marketing plan. Rather than just telling everyone about the plan after it has been developed, it is more effective to involve them along the way. Sport marketing strategies are more likely to be supported by the sport marketing team if all of its members have made a contribution.

Marketing leaders have to make decisions about how marketing activities should be delegated and what information should be provided to those empowered and responsible for tasks. Teams may need to be created, individuals may be given specific assignments and outside contractors may be engaged. The delegation of decision-making authority is delicate for sport marketers. Because of their centrality to the functioning of sport organisations, it is important that volunteers are given sufficient levels of responsibility to challenge and stimulate them. Equally, they should not be given roles which will burden them, or cause serious anxiety and stress. Most of all, volunteers should not be given tasks and responsibilities for which they do not have the authority to fulfil, or the accountability to answer for. The delegation of decision-making for marketing activities is therefore complex. A number of issues should be considered that are strongly connected with effective communication.

There are four preconditions to successful delegation. Delegation of marketing tasks can only work if leaders are: (1) receptive to the ideas of subordinates and volunteers, (2) prepared to let go of tasks, (3) willing to let others make mistakes and (4) ready to trust subordinates. However, even if marketing leaders are ready to delegate the performance of planned marketing tactics, subordinates and volunteers may not be ready. Resistance to delegation may arise from: (1) the fear of criticism over possible mistakes, (2) lack of confidence, (3) inadequate resources to do the job properly, (4) lack of an incentive and (5) already too much to do. If these concerns can be alleviated then delegation is workable. Since a sport marketing plan cannot be deployed without a significant amount of help from employed staff and volunteers, there is really no choice but to make it work.

Delegation is not just a way of involving more people in the implementation of sport marketing, it is a way of accessing a wider range of skills and abilities from those who want to contribute. Effective delegation will also lead to greater clarity about what needs to be done since the delegation process requires a clear statement of the jobs and responsibilities involved. It will also lead to faster decisions since those actually involved in the activity do not need to seek approval before they take action. Delegation allows staff and volunteers to act responsively when dealing with fans and consumers to improve customer satisfaction.

All activities within a sport marketing plan should be delegated or allocated to specific staff members or teams. If duties are not delegated, it becomes easy to assume that someone else is doing it. It is best to have a detailed job assignment which is put in writing after the marketing leader and the staff member or volunteer have agreed on the details. A detailed job assignment should address the following issues:

- Name: Name of the person responsible for project (job).
- Marketing plan: Short description of the relevant objective of the marketing strategy.

- Project title: Short, clear description of specific project (job) being delegated.
- Project description: Detailed description of each part of the project.
- Methods: Statement of *how* the staff member is expected to carry out the project (e.g. processes and techniques they should use).
- Reporting systems: Who staff member should report their progress to, how they should communicate it and how often they should do this.
- Performance measures: Indicators of performance.
- Timeline: Timeline for each stage of the project.
- Resources: What resources the staff member is able to use (e.g. money, materials, administration staff time, training).

It is also important to regularly communicate with other people in the organisation who are not in the marketing team. The more the employees and volunteers of a sport organisation who support the marketing plan, the more likely it is to succeed. This underpins the relevance of communicating the marketing plan internally within the organisation. Internal promotion and marketing means educating every staff member, volunteer and stakeholder about the contents of the plan.

> *Chapter Tool 13.2. Communication and Delegation*: Marketing leaders have to make decisions about how marketing activities should be delegated and what information should be provided to those empowered and responsible for tasks. Delegation of marketing tasks can only work if leaders are: (1) receptive to the ideas of subordinates and volunteers, (2) prepared to let go of tasks, (3) willing to let others make mistakes and (4) ready to trust subordinates. Resistance to delegation may arise from: (1) the fear of criticism over possible mistakes, (2) lack of confidence, (3) inadequate resources to do the job properly, (4) lack of an incentive and (5) already too much to do. A detailed job assignment should be created for every major marketing project or activity within the plan.

Teamwork and projects

The successful implementation of a sport marketing plan requires the involvement of a combination of staff and volunteers who have the right mix of skills, experience and attitudes. One of the most effective ways of ensuring that implementation is effective is to make project teams responsible for certain projects or groups of activities. Project teams are an indispensable tool for achieving quality service outcomes and sporting clubs in particular can make use of project teams because of the need to conduct events with a combination of paid and volunteer staff. A project team structure also has a fixed life and involves delegation, and is therefore a useful device for the organisation of special one-off functions at both the local level, and for larger, more complex events. For example, if a marketing plan includes a promotional barbeque, marketing leaders may decide to establish a special project team to conduct the event. The project team operates as long as it takes to organise, conduct and evaluate the event, after which time it disbands.

Not all marketing teams will produce high-quality outcomes in implementing their set projects and activities. However, the chances of a project team fulfilling its potential are dramatically increased when the following are in place:

- Agreement that the project is vitally important to the success of the marketing strategy.
- The project team has a guaranteed and appropriate lifespan.
- The team has a shared purpose.
- Realistic and concrete goals are agreed upon by the team.
- There is a common understanding on exactly what has to be done.
- Agreement that the rewards and accolades for successful completion will be shared.
- Unimpeded flows of communication, both within the team, and with marketing leaders.
- Strong working relationship with other related teams.

Part of building a team is choosing the right members who provide a mix of skills and abilities so that a team can tackle different kinds of marketing tasks. A mix of the following knowledge and skills is a good start for most marketing implementation teams.

Knowledge of	Skills in
The sport industry and marketplace	Communicating with staff, consumers and other groups
Marketing principles and concepts	Talking with the media
General business and management principles	Public speaking and hosting events
The target consumers, and sport consumers in general	Generating and developing ideas
The range of goods and/or services being offered	Problem-solving and negotiation
Specialist areas (e.g. contacts, sponsorship, event management and budgeting, risk management, facility development)	Organisation, time management and project co-ordination
	Personally promoting the value of the product and organisation
	Understanding market research and statistics

Chapter Tool 13.3. Teamwork and Projects: The successful implementation of a sport marketing plan requires the involvement of a combination of staff and volunteers who have the right mix of skills, experience and attitudes. Implementation teams work best when: (1) there is agreement that the project is vitally important to the success of the marketing strategy, (2) the project team has a guaranteed and appropriate lifespan, (3) the team has a shared purpose, (4) realistic and concrete goals are agreed upon by the team, (5) there is a common understanding on exactly what has to be done, (6) agreement that the rewards and accolades for successful completion will be shared, (7) there is an unimpeded flow of communication, both within the team, and with marketing leaders, and (8) a strong working relationship with other related teams exists.

Rewards and reinforcement

Whether the implementation of marketing strategy will be successful depends on the individual and team efforts of staff and volunteers. It can be helpful to put rewards into place for those who do a good job with implementing the strategy. Rewards can include positive feedback (e.g. praise, recognition), money (e.g. commissions, bonuses, raises) or other rewards like stock options or promotions and special assignments. It can be useful to offer smaller rewards along the way, as well as bigger rewards when major targets are achieved. Irrespective of their composition, the purpose behind all rewards is to reinforce the kinds of behaviours and actions that are conducive to effective plan implementation.

> *Chapter Tool 13.4. Rewards and Reinforcement*: It can be helpful to put rewards into place to reinforce the kinds of behaviours and actions that are conducive to effective plan implementation. Rewards can include positive feedback (e.g. praise, recognition), money (e.g. commissions, bonuses, raises) or other rewards like promotions, days off and special assignments.

Control and feedback

The final part of implementing a marketing strategy is to review and evaluate its outcomes on a regular basis. It is vital to keep track of how well the plan is going, and to make changes if things are not going as intended. This is such an important part of implementation that the next topic, the control process, is dedicated to it.

> *Chapter Tool 13.5. Control and Feedback*: Regular evaluation of the performance of a marketing plan is necessary in case corrections need to be made. This is achieved through the introduction of a control process.

Control process

Controlling a sport marketing strategy involves six steps which are summarised in Figure 13.3.

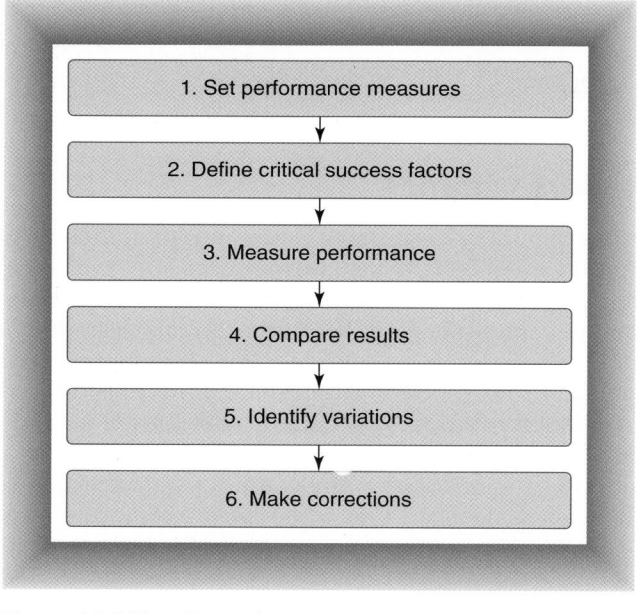

Figure 13.3 The Control Process.

Chapter Principle 13.3: Controlling a sport marketing strategy means keeping it on track, making sure that it is achieving what it set out to, and making changes to correct variations and problems. The control process involves six steps: (1) Set performance measures, (2) Define critical success factors, (3) Measure performance, (4) Compare results, (5) Identify variations and (6) Make corrections.

Set performance measures

Setting performance measures is the first step of the control process. Because setting performance measures is part of the strategic process, they should have already been determined in stage two of the Sport Marketing Framework. It might be advisable to re-read the section on setting performance measures in Chapter 5.

Define critical success factors

Critical success factors (CSFs) represent those marketing projects and activities most influential to the successful implementation of a marketing plan. CSFs are the critical actions in marketing that when appropriately implemented have the most impact on the success of the plan. CSFs are determined by asking the question, 'what must go right for the marketing plan to be successfully implemented?' The key to using CSFs is to prioritise them, thereby showing which areas demand the greatest implementation attention. For example, after some prioritisation it might become clear that the most important CSF is a new sponsorship deal. If this is the case, resources can be allocated towards the development of a proposal and the staff to personally sell it.

Measure performance

The next step is to put the performance measures identified in step one into action. How performance is measured will depend on the nature of the measures that were set. For example, if a performance measure was to increase membership numbers by 10 per cent in one year, then information on membership rates need to be collected. If a performance measure was to increase merchandise revenue to $120 000 by June 2009, then the relevant financial information needs to be acquired. With the before and after measures it is a simple task to determine the success of the marketing plan and its implementation in the next step. Obviously, an outcome of step two is to focus on the measurement of CSFs. Some further examples of performance measures and the corresponding information needed are given in Table 13.1.

Compare results

Comparing results means examining the outcomes of performance measurement *before* the marketing strategy was implemented and *after* it was

Table 13.1 Performance Measures and Required Information

Examples of Performance Measures	*Examples of Required Information*
To increase membership from 70 to 100 members by January 2008	Membership numbers
To increase the number of people who use our service to 50 customers per month by July 2008	Numbers of people who use the service
To increase spectator levels to an average of 25 000 spectators per game, by December 2008, as measured by ticket sales	Spectator numbers (e.g., ticket sales)
To increase customer satisfaction levels to 7/10 as rated by them on a customer satisfaction survey	Customer satisfaction levels (in this example a customer satisfaction survey is used)
To increase profit to $120 000, calculated at the end of the 2008 financial year	Profit figures
To increase the number of people who have heard of our club in this area to 1000, as measured by a phone survey	Survey responses of who has heard of the club

implemented. For example, if the performance measure of 'increasing profit by 10 per cent by the end of the financial year' was set, then the level of profit prior to the implementation of the marketing strategy (the previous year's profit level) should be considered against the measurements made at the end of the financial year in which the strategy was deployed.

Identify variations

To ensure that the objectives of the marketing plan are being achieved, it is necessary to find out if there are any variations between what was planned and what actually happened. Sport marketers usually call this *variance*. Sometimes the variance is positive because something beneficial occured that was not planned. For example, it is common in sport to sell more merchandise if a team performs unexpectedly well during a season. On the other hand, at other times the variance may be negative such as the sudden emergence of a scandal involving the behaviour of a prominent athlete. Variance can also been seen in the light of whether something can be done about it or whether it is unavoidable.

Once variation has been determined it can be classified as either acceptable or unavoidable. For example, membership numbers might actually increase to 25 per cent in a year even though the performance measure set was an increase of 10 per cent. Clearly, this is an acceptable variation as it has a positive impact on the achievement of marketing objectives. Other examples of acceptable variations could include good publicity that was not expected, or an offer of sponsorship that was unsolicited.

An example of an unavoidable variation might be a circumstance where membership numbers dropped by eight per cent because of a particularly bad season. Unavoidable variations are often random or infrequent events that cannot be foreseen or are difficult to plan for. Other examples of unavoidable variations could include negative publicity from alcohol overuse by players, or financial mismanagement. Part of the control process is to learn from these experiences and to try to improve them in the future. It is advantageous to measure performance as often as is practical to have time to take corrective action if something is going wrong.

Make corrections

The final step in the control process is to make changes if they are needed. This will depend on the types of variations noted in the previous step. If the variations are within acceptable limits, then no action may be necessary. But, if variations are significant enough, then corrective action will be needed to adjust the original plan to the new circumstances. For example, imagine that a performance measure reflected a goal to increase customer satisfaction ratings to 7/10 on a customer satisfaction survey by the end of June 2009. However, when June 2009 arrives, a new survey reveals that satisfaction actually dropped to 4/10. Naturally, this would constitute an unacceptable variance and it would be essential to immediately study the survey results to determine exactly what customers are unhappy about in order to take remedial action.

Sport marketing ethics

While the implementation of a sport marketing plan should align with an organisation's objectives, it should also fit within the broader boundaries of ethical behaviour. Ethics in sport marketing typically refers to whether the traditional four Ps of the marketing mix are deployed within a moral and professional code. Mostly these include issues associated with unsafe or poor quality products, deceptive or predatory pricing, misleading or dishonest promotions and exploitative or collusive distribution. In the sporting world, other major marketing issues are concerned with publicising the private lives of athletes, exploiting passionate fans and children who idolise sport stars through athlete endorsements of commercial products, the use of venues with unsafe facilities, unrealistic promises associated with health, fitness and weight loss products, and the overpricing of high-profile matches and special sport events.

One helpful view of marketing ethics was offered by Holley (1987), who proposed that there should be three basic tenets against which behaviour must be matched: (1) the buyer and seller must both be fully informed as to what is being purchased and what is being paid in exchange, (2) neither the buyer nor seller is compelled or coerced in their choices and (3) both buyer and seller are capable of making a rational decision concerning the transaction. In short, informed, autonomous decisions based on the faithful representation of the product features and its price lie at the core of responsible sport marketing.

> *Chapter Principle 13.4*: There are three basic tenets against which sport marketing behaviour must be matched: (1) the buyer and seller must both be fully informed as to what is being purchased and what is being paid in exchange, (2) neither the buyer nor seller is compelled or coerced in their choices and (3) both buyer and seller are capable of making a rational decision concerning the transaction.

It is probably reasonable to suspect that most sport marketers do not consider ethics directly in their daily activities until they are faced with a moral dilemma or an issue with ambiguous elements. For example, should a sponsor be told that a prominent player has tested positive to banned drugs?; is it right to sell a single ticket to a sport event for hundreds of dollars just because demand far exceeds supply?; are there circumstances in which ambush marketing is acceptable? It is for these difficult issues that sport marketers and

Table 13.2 Professional Code of Conduct for Sport Marketers

1. Products and services should be safe. Sporting venues and their facilities should meet all health and safety legislation requirements
2. All marketing communications honestly represent the products offered
3. The product-price exchange should represent fair value
4. Prices are transparent and clearly associated with products
5. Product features are clearly demonstrated and honestly represented
6. Sport marketers should not engage in price fixing or collusion outside of regulated practices
7. Marketing communications should not be coercive or manipulative
8. Athletes' and participants' private lives should not be used for marketing advantages without permission
9. Minors should not be exploited for marketing messages
10. Supply of sporting products should not be manipulated to influence pricing

organisations might elect to follow a professional code of ethics, which can be employed as a guideline for dealing with uncertain situations. In general, professional codes contain rules about norms of behaviour, ethical values and core principles such as honesty, responsibility and fairness. Table 13.2 provides a set of common professional guidelines for sport marketers.

Interactive case

The American Marketing Association provides a *Code of Ethics*, which provides an excellent example of professional guidelines for marketing behaviour (American Marketing Association, 2007). Log on to the following website to review the major elements and consider the extent to which they can be applied to the sporting context.
http://www.marketingpower.com/content435.php

Conclusion

This text has explored sport marketing over four levels. The most fundamental level describes the philosophy of sport marketing: to satisfy the needs of sport consumers. One of the features that makes sport marketing unique is the range and diversity of sport consumers' needs. Not only can sport products be offered in the form of goods and services, but sport itself can be both the target of marketing and a vehicle for marketing. Furthermore, sport consumers may be involved personally in the delivery of sport products, such as with sporting competitions, or may be passive recipients of an experience, such as spectators at a sporting contest.

At the next level—the process of sport marketing—this text has reviewed and explained the four stages of the Sport Marketing Framework. Stage one requires the identification of sport marketing opportunities. This is achieved through the assessment of the internal and external environment, the sport organisation, and the sport market and its consumers. After this information has been collected and analysed, it is possible to undertake stage two of the Sport Marketing Framework, and develop a sport marketing strategy. To construct a sport marketing strategy, sport marketers must make a series of decisions about the direction of the marketing programme, culminating in the formulation of marketing objectives and performance measures. Stage two also involves deciding on the core of the marketing strategy. This involves deciding exactly what products and services will be marketed to consumers (segmentation), and how the brand will be positioned in the marketplace against competitors. With a target market and a positioning strategy in place, stage three of the Sport Marketing Framework, planning the sport marketing mix, can begin. Here, tactics for marketing the sport product, price, distribution (place), promotion, sponsorship and sport services are established. It is imperative that these tactics are integrated and consistent with the chosen positioning strategy. Finally, stage four can be introduced, which requires the implementation and control of the sport marketing strategy. This means that plans are put into action using implementation strategies, and kept on track through a control process. Part of the control process re-engages the objectives and performance measures set in stage two, to see whether or not the targets set were achieved. In this final stage of the process it becomes transparent which parts of the marketing plan have been successful, and which parts require remedial action.

At the third and fourth levels of sport marketing are principles and tools, respectively. The principles of sport marketing represent the general rules and guidelines of good practice, while the tools of sport marketing are techniques that can be used to execute the principles. The principles and tools highlighted in the text are summarised in Appendix. The combination of the philosophy, process, principles and tools articulated in this text forge the relationship a sport brand enjoys with sport consumers.

Case Study—Fitness Centres for Kids

By Sharyn McDonald

Fitness centres continually look for innovative ways to improve in order to compete with their rivals. Some centres completely transform their operations to accommodate the changing needs of their market while others utilise promotional offers and marketing gimmicks. As there is considerable competition in the leisure industry, fitness centres can differentiate themselves by the activities they implement. While some centres try to keep up with the latest fitness trends and popular culture to attract and maintain the youth market, others consider the needs of the aging market. It is therefore important for fitness centres to consider the various life stages of consumers. Some centres try to find this balance by accommodating all age groups while others seek more specialised target markets.

Some innovative centres have provided fitness opportunities for the captive young audience placed in standard childminding facilities. While their active parents participate in fitness programmes, young children tend to be entertained with sedentary games and activities to pass the time. With the increasing problems associated with childhood health and physical inactivity, some centres have seen this as a unique opportunity to meet the needs of the next generation. The combination of potential obesity, sedentary lifestyles, diminished parental oversight and growing populations of children with special needs all drive an underserved market.

One centre in the United Kingdom has developed exercise classes as an extension product to their childminding service. Children from the age of two can participate in a thirty-minute exercise class developing their balance and hand–eye co-ordination, and from age four can use children's fitness equipment. Centres are now able to purchase gymnasium equipment specifically designed and engineered for young children. This equipment is often provided in a separate, child-specific room within a facility. Another centre in the United States has taken this concept one step further by designing a fitness centre exclusively for young children and 'tweens', who they see as one of the fastest growing populations of potential clients. The founder of Energym, Kevin Bolden, developed the unique concept to meet the market gap and to help encourage healthy habits. After seeing interactive videogames at a consumer electronic show, Bolden fused exercise with game technology known as 'Exergaming'. Realising that children spend a considerable part of their leisure time playing electronic games, Energym is filled with equipment that appeals to the youth market allowing them to exercise while having fun.

Already popular in game arcades, 'Dance Dance Revolution' shows participants dance moves on a floor pad. Children are also familiar with 'Eye Toy' technology, where the player uses digital technology to demonstrate kung fu on virtual opponents. In facilities like Energym, a host of innovative forms of interactive sports technology are employed, such as stationary exercise bikes and treadmills that control video games where the faster one pedals, the more speed their virtual game displays. Exergaming is not limited to individual workouts. For example, 'Sportwall' is a team game which requires players to track a ball, multiple targets, sounds, scores and a time clock all at the same time.

The success of Energym led to its first franchise named NexGym. The owners opened the new fitness facility for children by converting a childminding facility located next to an adult fitness centre. The convenience of being able to workout at a facility situated next to a fully supervised, child-friendly fitness centre is compelling parents to switch fitness centres. While Energym has capitalised on a market opportunity, their success has been a consequence of getting the implementation right.

For more information see:

Exeter Golf and Country Club (2007). *Keep Fit with the Pack*. Available at:
http://www.exetergcc.co.uk/index.php?page=kids-fitness.

NexGym (2006a). What We Offer. Available at:
http://www.nexgym.com/franchising/what_we_offer.html

NexGym (2006b). Nexgym, The Next Generation in Fitness for Kids. Available at:
http://www.nexgym.com

NexGym (2007). NexGym in the News. Available at:
http://www.nexgym.com/Nexgym_news.html

Principles summary

- Chapter Principle 13.1: Implementing a sport marketing strategy means putting the plans into action.
- Chapter Principle 13.2: The implementation success of a sport marketing plan is enhanced through the use of five implementation tools: (1) Leadership and commitment, (2) Communication and delegation, (3) Teamwork and projects, (4) Rewards and reinforcement and (5) Control and feedback.
- Chapter Principle 13.3: Controlling a sport marketing strategy means keeping it on track, making sure that it is achieving what it set out to and making changes to correct variations and problems. The control process involves six steps: (1) Set performance measures, (2) Define critical success factors, (3) Measure performance, (4) Compare results, (5) Identify variations and (6) Make corrections.
- Chapter Principle 13.4: There are three basic tenets against which sport marketing behaviour must be matched: (1) the buyer and seller must both be fully informed as to what is being purchased and what is being paid in exchange, (2) neither the buyer nor seller is compelled or coerced in their choices and (3) both buyer and seller are capable of making a rational decision concerning the transaction.

Tools summary

Chapter Tool 13.1. Leadership and Commitment
Chapter Tool 13.2. Communication and Delegation
Chapter Tool 13.3. Teamwork and Projects
Chapter Tool 13.4. Rewards and Reinforcement
Chapter Tool 13.5. Control and Feedback

Review questions

1. What is the difference between implementation and control?
2. Provide an example for each of the five implementation tools.
3. Outline the steps of the control process.
4. How can critical success factors be used to enhance the success of a control strategy?
5. Do you think there are any aspects of sport marketing which make the development of a code of professional marketing ethics different to mainstream marketing? If so, what are they and how should they be incorporated into a code?

Relevant website

http://www.marketingpower.com/content435.php (American Marketing Association Code of Ethics)

Further reading

Brinkmann, J. (2002). Business and marketing ethics as professional ethics. Concepts, approaches and typologies, *Journal of Business Ethics*, 41: 159–177.
Wood, G. (2002). A partnership model of corporate ethics, *Journal of Business Ethics*, 40: 61–73.

References

American Marketing Association (2007). *Code of Ethics* (revised ed.). American Marketing Association, Chicago, IL.
Holley, D.M. (1987). A moral evaluation of sales practices, *Business & Professional Ethics Journal*, 5: 3–21.

Appendix Text Principles and Tools Summary

Principles	Tools

Chapter 1. Sport Marketing Introduction

- Chapter Principle 1.1: Marketing is more than promotion, advertising, personal selling or sales gimmicks
- Chapter Principle 1.2: Marketing aims to create an exchange where the customer gives up something for a product or service
- Chapter Principle 1.3: Sport marketing is the process of planning how a sport brand is positioned and how the delivery of its products or services are to be implemented in order to establish a relationship between a sport brand and its consumers
- Chapter Principle 1.4: Sport marketing has two angles: one is the marketing of sport products and services, while the other is marketing through sport
- Chapter Principle 1.5: The philosophy of sport marketing is to satisfy the needs of sport consumers
- Chapter Principle 1.6: The process of sport marketing is the series of steps required to find opportunities, devise strategy, plan the tactics, and implement and evaluate a sport marketing plan
- Chapter Principle 1.7: Sport marketing can be described as a philosophy (an attitude towards marketing), a process (a series of activities), a set of principles (general rules and guidelines) and tools (recommended techniques)
- Chapter Principle 1.8: The principles of sport marketing provide the rules and guidelines for the implementation of the Sport Marketing Framework process, while the tools of sport marketing are specific activities designed to help execute the principles
- Chapter Principle 1.9: The Sport Marketing Framework provides a detailed explanation of the four stages of the sport marketing process: (1) identify sport marketing opportunities; (2) develop sport marketing strategy; (3) plan the marketing mix; and (4) implement and control the strategy

Chapter 2. Sport Markets

- Chapter Principle 2.1: Sport is a special form of business. A standard marketing approach does not always work in sport, so sport marketers must also understand the special features of the sport market
- Chapter Principle 2.2: Sport can elicit an emotional response in its consumers that is rarely found in other businesses. It can stimulate immense loyalty, but also strong attachments to nostalgia and club tradition
- Chapter Principle 2.3: Sport organisations measure their success both on and off the field of play. On-field success refers to achievement within sport competition. Off-field success refers to financial stability and profitability
- Chapter Principle 2.4: Sporting organisations that compete in leagues and competitions rely on the health of their competitors for their own success. Sport consumers are more attracted to attend games where there is a balanced competition
- Chapter Principle 2.5: Sport leagues and competitions implement policies to encourage competitive balance. Policies often include salary caps for players, rules about sharing revenues and regulations regarding how players are to be shared between teams
- Chapter Principle 2.6: Unpredictability can be advantageous in the competitive sport product because it makes sport more attractive
- Chapter Principle 2.7: In competitive sport there is a low cross elasticity of demand where it is difficult to substitute (or replace) one sport league, team, brand or competition for another
- Chapter Principle 2.8: Product loyalty is strong due to the emotional attachments that sport consumers develop to sport products and brands
- Chapter Principle 2.9: Sport consumers identify with teams, clubs, brands and athletes, and see them as extensions of themselves
- Chapter Principle 2.10: The competitive sport product is restricted by a fixed supply schedule making it difficult to change production rates in order to meet the demand of customers, but can be overcome through alternative distribution channels

(Continued)

Appendix (Continued)

Principles	Tools

Chapter 3. Sport Consumers

- Chapter Principle 3.1: A sport consumer is an individual who purchases sporting goods, uses sport services, participates or volunteers in sport, and/or follows sport as a spectator or fan
- Chapter Principle 3.2: Sport fan motives for consuming sport products and services can be summarised into three categories:
  (1) psychological motives,
  (2) socio-cultural motives and
  (3) self-concept motives
- Chapter Principle 3.3: Psychological motives for sport fans include the opportunity for stimulation, escape, aesthetic pleasure, and a sense of dramatic entertainment
- Chapter Principle 3.4: Socio-cultural motives for sport fans include the opportunity for family and social interaction, cultural connections and even economic benefit
- Chapter Principle 3.5: Self-concept motives for sport fans include the opportunity for belonging and group affiliation, tribal connections and vicarious achievement
- Chapter Principle 3.6: Fan motives for consuming sport are affected by their age, education, income, gender and race, but these demographic variables do not always influence motivation in a uniform or predictable way
- Chapter Principle 3.7: Sport fans can be classified according to the sources and dimensions of their attraction to the sport, and their frequency of attendance
- Chapter Principle 3.8: Fans' decisions to attend or view sport may be influenced by external factors, such as the type of sport involved, the balance of the competition, how uncertain the outcome is, the likelihood of their team winning, the venue and facilities, weather conditions, prices, personal income levels, special experiences that are being offered, promotional factors and the availability of alternative activities

Stage 1: Identify Sport Marketing Opportunities

Chapter 4. Sport Marketing Opportunities

- Chapter Principle 4.1: The Sport Marketing Framework describes the four stages of sport marketing including identifying sport marketing opportunities, developing a sport marketing strategy, planning the sport marketing mix, and implementing and controlling the sport marketing strategy

- Chapter Principle 4.2: The first step in identifying sport marketing opportunities is to analyse the internal and external environment using the tools of SWOT analysis (with external environment analysis) and competitor analysis (with the Five Forces analysis)

- Chapter Principle 4.3: The second step in identifying sport marketing opportunities is to conduct an analysis of the organisation. This requires four tools: Mission Statement; Vision Statement; Organisational Objectives; and Stakeholder Analysis

- Chapter Principle 4.4: The third step in identifying sport marketing opportunities involves acquiring information about the sport market and consumers. Market research is the process of collecting information in order to learn about the marketplace and what consumers in general, and a sport organisation's customers specifically, want. It involves two kinds of information: quantitative or numerical, and qualitative or non-numerical

- Chapter Principle 4.5: A market opportunity is a situation where a new or modified product or service can be introduced that meets an unfulfilled sport consumer need

- Chapter Tool 4.1. SWOT and External Environment Analysis

- Chapter Tool 4.2. Competitor and Five Forces Analysis

- Chapter Tool 4.3. Mission Statement

- Chapter Tool 4.4. Vision Statement

- Chapter Tool 4.5. Organisational Objectives

- Chapter Tool 4.6. Stakeholder Analysis

- Chapter Tool 4.7. Quantitative Market Research

- Chapter Tool 4.8. Qualitative Market Research

- Chapter Tool 4.9. Product-Market Expansion Grid

(Continued)

Appendix (Continued)

Principles	Tools
Stage 2: Develop a Sport Marketing Strategy	
Chapter 5. Sport Marketing Strategy	
● Chapter Principle 5.1: The second stage of the Sport Marketing Framework is to develop a sport marketing strategy. This requires two steps: (a) to develop a strategic marketing direction, and (b) to develop a sport marketing position	● Chapter Tool 5.1. Marketing Objectives
● Chapter Principle 5.2: Developing a strategic marketing direction involves constructing marketing objectives and setting performance measures	● Chapter Tool 5.2. Performance Measures
● Chapter Principle 5.3: Developing a sport marketing position involves four steps: market segmentation (1, 2), market positioning tactics (3) and devising the marketing mix (4)	● Chapter Tool 5.3. Market Segmentation
	● Chapter Tool 5.4. Market Positioning
Stage 3: Plan The Sport Marketing Mix	
Chapter 6. Sport Products	
● Chapter Principle 6.1: Sport goods may be differentiated from services on the basis of four factors: tangibility, consistency, perishability and separability	● Chapter Tool 6.1. Sport Product Continuum
● Chapter Principle 6.2: A sport product is the complete package of benefits presented to a sport consumer in the form of physical goods, services and ideas, or a combination of these to produce a sport experience	● Chapter Tool 6.2. New Product Development
● Chapter Principle 6.3: Sport products should be seen as a bundle of benefits comprising the core benefits, features of the product and augmented product. These three variables of the product are interrelated and should be manipulated as a group	● Chapter Tool 6.3. Product Life Cycle Stages

- Chapter Principle 6.4: In sport marketing, a new product can take many forms such as the improved performance of an existing product, new functions added to an existing product, a new way to use an existing product, combining existing products, or a new look or design for a product

- Chapter Principle 6.5: The term product life cycle refers to the stages that a product goes through from first being introduced onto the market to its decline. There are four stages of the product life cycle: introduction, growth, maturity and decline

- Chapter Principle 6.6: A sport brand is the symbolic representation of everything that a sport organisation seeks to stand for, leading to expectations about its value and performance. A brand can be portrayed as an identifying badge which triggers consumers to remember a product or an organisation. It can be a name, a design, a symbol (or logo), an image or a combination of these things. Branding is one of the key strategies that marketers use to help their product to stand out from the crowd by positioning it through associated ideas and concepts

- Chapter Principle 6.7: Building a brand is a process made up of four steps, including (1) establish brand awareness, (2) develop and manage a brand image, (3) develop brand equity, and (4) develop brand loyalty

- Chapter Principle 6.8: Brand equity increases when consumers rate products as high quality. There are different elements of product quality for goods compared with services. There are five elements of service quality: (1) reliability, (2) assurance, (3) empathy, (4) responsiveness and (5) tangibles. There are eight elements of goods quality, these are (1) features, (2) performance, (3) reliability, (4) conformity to specifications, (5) durability, (6) serviceability, (7) aesthetic design and (8) product warranty

Chapter 7. Sport Pricing

- Chapter Principle 7.1: Pricing communicates an important symbolic positioning message to consumers about a sport product

- Chapter Principle 7.2: The value of a sport product is the relationship between its price and the benefits a consumer believes they will receive from it

- Chapter Tool 7.1. Pricing Goals

- Chapter Tool 7.2. Price Sensitivity Analysis

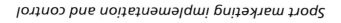

Sport marketing implementation and control

(Continued)

Appendix (Continued)

Principles	Tools
Chapter Principle 7.3: The price of a product is the amount of money a consumer must give up in exchange for a good or service. However, price also represents the value of a product. Although price is usually seen as an amount of money, it may also include other consumer sacrifices to acquire a sport product, such as time or social cost	Chapter Tool 7.3. Break-even Analysis
Chapter Principle 7.4: Revenue is the price that consumers pay for a product, multiplied by the number of units sold. Profit is revenue minus the costs of producing and selling the product	Chapter Tool 7.4. Assess Pricing Variables
Chapter Principle 7.5: The strategic pricing process provides a structure for setting price. The process involves: (1) setting a pricing goal, (2) determining price sensitivity, (3) conducting a break-even analysis, (4) assessing pricing variables, (5) selecting pricing tactics and (6) setting a price point	Chapter Tool 7.5. Select Pricing Tactics
	Chapter Tool 7.6. Select Price Point
Chapter 8. Sport Distribution	
Chapter Principle 8.1: A sport distribution channel is an organised series of organisations or individuals that pass a product from the producer to the final consumer	Chapter Tool 8.1. Distribution Issues Analysis
Chapter Principle 8.2: There are both direct and indirect distribution channels that vary in length. A direct distribution channel is short where the producer sells the product directly to the consumer. An indirect distribution channel is a long channel where there are a number of intermediaries involved along the way	Chapter Tool 8.2. Seating
Chapter Principle 8.3: A channel member is any organisation or individual that is involved in the sport distribution channel. Channel members may include wholesalers and retailers, as well as producers and consumers	Chapter Tool 8.3. Scoreboards and Signage
Chapter Principle 8.4: The sport facility is the most important distribution channel for sport activity services and professional sport events	Chapter Tool 8.4. Lighting and Sound Systems

- Chapter Principle 8.5: Sport marketers must consider four main aspects of sport facilities in which they can maximise the sport consumer experience: (1) location and accessibility, (2) design and layout (3) facility infrastructure and (4) customer service

- Chapter Principle 8.6: Ticket sales are one of the most important sources of revenue for sport organisations that conduct competitions or events. The smooth distribution of tickets is essential to the satisfaction of consumers and the maximisation of sales

- Chapter Tool 8.5. Transport

- Chapter Tool 8.6. Media and Broadcasting

- Chapter Tool 8.7. Childcare Facilities
- Chapter Tool 8.8. Merchandise
- Chapter Tool 8.9. Food and Beverages

Chapter 9. Sport Promotion

- Chapter Principle 9.1: Promotion can be defined as the way that sport marketers communicate with consumers to inform, persuade and remind them about the features and benefits described by a sport product's positioning

- Chapter Principle 9.2: The promotions mix consists of four marketing tools: (1) advertising, (2) personal selling, (3) sales promotions and (4) public relations

- Chapter Principle 9.3: Promotional elements should be combined in order to complement one another in order to achieve a promotional goal that is consistent with the overall marketing and positioning strategy

- Chapter Principle 9.4: There are three main objectives of promotion: (1) to inform, (2) to persuade and (3) to remind

- Chapter Principle 9.5: Promotions that inform aim to communicate the product's existence, its benefits, its positioning, and how it can be obtained. Promotions that aim to inform consumers are usually undertaken during the early stages of the product life cycle

- Chapter Principle 9.6: Persuasive promotions are utilised when trying to give consumers good reasons to buy a sport product. Persuasive promotions are more common when a product enters the growth stage of the product life cycle

- Chapter Tool 9.1. Advertising

- Chapter Tool 9.2. Personal Selling

- Chapter Tool 9.3. Sales Promotions

- Chapter Tool 9.4. Public Relations

- Chapter Tool 9.5. Align with Marketing Objectives

- Chapter Tool 9.6. Consider the Target Market

(Continued)

Sport marketing implementation and control

Appendix (Continued)

Principles	Tools
• Chapter Principle 9.7: Reminder promotions aim to keep a product or brand name prominent in consumers' minds. Reminder promotions are most common during the maturity stage of the product life cycle	• Chapter Tool 9.7. Set Promotional Objectives
• Chapter Principle 9.8: A promotional strategy is a plan that aims to use the elements of the promotions mix for the best results. The promotions planning process involves five steps: (1) Align with marketing objectives, (2) Consider target market, (3) Set promotional objectives, (4) Set promotional budget and (5) Develop promotional mix	• Chapter Tool 9.8. Set Promotional Budget
	• Chapter Tool 9.9. Develop Promotions Mix
Chapter 10. Sport Sponsorship	
• Chapter Principle 10.1: The term sport property refers to the recipient of the sponsorship. This could be an athlete, team, event, venue, association, cause or competition	• Chapter Tool 10.1. Sponsorship Proposal
• Chapter Principle 10.2: Sport sponsorship is a business agreement where one organisation provides financial or in-kind assistance to a sport property in exchange for the right to associate itself with the sport property. The sponsor does this to achieve corporate objectives (such as enhancing corporate image) or marketing objectives (such as increasing brand awareness)	• Chapter Tool 10.2. Sport Sponsorship Rights
• Chapter Principle 10.3: Sport sponsorship generates goodwill among consumers. The amount of goodwill generated can vary depending on the kind of sport property being sponsored, the degree of involvement that consumers have with the sport property, the time at which the sponsor becomes involved, and when and how the sponsor ceases the sponsorship	• Chapter Tool 10.3. Sponsorship Leveraging

- Chapter Principle 10.4: Fan involvement is an important consideration in sponsorship because a consumer's response to a sponsorship is driven by the level of involvement that he/she has with the sport property

- Chapter Principle 10.5: The objectives of sponsorship can vary greatly, depending on the size of the partners, the type of sponsorship and the type of sport property being supported. Some common objectives for the sponsor are to enhance sales, to promote the public image of its brand, to increase consumer awareness, to modify its brand image, and to build business relationships

- Chapter Principle 10.6: The objectives of sponsorship for the sport property will vary. In addition to attracting financial support, objectives include increasing credibility, increasing awareness, and managing brand image

- Chapter Principle 10.7: Sponsorship affinity refers to whether there is a good fit or match between the sponsor and the sport property. Two factors are particularly important for ensuring a good match: (1) an overlap of target markets and (2) a match up of brand positioning strategies

- Chapter Principle 10.8: To be able to demonstrate that sponsorship has a positive outcome for corporations is the best way to legitimise it as a marketing technique, and to attract and retain sponsors

- Chapter Principle 10.9: Ambush marketing refers to a strategy where a company (other than an official sponsor, and often a competitor to the official sponsor) creates the impression that it is associated with the sport property. This is achieved by attracting attention and by giving the false impression of a relationship with the sport property

Chapter 11. Sport Services

- Chapter Principle 11.1: There are four characteristics which illustrate the difference between sport goods and services: tangibility, consistency, perishability and separability. Sport services are intangible because they exist only as an experience. Sport services tend to be inconsistent because they are affected by variables that are difficult to control. Sport services are perishable because they can only be offered and experienced once at any point in time. Sport services are inseparable because they are consumed at the same time as they are produced

- Chapter Tool 10.4. Sport Sponsorship Evaluation

- Chapter Tool 10.5. Ambush Marketing Methods

- Chapter Tool 10.6. Sport Sponsorship Evaluation

- Chapter Tool 11.1. Service Quality Gaps

(Continued)

Appendix (Continued)

Principles	Tools
● Chapter Principle 11.2: The sport services mix is made up of participants, physical evidence and processes. Participants are those people involved in delivering and receiving a sport service. Physical evidence is the tangible or visual elements of a service such as a sport stadium. Processes represent the steps involved in delivering a sport service ● Chapter Principle 11.3: There are three key principles behind the successful marketing of sport services: service quality, customer relationship building and customer satisfaction ● Chapter Principle 11.4: Sport consumers are more likely to be loyal to a service if they perceive it to be of high quality ● Chapter Principle 11.5: Service quality can be seen as the degree to which a service meets the needs and expectations of consumers ● Chapter Principle 11.6: There are five areas that are commonly used to describe expectations of service quality. These five areas are reliability, assurance, empathy, responsiveness and tangibles ● Chapter Principle 11.7: Customers will make a judgement about whether a service is meeting their expectations at two points in time: first, they will evaluate what the service delivered after it has been consumed (outcome quality); and, second, they will evaluate how the service is delivered during consumption (process quality) ● Chapter Principle 11.8: The service quality elements of empathy, assurance and responsiveness are particularly important to customers' evaluations of process quality. Tangibles and reliability are particularly important to customers' evaluations of outcome quality	● Chapter Tool 11.2. Customer Relationship Marketing Process

- Chapter Principle 11.9: Relationship marketing involves creating, developing and maintaining a connection between sport organisations and sport consumers that leads to interactive, rewarding and long-term exchanges. Relationship marketing recognises the importance of keeping current customers, as well as attracting new ones, and highlights that the relationship with customers needs to be managed well to encourage loyalty

- Chapter Principle 11.10: CRM involves the use of information technology to create and maintain ongoing, long-term relationships with sport consumers, leading to high levels of loyalty, and improved sales

- Chapter Principle 11.11: Customer satisfaction is a judgement which customers make after they have experienced a sport service where they compare what they expected from it with what they believe they actually received. When expectations are met or exceeded, customers are satisfied, and when expectations are not met, customers are dissatisfied

- Chapter Principle 11.12: Focusing on customer satisfaction ensures that sport marketers make the needs and perceptions of their customers a priority, which in turn leads to stronger loyalty to the sport organisation and its products

- Chapter Principle 11.13: Customer delight occurs when a customer's expectations are exceeded to a surprising degree, resulting in an extremely positive emotional state. Delight transpires when the customer is more than just satisfied. This can happen when a service exceeds a customers' expectations of what they think is normal or reasonable from that particular sport service

- Chapter Principle 11.14: Providing customer delight in a sport service can lead to higher levels of loyalty, word of mouth promotion and an advantage over competitors. However, it is essential to know how customer satisfaction/delight influences customer behaviour. It is also important to consider how capable competitors are of copying any innovative service features. It is usually better to invest resources in decreasing customer dissatisfaction than in increasing customer delight

(Continued)

Principles	Tools
Chapter 12. Sport Marketing and the New Media	
● Chapter Principle 12.1: New media refers to communications that are generated by electronic means, or through recent technological platforms. It refers to technologically sophisticated platforms or vehicles for transmitting and communicating information	● Chapter Tool 12.1. Internet-Driven Platforms
● Chapter Principle 12.2: New media is represented numerically, and it is modular, automated, variable and transferable to differing file formats and able to be customised	● Chapter Tool 12.2. Mobile Communications
● Chapter Principle 12.3: New media technologies provide sport marketers with new ways of communicating with consumers and novel approaches to their marketing activities. Many of these approaches are far more rapid, responsive, interactive and inexpensive when compared with other marketing strategies; they are also more able to be customised to key target audiences	● Chapter Tool 12.3. Upgraded Conventional Technologies
● Chapter Principle 12.4: New media sport marketing is customised communication with targeted sport consumers that is generated by electronic means or through technologically sophisticated platforms that facilitate the transmission of information	● Chapter Tool 12.4. Hardware
● Chapter Principle 12.5: New media marketing is targeted and personalised interaction which is based on the principles of customisation, modularity, sticky branding, networked communication and permission	● Chapter Tool 12.5. Software
● Chapter Principle 12.6: New media sport marketing messages should be customised or targeted and adapted to specific consumers and their needs	
● Chapter Principle 12.7: A modular new media marketing programme (including product design) is the one structured in a standardised and automated way which incorporates flexibility, responsiveness to changes in demand and ease of transfer	
● Chapter Principle 12.8: Sticky branding occurs when new media sport marketing ideas take hold in consumers' minds in ways that are consistent with the positioning strategy for the brand	

- Chapter Principle 12.9: Networked communication is based on the idea that instead of telling consumers about products, it is more productive to get consumers to talk to each other about them
- Chapter Principle 12.10: Inclusivity refers to the use of new media marketing to fulfil the need to 'belong', which in turn fosters the development of identity. New media marketing can be conducted in such a way that sport consumers feel 'included' in virtual groups
- Chapter Principle 12.11: Permission in new media sport marketing refers to the effectiveness of communicating with consumers who have consented to receive customised messages, rather than to send random, untargeted and uninvited marketing communications

Stage 4: Implement and Control the Sport Marketing Strategy

Chapter 13. Sport Marketing Implementation and Control

- Chapter Principle 13.1: Implementing a sport marketing strategy means putting the plans into action
- Chapter Principle 13.2: The implementation success of a sport marketing plan is enhanced through the use of five implementation tools: (1) Leadership and commitment, (2) Communication and delegation, (3) Teamwork and projects, (4) Rewards and reinforcement, and (5) Control and feedback
- Chapter Principle 13.3: Controlling a sport marketing strategy means keeping it on track, making sure that it is achieving what it set out to, and making changes to correct variations and problems. The control process involves six steps: (1) Set performance measures, (2) Define critical success factors, (3) Measure performance, (4) Compare results, (5) Identify variations and (6) Make corrections
- Chapter Principle 13.4: There are three basic tenets against which sport marketing behaviour must be matched: (1) the buyer and seller must both be fully informed as to what is being purchased and what is being paid in exchange, (2) neither the buyer nor seller is compelled or coerced in their choices and (3) both buyer and seller are capable of making a rational decision concerning the transaction

- Chapter Tool 13.1. Leadership and Commitment
- Chapter Tool 13.2. Communication and Delegation
- Chapter Tool 13.3. Teamwork and Projects
- Chapter Tool 13.4. Rewards and Reinforcement
- Chapter Tool 13.5. Control and Feedback

Index

319